D0154453

SAINTS AND STRANGERS

*Regional Perspectives on Early America*

JACK P. GREENE AND J. R. POLE, ADVISORS

# Saints and Strangers

NEW ENGLAND
IN BRITISH NORTH AMERICA

Joseph A. Conforti

THE JOHNS HOPKINS UNIVERSITY PRESS
BALTIMORE

The Johns Hopkins University Press
2715 North Charles Street
Baltimore, Maryland 21218-4363
www.press.jhu.edu

LIBRARY OF CONGRESS CATALOGING-IN-PUBLICATION DATA

Conforti, Joseph A.
    Saints and strangers : New England in British North America /
Joseph A. Conforti.
        p. cm. — (Regional perspectives on early America)
    Includes bibliographical references and index.
        ISBN 0-8018-8253-2 (hardcover : alk. paper) — ISBN 0-8018-8254-0
(pbk. : alk. paper)
        1. New England—History—Colonial period, ca. 1600–1775.
    2. Puritans—New England—History.  I. Title.  II. Series.
F7.C74 2006
974—dc22            2005013362

A catalog record for this book is available from the British Library.

*For Dorothy*

# *Contents*

# Acknowledgments

THIS BOOK EXAMINES colonial New England as a region within British North America. It builds on the work of scores of historians and other scholars who have made early New England one of the most examined subjects of the American past. Robert J. Brugger invited me to write this volume while I was finishing another book on New England. He waited patiently for me to get started and then offered much encouragement and advice. At the Press Amy Zezula responded thoroughly and efficiently to my inquiries. Juliana McCarthy oversaw the transformation of the manuscript into the book. I would like to thank Martin Schneider for his superb copyediting. Robert Imholt read an early draft of the manuscript and reminded me that it has been decades since the publication of the last overview of colonial New England.

I completed this volume during a yearlong leave. I want to thank the University of Southern Maine for awarding me the annual Trustees' Fellowship and a sabbatical. Interim Dean of the College of Arts and Sciences, Luisa Deprez, approved the funds that supported my research. Robin O'Sullivan, my graduate assistant, provided valuable help, from checking quotations to working on maps. Two other graduate students, Rosemary Mosher and Kirsten Boettcher, prepared the final version of the maps. Without Madeleine Winterfalcon, departmental administrative assistant, this book would have progressed much more slowly. She worked through many drafts and in a variety of ways proved indispensable to the book's completion.

I dedicate this book to my wife, a native New Englander whose ancestors, like mine, arrived in the region long after the Colonial Era.

*Note to the Reader:* Citations in the text refer primarily to direct quotations from original sources. I have modernized some of these quotations for clarity. The essay on sources at the end of the book acknowledges my debt to many scholars and offers suggestions for further reading.

# SAINTS AND STRANGERS

# City upon a Hill

"COLONIAL NEW ENGLAND" evokes some of the most familiar, even notorious, images in American history and mythology. We think of early New England as a world of Pilgrims and the first Thanksgiving, of clustered villages and white steepled churches, of pious founders and stern fathers, of the tormented souls of Nathaniel Hawthorne's fiction and the witchcraft mania of Salem, of unquiet Yankees and brooding "sinners in the hands of an angry God." We also identify colonial New England in terms of the famous phrase of one Puritan leader—Massachusetts Bay Colony Governor John Winthrop's likening of the new American settlement as a "city upon a hill."

Though not a minister, Winthrop delivered the sermon in 1630 to prospective colonists in England while his assistants sifted through recruits and readied to depart for Massachusetts. The governor admonished the settlers to be "knit together in this work as one man." He reminded them that God in his Providence had so arranged the world "as in all times some must be rich, some poor, some high and eminent in power and dignity, others mean and in subjection." Winthrop sketched a hierarchical social vision for Puritans who aimed to move from a dissenting religious minority in England to the governing majority in America. He challenged the would-be colonists: "We shall find that the God of Israel is among us, when ten of us shall be able to resist a thousand of our enemies, when he shall make us a praise and glory that men shall say of succeeding plantations, 'the

Lord make it like that of New England.' For we must consider that we shall be as a city upon a hill. The eyes of all people are upon us."[1]

The birth and development of Puritan New England resembled a city upon a hill because the region differed so much from the settlements in England's mid-Atlantic, southern, and Caribbean colonies. Unlike the young, poor, indentured white males of Chesapeake's tobacco colonies, for example, it was middle-class families that dominated the Puritan settlement of Massachusetts and Connecticut. With widespread property ownership among a free white population of farmers, artisans, and merchants, New Englanders formed British America's most solidly "middling" colonial society. Town-centered settlement patterns further distinguished early New England from other parts of British America. Local institutions—town meetings, self-governing churches, public schools—fostered early America's most fully developed civic culture. Indeed, the evolution of these autonomous political institutions and practices in New England distressed royal officials in England. They repeatedly attempted to "reform" the region's governments because they boasted the strongest representative elements in British America.

Through comparisons with other British American regions, this book examines many distinctive aspects of New England as a colonial world. Some of these differences sowed an image of the region as an inhospitable place—and not simply because of the climate, so much harsher than that of England. Connecticut and Massachusetts achieved notoriety as the only colonies that executed witches. Puritan writers cultivated a sense of New England's moral and intellectual superiority over other regions. High rates of literacy and the establishment of the first two print shops in the colonies (1640 and 1675) enabled Puritans to forge a powerful regional identity. New England surpassed all other British regions in the development of a historical consciousness and a collective, if exclusive, identity. Seventeenth-century writers produced the first Puritan-centered histories of New England, launching a religion-driven deluge of printed words that has shaped how we have come to understand the region's storied colonial past.

The famous image of the city upon the hill, then, is a helpful reminder of Puritanism's weighty influence on New England and of the region's differences from other corners of British America. But Winthrop's words have often been used to explain how the founding of Puritan New England launched an *American* sense of mission. In this familiar vein, their city upon the hill served as a moral beacon to the world. This book moves beyond such customary but often limited images of early New England to examine the region's founding and early history in a colonial context rather than as a precursor to later historical developments like the rise of the achievement of American independence or the American sense of mission abroad.

Common activities and monumental events in colonial New England took place in a heavily transatlantic and British context. As they made strides toward creating a distinctive regional culture, New England's Puritan founders remained above all transplanted Englishmen and -women with strong bonds to their mother country. The very name of the region signaled a hope for cultural continuity with the homeland. Many original settlers returned to Britain during the first decades of settlement, disappointed that the region did not resemble a "new" England or else drawn home by the temporary triumph of Puritan forces under Oliver Cromwell at midcentury. In the eighteenth century, colonial New Englanders relied on new sources of British identity and pride. It was unusual for an imperial power to have limits on the monarchy and constitutional protections for the civil and religious rights of its citizens both at home and in its colonies, as England did; British Protestants on both sides of the Atlantic did enjoy freedom of worship. For such reasons, British patriotism swept through eighteenth-century colonial America. New England's confrontations with French political and religious absolutism in nearby Canada inflamed the region's pride in its British heritage.

In other words, colonial New England was not an insular American city upon a hill, either at the time of its founding or in the course of its colonial development. Even as New Englanders adapted their English heritage to New World circumstances, they inhabited a transatlantic realm whose religious movements, commercial exchanges, and imperial demands shaped regional life. Indeed, colonial New England prospered into British America's preeminent mercantile region, a maritime "nation" within the imperial domain. New England merchants quickly saw or created opportunities in coastal and transatlantic trade. Rather than isolating New England from the outside world, the Atlantic Ocean served as a watery frontier, a highway of commercial and cultural encounter and exchange. The ocean linked New Englanders not only to English people in other colonies and in the homeland but to racial and religious "strangers" throughout the Atlantic world.

Strangers to Puritanism participated in the creation of colonial New England. In Puritan usage, *stranger* might identify someone who was non-English, non-Christian, non-Protestant, or nonwhite. Most commonly, *stranger* referred to all non-Puritan inhabitants, whether white, black, or Native American. The image of the city upon the hill has become historical shorthand for Puritan New England, an image that tends to distill the chronicle of the Colonial Era into an exclusively Puritan historical drama—the story of pious "saints." Yet within and beyond the Puritan Bible commonwealths of Massachusetts and Connecticut, strangers fashioned their own subcommunities. From the region's origins to the end of the Colonial Era, profane or nominally Protestant white settlers posed ongoing problems to pious New Englanders. In spite of disease and bloody early encounters with English colonists, Native people were not erased from the regional landscape. Whether as military allies, bound laborers, or subjects for religious conversion, Natives endured as participants in New England colonial life. By the mid-eighteenth century, New England merchants came to dominate the American phase of the Atlantic slave trade. As a consequence, the region's leading seaports hosted large, vital African-American communities.

Of course, unlike other parts of British America, racial and cultural diversity altered rather than transformed colonial New England. From its founding through the eighteenth century, New England persisted as the most Anglo region of British America. In fact, English origins rather than Puritan piety defined the most inclusive category of identity in colonial New England. Still, the region was far from the homogeneous Anglo world that the dominant images of Pilgrims, Puritans, and Yankees suggest. This book examines New England as a distinctive section of British North America, assessing the scope of Puritanism's influence in the region and exploring colonial New England's history beyond its overemphasized image as the city upon the hill.

# ONE

# Native New England

## From Precontact to Colonial Beginnings

NEW APPROACHES TO THE study of Native American life have revealed its complexity before and after contact with Europeans. Ethnohistory has made the study of Native ways more cultural and anthropological. Drawing on archaeological evidence and European reports, historians now examine Native culture in its own context. Ethnohistorians also focus on changes in Native material artifacts, trade, and warfare as a result of contact with European explorers and settlers. At the same time, the emergence of environmental history has encouraged historians to study Native ecological practices and to document the major alterations of the New World landscape that preceded the arrival of European settlers.

Ethnohistory and environmental history have helped transform our view of Native Americans. Consider New England. We no longer see its Natives as members of wandering warrior societies or as unchanging, seemingly "natural" inhabitants of a howling wilderness. Natives had their own history and did not enter the story of New England only as a consequence of their encounter—sometimes violent—with English colonists. Yet, through these encounters, Natives participated in the making of early New England. Colonists founded and developed a "new" England, an English cultural region. They did so only with crucial assistance from Native people. Colonists erected towns on sites where land had been cleared by agricultural tribes. Native food and farming practices sustained early settlers. Their trade with Indians advanced the commercialization of the regional economy. The English colonists also relied heavily on Indian military allies, guides, and mapmakers. Native Americans did not simply present an obstacle to New England's settlement; they also proved essential to the region's colonization and survival.

## NATIVE PEOPLE NORTH AND SOUTH

We do not have precise figures on the size of New England's Native population before contact and colonization in the seventeenth century introduced European diseases that devastated the region's aboriginal people. Estimates of Native population range widely, from 75,000 to over 140,000. In spite of these epidemics, the tribes were a major presence in New England up to the outbreak of King Philip's War (1675–78). In 1670, Native Americans still constituted nearly one quarter of the region's approximately 68,000 inhabitants. This figure suggests that the precontact Indian population may have been closer to the high estimate of more than 140,000.

New England's Algonquian people shared linguistic and cultural ties with Natives as far south as Virginia. But even within New England, Algonquians spoke in varied dialects. Moreover, they adapted in divergent ways to the region's landscape and climate. It is customary to describe New England's Native people, from north to south, as nomadic hunter-gatherers and semi-sedentary agriculturalists. Well before 1600, however, the eve of sustained European-Indian contact, agriculture had become quite developed in northern New England. An exclusive hunter-gatherer way of life prevailed only in parts of northern New England, such as east of the Kennebec River in central Maine, where the growing season was too short to support an agricultural way of life. In these northern climes, Natives moved their camps frequently in their pursuit of moose, bear, caribou, deer, and beaver. Through the dark and protracted winter, they tracked large prey on snowshoes with the assistance of dogs, the one animal that precontact Algonquians had domesticated. In other seasons, they gathered wild fruit, nuts, seeds, and roots; along the coast they hunted fowl, harvested shellfish (including lobster), and killed seals and whales. Indeed, Natives in the north and south were New England's first whalemen, an often romanticized and heroic "Yankee" livelihood that employed large numbers of Indian men even after English colonists organized whaling into a commercial enterprise.

The Algonquians of northern New England were known as the Abenaki, "people of the dawn or first light," so named by interior tribes, who saw them as eastern people. The eastern Abenaki homeland extended from northern Maine to Nova Scotia. The western Abenaki inhabited much of New Hampshire, Vermont, and Maine. By 1600, the bulk of the western Abenaki had become agriculturalists, incorporating hunting, fishing, and gathering into a semisedentary way of life. New England's geography, as well as its climate, shaped Native life. The region was not endowed with rich natural resources, though the colonists exploited abundant supplies of timber and fish. New England's rocky, thin soil challenged farmers, Native and English alike. But in addition to the bounty of forest and ocean, New England contained abundant river systems and lakes, many of which bordered fertile valleys. Throughout the region Natives established their villages on the coast, in river valleys, and adjacent to lakes and ponds. In northern New England, Abenaki clustered at sites along the Saco, Kennebec, and Androscoggin Rivers in Maine, the Lake Champlain Valley in Vermont, and the Connecticut River and Lake Winnipesauke in New Hampshire. Given the importance of waterways to Indian sustenance and trade, it should not be surprising that even today, from the Housatonic in western New England to the Penobscot in eastern Maine, the region's major rivers are dominated by Native names (fig. 1).

French explorer Samuel de Champlain published a detailed map of the Indian village at the mouth of the Saco River in Maine (see fig. 2). Champlain explored the northeast coast between 1604 and 1607. His depiction of the Saco village was part of a larger mapping of the region. Champlain benefited from Abenaki informers, who probably outlined the geography of the interior on bark or on the ground. That map reveals a cultivated landscape with open fields on both sides of the river, a terrain where corn grows in abundance (*C*). Wigwams and long houses huddle near the fields (*E*). The river offers access to the interior and its hunting grounds. Champlain describes what he labels *H* as "a large point of land all cleared except [for] some fruit trees and wild vines." The map also reveals a fortress (*B*) built for protection against raiding hunter-gatherers from further north.[1]

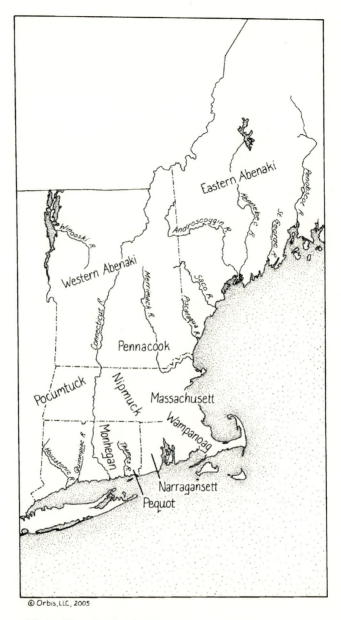

FIG. 1 Native New England, ca. 1600

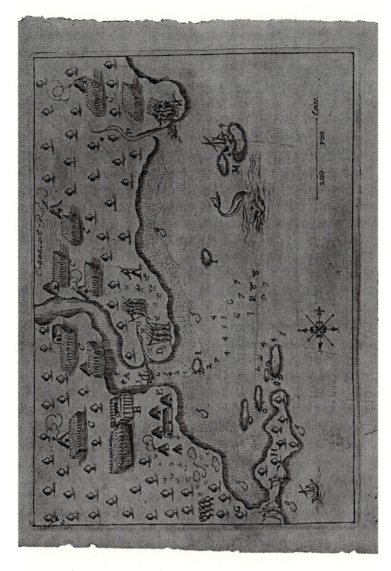

FIG. 2  Champlain's detailed map of the Native village of Saco, Maine. This is a 1635 version of the map that originated from the French explorer's travels three decades earlier. Courtesy of the Osher Map Library, University of Southern Maine, on loan from William Browder.

In southern New England, with its larger and much denser indigenous population and a longer growing season than the north, agriculture was even more critical to Native survival. We tend to be familiar with tribal names in the south, not only because they have been the focus of the attention of colonial historians but also because these groups served as the allies, neighbors, trading partners, and enemies of a land-hungry colonial population that grew rapidly and incited major conflict. The Wampanoag of Plymouth Colony, the Massachusett and Nipmuck in the Puritan Bay Colony, the Pennacook of New Hampshire, the Mohegan and Pequot in Connecticut, and the Narragansett in Rhode Island constituted the largest and most dominant tribes in presettlement central and southern New England.

These semisedentary agricultural Natives cleared extensive tracts of land. European explorers marveled at the openness of coastal terrain. As Champlain reported, "All along the shore there is a great deal of land cleared up and planted with corn." He described the New England coast as "very pleasant and agreeable." The adventurer John Smith, who bestowed the name "New England" on the region, recorded similar impressions of the Massachusetts coast. On a voyage in 1614, he found "great troupes of well proportioned people and large corn fields."[2] Such testimony confirms that coastal Natives had dramatically altered the landscape, so that neither explorers nor early coastal settlers encountered what later generations claimed was a thick, unbroken wilderness. Of course, New England was heavily forested, and a swarming colonial population did hack its way through woods. Yet from the coast to the Connecticut River Valley and beyond, semisedentary Native agriculturalists cultivated vast tracts of land that became choice sites for colonial settlement. In the spring and again in the fall, Indian villagers set controlled fires to burn underbrush, saplings, and deadwood. This practice opened the landscape and facilitated the hunt for foraging animals. Controlled burning also significantly reduced the risk of massive fires, an effective practice that has been acknowledged in recent years by the United States Forest Service, whose restraint has contributed to historic conflagrations in the west.

Besides clearing swaths of the forest, the large semisedentary Native population altered the landscape in other ways that ultimately aided the colonists' "conquest" of the wilderness. An elaborate system of Native trails crisscrossed the region. Seldom more than two feet wide, these trails enabled Natives to move "Indian file" through woods on hunting, trading, diplomatic, and military journeys. Trails intersected and traveled in many directions. Natives, like modern hikers, often depended on marked trees to find their way. Indian trails facilitated the colonists' movement through New England forests. Some trails, such as the Bay Path near Springfield, Massachusetts, were given names that obscured their Native origins. Today, not just the Bay Path but also the Mohawk Trail, the Wampanoag Trail, and the Old Connecticut Path remind us that Native people, not just the colonists, blazed their way through New England's forests, tilling acres of corn within a village landscape.

## VILLAGES, GENDER, AND FOODWAYS

Trails and paths linked the rotating villages that semisedentary Natives inhabited. Seasonal settlements for farming, fishing, and hunting sustained Indian life. For most of the year, from early spring through late fall, the vast majority of New England Indians lived in agricultural villages. Corn, beans, and squash were the staples of their diet. Native people also cultivated pumpkins, Jerusalem artichokes (a sunflower-like plant with edible roots), and tobacco. A division of labor separated villagers by gender. Beyond their childrearing responsibilities, women planted and cultivated village fields. They relied on trained hawks to protect crops from birds. Native women harvested, prepared, and preserved their produce. They also gathered wild fruit, nuts, and roots, and wove baskets and mats. Early colonists deplored what they saw as the servile burdens that Native women bore while their men appeared shiftless, especially during the summer months. "The men employ themselves wholly in hunting and other exercises of the bow, except at some times take some pains in fishing," one Plymouth leader grumbled. "The women live a most slavish life."[3] We do not know whether Native women saw their lives that way. The labor of Indian men varied according to the seasons, but it did involve periods of intense activity. Beyond hunting and fishing, men fought enemies, built dugout canoes, and fashioned stone tools and weapons. Some historians have suggested that the burdens of colonial New England women were not radically different from what Native women confronted. After all, colonial "good wives" gave birth to numerous children (seven or eight was common), cultivated house gardens, and faced an array of domestic responsibilities from food preparation to homespun clothing. They did not perform sustained agricultural labor, however. Furthermore, Native women participated in many "manly" activities, from building wigwams and sewing bark canoes to processing products of the hunt that further distinguished their labor from the work of colonial goodwives.

The land that women cultivated was assigned by a sachem, the leader of a band or tribe. Sachems saw land as sovereign tribal territory, but Natives did not possess individual ownership of their fields. They did not share the English idea of land as private property. Natives "owned" the right to use their fields. As long as families cultivated their land, it belonged to them. Indians did not raise the domestic animals whose manure could have renewed corn fields. Approximately every decade, agricultural villages were moved as the soil became depleted. Abandoned land reverted to the tribe. Natives moved to more fertile ground where the sachem would have to assign land again.

During the first years of settlement, when survival hung in the balance, English colonists did adopt Native agricultural practices, a development epitomized by the famous story of Squanto, who supplied the Pilgrims with corn seed and taught them how to plant it in hills. Squanto had been captured by English traders in 1614, part of a group of Patuxet (from the site of the Plymouth colony soon to be created), some of whom were sold into slavery. During the contact decades, Native agriculturalists along the coast were often captured for the slave market or carried to England where they were held in preparation for service as guides and interpreters in future English expeditions. Squanto spent time in Spain, by 1617 had escaped to England, finally returning to his homeland in 1619 after jumping from an English ship. Squanto served Plymouth not only as a teacher of Native corn culture but also as a guide, interpreter, and Indian-English mediator. Though it has often been characterized as a legend, he did teach the colonists how to use fish as fertilizer. Nevertheless, this indigenous, labor-intensive practice was not widely employed by New England Natives.

Other Indian teachers followed Squanto. One early New England writer described how the Natives were "our first instructors for the planting of the Indian corn, by teaching us to cull out the finest seed, to observe the fittest season, to keep distance for holes, and fit measure for hills, to worm it, to prune it, and [to] dress it as occasion shall require."[4] Still, once New England colonists survived their "starving times," they reverted to familiar English ways. The plow replaced the Indian hoe; the ox and horse enabled more land to be cultivated with less labor; and manure turned the colonists away from fish. During spring planting and fall harvesting, New England's chronic labor shortage often compelled farmers to rely on Native indentured laborers who tilled the soil in English ways.

Pioneering colonists did rely on Native foods, some of which were assimilated into the New England diet. An abundance of corn, beans, squash, pumpkins, and maple sugar, for example, influenced regional foodways: the process of acquiring, preparing, and serving food. In 1643, Edward Johnson, Puritan founder and first historian of Massachusetts, satirized critics who complained that the colonists' diet had become too savage and Indianized:

Instead of pottage and puddings, and custard and pies,
Our pumpkins and parsnips are common supplies;
We have pumpkin at morning and pumpkin at noon,
If it was not for pumpkins we should be undone.[5]

Native foods enriched rather than revolutionized the New England diet. Now familiar fare such as corn bread and corn chowder derive from Indian foodways. Even the fabled New England baked beans have an aboriginal parallel; Natives also sweetened their beans with maple sugar and syrup.

Yet, as Edward Johnson suggested, for all their early reliance on pumpkins, corn, beans, and squash, the English colonists did not abandon pottage, puddings, custards, and pies—that is, their inherited foodways. We have long known that immigrants to a new world cling to familiar foods as "ethnic" touchstones. It should not be surprising, then, that New England farmers reduced their dependence on Indian corn and increased the cultivation of English grains. The early intimacy and interdependence of Natives and colonists does not obscure the fact that most English newcomers viewed aboriginal people as savages. Indeed, the fear of "Indianization" imposed limits on cultural exchange, including foodways. Dread of Indianization shaped public policies, which included banning intermarriage and laws, like the one passed in Connecticut in 1642, that established severe punishment for "persons [who], depart from amongst us, and take up their abode with the Indians, in a profane course of life."[6] The threat of Indianization preoccupied colonial writers and preachers. In other words, the colonists' fear of "going native" operated not only in everyday life, where Squanto's successors lived closely and often cooperatively with the English. The specter of Indianization also infiltrated the colonial New England imagination, where Natives resided as savage threats to English culture and identity.

The Indians' system of rotating villages contrasted sharply with the English cultural and economic investment in fixity, private property, and livestock (horses, cattle, sheep, chickens, and pigs). In addition to their agricultural villages, Natives inhabited summer fishing camps and winter hunting sites. Natives throughout New England consumed fish, many taking advantage of spring fish runs up the region's rivers. But it was along the coast that the Indians enjoyed a wide variety of seafood: clams, oysters, lobsters, crabs, and bluefish, for example. During the summer months, while planted crops grew, Natives erected temporary fishing camps where they feasted on the bounty of the sea and smoked seafood for later use. Men and women fished, and the latter were responsible for preserving and storing part of the catch. One English observer described Native women lobsterers, who dove for their catch: "The tide being spent, they trudge home two or three miles with a hundred weight of lobsters at their backs."[7] Native women stored smoked fish and clams as well as dried meat, vegetables, nuts, and berries in underground caches lined with birchbark or woven mats.

Coastal Indians introduced New World shellfish to English colonists. In fact, along with Indian corn, shellfish became critical to the survival of early colonists. The storied New England clambake has its origins in Native practices at their summer fishing camps. Late eighteenth- and nineteenth-century New Englanders "invented" the clambake to commemorate the heroic survival of the region's founders. Colonial New Englanders, however, were slow to adopt "Indian" shellfish as a staple of their diet. Sachems complained, for instance, that colonists allowed their pigs to root on Native clam banks. With shellfish as with Indian corn, once their survival was assured, colonists reaffirmed traditional foodways.

Beyond food, summer coastal villages also supplied some tribes with the raw material to make wampum. Long Island Sound and Narragansett Bay teemed with quahogs, large clams with purple and white shells. These shells were fashioned, often by the skilled hands of women, into beads, which were then strung together to create a wampum belt. Algonquians throughout New England and Iroquois in New York and Canada greatly valued wampum for ceremonial and religious purposes, and also used it as tribute. The sachem and the village powwow, or holy man, typically wore the most impressive wampum belts. Since southern New England coastal tribes controlled access to quahogs, wampum became a valued trade item for Native people. The English colonists transformed wampum into a kind of money, a medium of exchange. Because of its value to Indians and its purchasing power for Native goods, wampum circulated as money in the hands of early New Englanders.

English traders acquired wampum from southern tribes and then used it to obtain beaver pelts from inland and northern Indians. The commercialized beaver hunt disrupted longstanding Native hunting practices. In the winter months, semisedentary Indians moved to another seasonal village on tribal hunting grounds. Natives built sturdy wigwams and longhouses at these winter sites, and women labored on their construction. Like the hunter-gatherers of the far north, in the winter the semisedentary Algonquians pursued large and small game on snowshoes. Men bore the burden of the hunt, but women dressed, smoked, and froze the meat and processed animal hides for domestic use. Due to spiritual beliefs, the Natives limited the scale of the hunt to subsistence needs. Respect for the animal world and fears that the spirits would punish them for killing more than they needed encouraged Natives to limit the scope of the hunt.

The European commercial quest for beaver pelts undermined customary Native hunting practices. New Englanders manufactured wampum rather than simply depending on Indian sources. Fur-trading posts sprang to life from the Connecticut River to the Kennebec River. Traders sought the thickest, most valuable beaver pelts from the region's coldest locations. Natives were drawn into a commercial network that linked southern and northern New England and tied the region to European markets. With their traps, nets, and bludgeons, Indians slaughtered beaver in unprecedented numbers.

Precontact Natives did not inhabit a static world. The expansion of semisedentary agricultural villages and shifting patterns of intra-Native trade, tribute, and tribal power preceded European contact. Natives continued to live in seasonal hunting, fishing, and farming villages, but their precontact way of life was irretrievably altered after traders and then settlers invaded New England. Hunting became more commercial and deadly. English pigs foraged at Native shellfish sites. The colonists' livestock trampled unfenced Indian corn fields. From material to spiritual life, the European presence in New England posed challenges to Algonquians' precontact ways.

## NATIVE MATERIAL LIFE

Precontact Algonquian society has often been characterized as egalitarian, free of the material accumulation and class distinctions that divided European settlers. Material acquisition hindered the movement of both hunter-gatherer and semisedentary Indians. Intertribal trade and tribute, like Native "ownership" of the land, were not imbued with the acquisitive, commercial values that Europeans introduced to the New World. Yet traditional Algonquian communities institutionalized their own social differences that were reflected in material comfort and display.

Sachems sprang from highly respectable families and established a hereditary claim on succession. They lived in the largest wigwams and accumulated tribute. They wore the most impressive wampum belts, dress, and jewelry. Sachems' advisors, powwows, and distinguished warriors were also high-ranking Natives whose status was similarly reflected in dress and ornamentation. Men and women from common families filled the membership of local bands. From contact to colonization, European technology and commercialism made major inroads into Algonquian material life, affecting all segments of Native society.

New England's semisedentary Indians lived in wigwams and longhouses like those depicted in Champlain's map of the Saco village in Maine. Natives constructed conical wigwam frames by bending poles that were buried in the ground. This hutlike frame, designed to house a single family, was then covered with a variety of material—most commonly bark, woven mats, and animal skins. Women played a major role in the construction of wigwams. For instance, they sewed together the bark strips that formed the walls and roof of the wigwam. An opening in the roof admitted light and allowed smoke to leave the dwelling. Longhouses were much larger multifamily structures. Some reached one hundred feet in length and thirty feet in width; they housed kin who often spanned three generations.

Native women lined and decorated wigwam and longhouse interiors. They covered walls with fur and deerskin. They used berries and roots to paint mats and add color to the interior. They stored goods in an assortment of hanging baskets. Totems—images of animals and birds of prey that clans adopted as spiritual guardians—reminded Natives of blood relations and of their kinship with the natural world. Winter wigwams and longhouses were particularly sturdy, well-lined dwellings. English visitors found Indian homes at once cozy and wanting. One early English observer claimed that they were "warmer than our English houses." He also ridiculed them as "smokey dwellings." When the Indians stoked their fires, he reported, "they are not able to stand upright but lie all along under the smoke." Still, early New England settlers temporarily adopted wigwam construction, though complaints of porous walls and roofs suggest that the colonists failed to master Native building techniques. Puritan historian Edward Johnson noted that "all the wigwams, huts, and hovels" of pioneering colonists were replaced by well-constructed, framed English houses.[8] Wigwams—like Indian corn, pumpkins, and shellfish—aided the birth of New England, offering temporary shelter before the colonists reaffirmed familiar English customs.

New England Natives continued to live in wigwams and longhouses throughout the colonial period and well beyond. Trade and early colonization initiated changes that affected not so much architecture as other aspects of Native material life. The proliferation of European trade goods—domestic artifacts, tools, weapons, and alcohol—did more to transform Native ways.

Prior to European contact, Indians in the New England region relied on domestic items such as clay pots, hollowed-out wooden bowls, and birch bark containers. Traders introduced products made of brass, copper, and iron that Natives often adopted for their own cultural purposes. A brass item, to cite one example, might be forged into a beautiful ornament that could be worn around the neck. As colonists noted, Native material life, from dwellings, tools, and weapons to the cultural adaptations of English goods, revealed Indian ingenuity. This resourcefulness predated New England's more famous Yankee inventiveness. With colonization, the widespread availability and durability of European goods increasingly led Natives to use brass, copper, and iron pots and utensils in English ways. Similarly, New England Indians adopted woolen cloth and blankets, which decreased the traditional domestic use of animal skins.

European trade also transformed Native tools and weapons. Precontact Indians possessed a variety of utensils—simple implements and clever items fashioned from stone, flint, bones, and shells. They created axes of varying sizes by strapping grooved stones to wooden handles. Flat, pointed stones and flint attached to wooden handles served as knives, chisels, and scrapers. The shoulder blades of moose and deer as well as large clam shells functioned as hoes. Labor-saving iron tools of European traders and settlers invaded Native villages. This new technology altered Native ways of cutting and scraping animal skins, felling trees, building dugout canoes, and cultivating the land. Over time, some Natives, amply supplied with iron tools, even adopted English ways of preparing the ground for planting.

Native weapons were also Europeanized. Indians in New England possessed firearms before the arrival of large numbers of Puritan-led colonists beginning in 1630. But, as one ethnohistorian has aptly put it, "the introduction of metal cutting edges" Europeanized Native hunting and warfare more than guns did.[9] Iron replaced stone in war clubs and hatchets. Brass-tipped arrows proved deadlier than traditional flint or the antlers, eagle talons, and horseshoe crab tails that some inventive Indians used. Trade provoked what has been described as a Native "arms race." This demand for new weapons was part of a larger Native appetite for European goods—a new consumption and commercialism stimulated by presettlement and then colonial trade.

Natives came to crave alcohol along with an array of practical European trade items. At first Indians adopted alcohol for their own religious purposes: it helped produce the visions and dreams that were so central to Native spirituality. In the face of an abundant supply, however, religion failed to regulate the consumption of alcohol. Unaccustomed to intoxicants, Indians were easily inebriated, even with often watered-down goods. Traders and colonists capitalized on the growing alcohol dependence of many Natives to acquire fur, wampum, land, and labor. A new wave of alcohol-induced violence, including domestic violence, wracked Indian villages. Alcohol emerged as a critical European "material" item for Indian trade and exploitation.

The study of material culture embraces a broad range of utilitarian, expressive, and decorative objects. It also includes bodily ornamentation and dress. Iron tools accelerated the production and display of wampum and brass jewelry. Natives valued imported shirts, though European clothing did not completely replace traditional dress or make the Indians' appearance any more acceptable to most whites. Native people's physical features and migratory habits led an early New England writer to compare them to English gypsies. Other writers described the red and black tattoos that Natives imprinted on their faces, arms, and chests. Some males wore totemic clan images on their cheeks— "portraitures of beasts, as bears, deers, mooses, wolves . . . eagles [and] hawks."[10]

Such "devilish" ornamentation repulsed the Puritan settlers in particular. For their own part, despite their demand for imported clothing and other trade goods, Natives did not find Europeans physically appealing. New England Indians were repelled by the hairiness of the English, especially their thick beards. Some colonial accounts indicate that Indians were taller than the English colonists. The Natives' high-protein diet seems to have contributed to this physical difference. John Smith, the famed Virginian Indian fighter and New England explorer, stood just over five feet—a height that approximates the average size of early English colonists. Miles Standish, the mythologized military leader of Plymouth, may have been shorter than Smith. One of Standish's Indian foes described him as "a great captain, yet he was but a little man."[11] Outfitted in armor and equipped with European weapons, the short, bearded Standish resembled a conquistador. Superior technology rather than physical strength or stature propelled English military victories over Native people.

Fishermen, traders, and would-be colonists encountered large and prominent tribes in early seventeenth-century New England. These tribes were the products of historical developments that shaped Native life before European contact: migration, the expansion of agriculture, and intertribal trade, warfare, diplomacy, and tribute. The label *tribe* is customary, but it is not the most historically accurate way to characterize the social and political organization of Native life. From the hunter-gatherers of the far north to the semisedentary agriculturalists of the south, it was the band that served as the fundamental unit of Native survival.

In most of New England, a band consisted of two to three hundred Indians who occupied an agricultural village and hunted, gathered, and fished at common locations. Daily and seasonal activities revolved around the local band. Extensive kinship networks, symbolized by clan totems, unified villages. Kinship and marriage facilitated movement among bands. Thus, a tribe consisted of a collection of semi-autonomous local bands linked by kinship, dialect, trade, and self-defense. These ties, however, did not preclude interband feuds and violence.

Local bands were led by their own sachems, typically men whose positions of leadership were inherited. Sachems governed their bands in consultation with a council of local leaders that included powwows and distinguished fighters. Sachems received tribute such as food and fur from their people, but they also bestowed gifts on their "subjects." Native leaders remained in power as long as they ruled by consensus and discharged their numerous duties satisfactorily. They were responsible for the assignment of land, the resolution of conflicts between band members, and the conduct of trade, diplomacy, and warfare. Disgruntled Natives were free to withdraw from one band, join clan members in another village, and pledge loyalty to a new local sachem. In the case of a successful sachem who retained his position until death, the leadership would pass to his eldest son. In the absence of a male heir, a deceased sachem's sister or daughter—women of "royal" blood—might succeed him. Women sachems were not common, though several appear in the records of early New England. One "queen," Awashunkes of the Sakonnet on the east side of Narragansett Bay, was pressured by the English to keep her people out of the Wampanoag uprising sparked by sachem King Philip. Weetamoo, a neighboring female sachem of the Wampanoag band of Pocassets, supported King Philip.

English colonization complicated the leadership of sachems in New England. The "chief" sachems who appear in colonial annals and in modern history books—Massasoit and Philip of the Wampanoag, Miantonomi of the Narragansett, and Uncas of the Mohegan, for example—were leaders of large bands who secured tribute from lesser bands. Colonization required these sachems to supervise trade, diplomacy, and warfare with the English and not just with other bands and tribes. Natives formed client relationships with European colonists, whether English, French, or Dutch, for the exchange of goods. Sachems also negotiated political and military alliances with colonists that served mutual interests. Sachems were not inexperienced negotiators with primitive diplomatic skills who were easily outwitted, as suggested by the tale of Manhattan's purchase by the Dutch for the equivalent of twenty-four dollars.

In diplomacy with the early colonists in New England, sachems pursued their own agendas. It is well documented that Massasoit accepted the arrival of Plymouth settlers and signed a peace treaty with them because his Wampanoag had been depleted by disease and needed protection from their tribal enemy, the Narragansett, across Mount Hope Bay. After the Narragansett were victimized by smallpox in 1633, they too accepted cooperation with the English to counter the power of rival eastern Connecticut tribes. Uncas, chief sachem of the Mohegan, pursued his own goal in aligning with the English: to dominate Native Connecticut and control access to wampum. Tribal rivalries, the political calculations of sachems, and colonial ambitions to open Connecticut to English settlement created a confluence of Native-white interests that led to the Pequot War of 1637, the first major Indian conflict in New England. An Anglo-Native force of Narragansett, Mohegan, and colonial warriors surrounded the Pequot village on the Mystic River, set fire to wigwams, and killed or captured those who were not consumed in the inferno.

The Pequot massacre illustrates patterns of Native-English

warfare in early New England. First, it reminds us that major confrontations did not simply pit white colonists against Native people. Warriors fought right alongside the English against their Native rivals. In fact, Indians comprised up to one quarter of colonial armies in the seventeenth century. They also served the English as military advisers and guides. Natives urged the colonists to launch the surprise attack on the Pequot and to do so at night. But the massacre also revealed conflicts between Native and English ways of war. Some Puritans did express moral reservations about the needless bloodletting and the incineration of old people, women, and children. Most, however, probably agreed with Plymouth governor William Bradford, who described the stench of Indian flesh "frying in the fryer" and deemed the war "a sweet sacrifice." In contrast, one Narragansett participant protested "the manner of the Englishman's fight . . . because it is too furious and slays too many men." The captain of the Massachusetts troops at the assault recalled an earlier military clash between the Pequot and the Narragansett, who appeared to fight "more for pastime than to conquer and subdue enemies."[12]

The Algonquians of New England were unaccustomed to the kind of European total war that was waged on the Pequot. Feuds and violence among kin, bands, and tribes did permeate Native life long before English settlements took hold. Precontact Natives found plenty of reason to fight—revenge, defense, and control over tribute and trade, for instance. But inter-Indian warfare seldom took the form of major battles in open fields. What the colonists described as the Natives' "skulking way of war" involved ambushes in the woods or quick raids on villages. Some raiding parties sought captives—women and children who could be incorporated into a band to replace losses. Rhode Island's Roger Williams, an astute observer of the Narragansett, reported that Indian conflicts were "far less bloody and devouring than the cruel wars of Europe."[13]

Of course, Native warriors were known for their ritualized torture of enemies, through which the killers claimed to acquire their rivals' spiritual power. Pre-Columbian archaeology also confirms that scalping was an indigenous New World practice. New England Indians took human "trophies" in battle. If warriors fought too far from home, they scalped victims rather than lugging home entire heads. One might conclude that, in spite of the relatively small scale of Indian war in comparison to the Pequot massacre, Native people were particularly cruel. Yet seventeenth-century European warfare and criminal justice harbored its own brutality. The public display of enemy and criminal heads was common, a spectacle the colonists would later make of King Philip's body. Furthermore, though scalping originated with Native people, colonists encouraged and commercialized it. Authorities paid client tribes bounties for the scalps of Native and eventually French enemies.

Such changes in scalping represented only one of the ways that the colonists altered Indian warfare. Armed with European weapons, Native combat became more deadly. Fighting shoulder to shoulder with the colonists, large numbers of New England Indians were introduced to, and even intimidated by, European military tactics. Still, the cultural exchange on the battlefield was not unidirectional. Colonists would adopt aspects of the skulking way of war and a century later draw the derision of British soldiers for fighting "Indian style."

## PLEASING THE SPIRITS

Spiritual beliefs informed Native torture, execution, and scalping of enemies. Religion pervaded Indian warfare. Powwows led pre-battle ceremonies that invoked gods who would ensure victory. These practices reflected the cornerstones of Native spirituality: animism and polytheism. New England colonists sneered at Native religion, dismissing it as superstitious, even Satanic.

What settlers perceived as diabolical religion began with the Native belief that the entire physical world—human and natural—was inhabited by spirits. Kinship totems displayed in wigwams or worn as tattoos conveyed this belief. Animals, plants, trees, and stones possessed spiritual power. The New England Puritan belief in the supernatural, transcendent power of a single god held little meaning for Natives, who saw spirits inherent in the physical world. They summoned the power of these spirits for success in warfare, hunting, and farming. Natives could also antagonize the spirits that dwelled in nature. Overhunting, for instance, might provoke the spirits to make animals scarce. Animistic beliefs encouraged Indians to establish a balanced, respectful relationship with nature. Because of this, Natives have often been depicted as America's first ecologists. This ahistorical label obscures the ways in which they were not environmentalists in any modern sense. Animism fostered whatever restraint Natives practiced in their use of nature.

In the Algonquian language, the word *manitoo* referred to the spirit that dwelled in living and inanimate things. Roger Williams reported that it was the "general custom" of the Narragansett "to cry out *Manitoo*" whenever they saw "any Excellency in Men, Women, Birds, Beasts, Fish, etc."[14] Williams equated manitoo with God, rather than with the expression of divine spirit in all of its worldly forms. New England Algonquians communed with many deities that governed the workings of manitoo. Algonquians worshipped gods of animals, the sea, the sky, and the earth. Williams noted that the Narragansett had names for thirty-seven gods. Southern New England Indians, especially the Narragansett, exalted Cauntantowwit, who created the first people from wood. They buried their dead with their heads oriented to the southwest, the direction of Cauntantowwit's home. The Abenaki of northern New England did not worship a god like Cauntantowwit. They still fashioned an origins narrative—Gluskap, physical giant and Abenaki cultural hero, did not bring the world into being, but he did create all living things.

Manitoo enchanted the world; many gods inhabited the earthly temple; particular deities or cultural heroes created life; and powwows appealed to the god-spirits for Indian betterment. New England Puritans scorned the "diabolical" beliefs and practices of Native religion. Powwows were equated with witches, and the framework of Indian belief was disparaged as little more than devil worship. Allies in trade and war, Natives and colonists found little middle ground on matters of the spirit. New England's aboriginal people fell victim to imported diseases by the thousands, which the colonists saw as providential intervention that confirmed the superiority of their God.

### DISEASE AND DEPOPULATION

European diseases doomed far more Native people than firearms and severely undermined tribal life. Unable to halt the spread of disease, powwows found their authority drastically diminished when traditional rituals and remedies failed. Powwows themselves even fell victim to epidemic disease. Depleted bands and tribes scrambled to reconstitute themselves as functioning economic and political entities. Some formed alliances with English colonists; others pursued new ties with bands and tribes that had been spared from the initial epidemics. New England authorities and settlers typically welcomed the extermination of Indians as God's handiwork that served the biblical command to multiply and subdue the earth.

New England's coastal Natives were the first to be devastated by European diseases. Coastal tribes experienced the earliest contact with European fishermen, traders, and explorers—contact that quickened after 1600, when the English and French increasingly awakened to the prospects of New World settlement. Their fishing fleets, along with Portuguese and Basque ships, were visiting Newfoundland regularly by the 1580s and gradually pushed southward toward rich codfish grounds. In 1602, Bartholomew Gosnold commanded a major English exploratory voyage along the New England coast. He encountered a Basque shallop manned by eastern Abenaki in Maine waters. One Native, crew members recorded, was outfitted in European dress: "a waistcoat and breeches of black serge . . . [and] hose and shoes on his feet."[15] Gosnold sailed south, acquired geographical information from coastal Natives, and arrived at a teeming fishing area that members of his crew named "Cape Cod." Gosnold established a short-lived island settlement and traded with Indians on the mainland.

Gosnold's expedition suggests how Native people of New England increasingly came into contact with English—and French—explorers, traders, fishermen, and would-be settlers after 1600. These voyages furnished the home countries with new knowledge about the coast, especially its fertile fishing banks. Between 1600 and 1630, fishermen established seasonal camps on islands off the coast, from Monhegan to the Isles of Shoals and then, on the mainland, from Pemaquid in Maine to Cape Ann in Massachusetts. Some fishermen became year-round "settlers" at these sites. Well before boatloads of colonists arrived on New England's shores, then, coastal Natives had participated in numerous and varied encounters with Europeans. This early contact introduced deadly diseases to which Indians had not been exposed and against which they had not acquired immunity.

Historians and anthropologists have cited Native Americans'

migration to and isolation in the New World as explanations for their vulnerability to European contagions. Native creation myths held that aboriginal people had emerged in the New World. But scholars have documented how Siberian hunter-gatherer bands crossed into what is now Alaska thousands of years ago. Over generations, subarctic life served as a screen that filtered out pathogens. Separated from Europe by an ocean and isolated in the New World for centuries, Native Americans were not exposed to the epidemic diseases that ravaged the heavily populated Old World: bubonic plague, smallpox, measles, cholera, influenza, and dysentery. Even Native dogs succumbed to European canine microbes that the colonists' pets brought to the New World.

Of course Native populations hosted their own diseases. Archaeologists specializing in human biology have found tuberculosis, syphilis, intestinal infections, hepatitis, polio, and rheumatoid arthritis in Native remains. Infant mortality and dental problems appear to have been common as well. One reason Natives smoked, according to Roger Williams, was to relieve tooth pain. Still, European contagions proved far more destructive of Native lives than indigenous diseases and ailments.

Before permanent settlement clung to the shoreline, English and French contact infected Indian tribes from Maine to Massachusetts with pathogens that bred epidemics. In some locales, 75 to 90 percent of the Native population perished. Between 1616 and 1618, what was probably the plague devastated tribes from Massachusetts to Maine. Decimated by disease, the Massachusett, or "people of the great blue hill," mustered only minor resistance to the English settlers swarming over their land. The once powerful Wampanoag, who may have numbered fifteen thousand, shrank to approximately one thousand by the time the Mayflower dropped anchor. Nearly wiped out during the epidemic, Squanto's Patuxet left behind cleared fields surrounding Plymouth Harbor. A similar setting greeted a traveler in Agamenticus (York), Maine, several years after the epidemic of 1616–18. Forlorn Plymouth and Agamenticus were two of the many Indian "ghost" villages that attracted English colonists.

The human devastation that the epidemic visited on Native people posed unprecedented challenges to their leaders, challenges that extended beyond negotiating new alliances with the

English or stronger rival tribes. Faith in powwows eroded as their rituals and remedies failed to stem the trail of death. Remnant bands and tribes had to reconstitute themselves. Squanto unsuccessfully tried to revive the Patuxet, even as he served as an English-Wampanoag emissary and manipulated both sides. Other remnant bands blended together and reestablished villages. Disease, depopulation, and the arrival of English colonists transformed New England's diplomatic landscape into treacherous terrain. Historic antagonisms precluded pan-Indian alliances throughout the Colonial Era. One early sachem, the Narragansett's Miantonomi, did propose such an alliance; he was murdered by his Mohegan rival Uncas, with the complicity of English authorities, in 1643.

Disease and depopulation, along with their destabilizing effects on Native life, traveled from the coast toward interior villages. Epidemics often disrupted spring planting and fall harvest-ing; they affected cycles of fishing, hunting, and gathering. The resulting malnourishment increased Natives' susceptibility to disease, as did the overconsumption of alcohol. Early colonial writers recorded graphic descriptions of Native casualties Squanto and two Plymouth emissaries journeyed forty miles through Wampanoag country to meet with Massasoit in 1621. They reported that so many Natives had died from the epidemic of 1616–18 that survivors had not yet buried all the remains: "Skulls and bones were found in many places lying still above ground where their houses and dwellings had been; a very sad spectacle to behold."[16] Seeking to encourage prospective colonists to settle in New England, promotional writers stressed both the region's open landscape and the demise of the Native people who had cultivated the treeless fields.

Colonial New Englanders attributed the Indians' fate to providential design. "It pleased God to visit these Indians with a great sickness," noted Governor Bradford with gratitude. A Puritan poet boasted that epidemics constituted God's "fatal broom" that provided his people with "elbow room." This providential explanation for what historians define as ecological imperialism was not confined to Puritan New Englanders. Thomas Gorges, the Anglican deputy governor of Maine, found coastal Natives cooperative because "the Lord sent his avenging Angel and swept the most part away."[17] Disease, land hunger, and religious triumphalism propelled colonial settlement of Native land. In drastically reduced numbers, however, bands and tribes did survive the invasion of pathogens and people. Native people persisted as allies, enemies, and laborers. Weakened tribes also furnished subjects for Puritan missionaries to convert.

## FROM THE NATIVE SENSE OF PLACE
## TO "NEW ENGLAND"

New England Natives were linked by language and custom, but they displayed little sense of a pan-Algonquian identity, much less a pan-Indian one. Moreover, Native people did not perceive territory in terms of a regional identity like that expressed by the English with the name "New England." Yet Natives possessed a strong sense of place—the insiders' knowledge of, experience in, and bond to tribal homelands.

Migration, seasonable adaptation, and intertribal exchange deepened Native geographical knowledge of New England, which aided European explorers, traders, and settlers. Algonquian place names mapped the physical geography of tribal land and identified its natural resources. In Maine, Passamaquoddy referred to a place where pollock were abundant. New Hampshire's Amoskeag described the site of large waterfalls. In Rhode Island, Apponaug designated a spot abounding with shellfish, and Wabaquasett signaled a place where plants for making mats were found. Pokanoket identified cleared land in Plymouth. Agawam referred to sites in Massachusetts that were good for curing fish. Native place names charted the physical geography of tribal land and recorded how natural resources were used to sustain Algonquian life. Colonists often obtained "Indian deeds" fraudulently, but these documents were frequently filled with Native place names and landmarks (rock formations, special trees, water) that conveyed to the English an indigenous peoples' detailed knowledge of tribal terrain.

Petroglyphs and oral tradition also contributed to a Native sense of place. On cliffs and large rocks, many of them near important natural resource sites, Algonquians carved symbols, maps, and images of humans, animals, and objects such as canoes. These petroglyphs inscribed the Native experience in stone and imparted information to Indian travelers. Other inscriptions on the landscape recorded Natives' experience in that place. One Plymouth leader noted that his Indian neighbors dug holes in the ground "where any remarkable act is done." When the holes began to fill up or to become overgrown, "they will oft renew the same; by which many things of great antiquity are fresh in memory."[18] Individual and tribal lore fostered a narrative sense of place. Stories and legends endowed the spirit-imbued tribal landscape with historical and cultural importance. Oral tradition transmitted knowledge of the Native experience in warfare and hunting across generations. Legends and creation stories attributed physical features of tribal land to the heroic labors of Gluskap, the subject of a rich body of lore.

Oral tradition, petroglyphs, physical inscriptions, and place names all shaped a Native sense of place. In turn, English colonial promoters and settlers advanced an imperial conception of the New World landscape. They initiated a regional identity. "New England" summed up their vision for the territory long held by Algonquians.

Following historical convention, the preceding pages have employed the name New England to refer to the region from the precontact period forward. In fact, New England—both the name and the geocultural concept—was coined only shortly before permanent colonization began. Captain John Smith christened the Algonquian domain "New England." In 1616, Smith published his influential *Description of New England,* a promotional account of his coastal voyage between Monhegan Island and Cape Cod two years earlier. "New England" distilled Smith's geocultural vision of the region. Through the labor of industrious English colonists, the Natives' abundant, fertile, and seemingly underutilized land and open coastal fields would be transformed into a second England—a prosperous, pastoral, cultural extension of the homeland. Smith's promotional tract included a map that projected an imperial conception of the region (see fig. 3). Smith's map substituted English toponyms for Native American place names. The Charles River, Cape Ann, and Cape Elizabeth, for instance, honored members of the English royal family. As historical geographers have argued, naming a colonial land is among the first acts of imperialism. In this sense, Smith's New England paralleled New France and New Netherland; the

FIG. 3 John Smith, "New England," a label that originated as a cartographic and promotional idea that Smith publicized. This is a 1635 version of Smith's map, which was first published in 1616. Courtesy of the Osher Map Library, University of Southern Maine.

renaming of regions earmarked for colonial enterprise during the 1620s helped launch imaginative and then physical possession of Native territory.

Smith, the self-described "Admiral of New England," promoted his vision for Algonquian territory from 1616 to his death in 1631. Emphasizing the economic promise of the region, Smith described the sculpted Native coastal landscape as a "vacant" terrain that beckoned English settlers. Fertile soil, impressive stores of fish, abundant timber, a temperate climate in southern parts—these attributes of the Algonquian realm fired Smith's imagination for the creation of a productive English shire in the New World.

The "Admiral" conferred with John Winthrop before the Puritan leader set sail for New England in 1630. For the imperial Smith and the reformist Puritan governor alike, the name "New England" announced a quest for cultural continuity with the homeland. The region would be a second England—a productive, prosperous English world. Smith praised the Puritans as the embodiment of "Industry herself." He also recorded his hope that "my aged endeavors" will now be fulfilled.[19] But for the Puritans, Native land loomed not just as an economic prospect but as a moral terrain. They imagined New England as a terra firma for glorifying God, purifying the Church of England, and forging a reformed new English social order.

"New England" and other English place names set in motion

FIG. 4 Seal of the Massachusetts Bay Colony. Courtesy of Massachusetts Archives.

an imaginative displacement of Native people from their homeland. Yet not even so formidable a confluence of factors managed to erase Indians from the regional landscape, not new geographical labels, disease, war, not the invasion of land-hungry, trade-oriented, and religiously motivated colonists. The official seal of the Massachusetts Bay Colony depicted a "savage" Native warrior appealing to the English, in language from the book of Acts in the Bible, "Come Over and Help Us" (see fig. 4). This image recalls the Puritans' limited success in Christianizing Native people, one of the goals of colonization. It also suggests how throughout the seventeenth century and beyond, Natives persisted in New England not only as prospective converts but as neighbors, allies, enemies, laborers, whalers, and figures in the regional imagination.

# TWO

# Puritan New England, 1620–1660

THE BIRTH OF COLONIAL New England was very distinctive. Between 1620 and 1642, more than twenty-one thousand settlers landed on the region's coastlines. The bulk of these colonists journeyed to New England during the "Great Migration" that persisted for nearly a decade and a half beginning in 1629. Though the migrants were a mix of "saints" and "strangers," Puritans constituted the clear majority. They shaped the settlement of Massachusetts Bay and Connecticut, the region's largest colonies. The religious/cultural values and demographic characteristics of New England's Puritan settlers distinguished the two Bible commonwealths from all other New World colonial societies.

The Puritan participants in the Great Migration represented unusually rich "human capital" for a colonial people.[1] Their piety encouraged worldly activity and improvement. Religious idealism fostered industry and enterprise. Work was understood as a "calling" or vocation that glorified God. Puritanism enshrined self-discipline, the stewardship of wealth, and competency—the pursuit of a middling or "sufficient" level of prosperity. A religion of the printed and spoken word rather than of sacraments, ceremony, and churchly sensualism, Puritanism promoted literacy, education, and what became the best-developed collective identity of any English colonial region. During the course of the first generation, a distinctive civic culture emerged from colony-wide and town-based governments with strong representative elements. The growth of locally controlled churches and schools further strengthened civic life.

Beyond such religious/cultural resources, the demographic characteristics of the Puritan migration also defined New England's distinctive origins and early history. In contrast to other New World settlements, families of the "middling sort" sustained the Great Migration, not impoverished single young men. From its founding, New England's population was far more gender-balanced than England's Chesapeake and Caribbean colonial societies. With its temperate climate, New England also proved to be much healthier. The region's population swelled as a result of the high birthrate and low death rate. Large, healthy families made the region's population more youthful than other English colonies. In sum, a distinctive demography, a dynamic religious culture, and an evolving civic order set Massachusetts and Connecticut apart from other colonial societies.

## PURIFYING OLD ENGLAND

The religious dissenters and reformers in the homeland, many of whom journeyed to the New World, did not identify themselves as "Puritans." Their opponents minted that label; it ridiculed dissenters in the Church of England, depicting them as moral "precisionists," that is, perfectionists. Reformed Protestantism acquired its own dynamism. In this religion of "protest," dissent begat new dissent; reformers disagreed over theology, church governance, and their relationship to England's religious establishment. Some historians question whether a coherent "Puritan movement" ever really existed in England. Despite the diversity of the reformers and the scornful origins of the term, "Puritanism" suggests common elements shared by English religious dissenters in both England and New England. As English historian William Hunt has aptly put it, a "Puritan who minds his own business is a contradiction in terms."[2] Puritans were reformers, improvers, activists; their "purifying" impulse extended well beyond the established church. The Puritans who eventually made their way to New England sought nothing less than the moral renovation of a troubled English nation. They longed to fulfill the promise of the Protestant Reformation and also to restore a stable, industrious social order that Puritan reformers associated with an idealized English past.

The century that followed King Henry VIII's repudiation of the Roman Catholic Church in 1534 brought repeated disappointments to religious reformers in the homeland. The king assumed leadership of the independent Church of England, but the Romish trappings of the old religious establishment persisted. A powerful religious hierarchy, for example, dominated the Church. The English king replaced the Pope as the head of the Church. Monarchs installed archbishops and bishops and, through them, controlled parish appointments. This state-church alliance regulated religious life and stifled dissenters, who advocated the continuing de-Romanization of the Anglican establishment. Moreover, the Church became a political arm of the crown; the king often directed the clergy to preach in support of specific royal positions.

Beyond hierarchy, other Roman Catholic vestiges continued to define worship in the Church of England. Puritan reformers rejected the mechanical recitation of official prayers. They objected to the role of rituals, icons, and symbols, such as making the sign of the cross or displaying the crucifix during worship. They also scowled at priestly vestments and organ music. "We call you Puritans," one English clergymen proclaimed, "not because you are purer than other men ... but because you think yourselves to be purer."[3]

Yet English Puritanism was not simply a movement based on being holier-than-thou. Puritan dissenters possessed their own powerful and appealing vision of a reformed church. They stressed the role of direct communication between the individual and God. This "priesthood of all believers" reduced the role of sacraments, clergy, and ritualized formal worship as a means of attaining God's grace. Puritans envisioned a "primitive" and apostolic church shorn of the entrenched human accretions that had corrupted both Roman and Anglican establishments. Puritans put preaching rather than ceremony at the center of public worship. They encouraged believers to read the Bible and rely on individual and voluntary group prayer to cultivate personal piety. Indeed, Puritanism redistributed religious authority away from the institutional church to the individual, away from ceremonial public worship to the personal and interior spiritual lives of believers. Sermons by educated Puritan clergy clarified the meaning of the Bible and promoted the practice of piety.

And salvation resulted from a person's direct encounter with God.

Following the teachings of John Calvin, the sixteenth-century Swiss reformist theologian, Puritan clergy preached the need for a transforming spiritual rebirth, not the more gradual accumulation of grace through churchly sacraments and practices. As "Calvinists," Puritans emphasized humanity's morally fallen status, as derived from Adam's original sin. They also exalted God's absolute sovereignty in determining the recipients of saving grace. But since no one knew for certain who would be saved, Puritans were encouraged to strive in the hope that they would be among the chosen. Life, then, was conceived as a pilgrimage—a journey through the world, with all of its temptations, that could lead to the city of God.

Some English religious dissenters, like the "Pilgrims" who settled in Plymouth, had lost hope for reform within the Church of England and turned to "Separatism." Most English Puritans, including the preponderance of those who settled in New England, were nonseparating reformers. They imagined that the purification of the established church would proceed from local congregations. Puritans asserted the rights of local bodies of worship and resisted the intrusion of the state-church hierarchy. After decades of persecution and then accommodation, Puritan reformers confronted renewed displays of state-church authority during the years surrounding the Great Migration.

In 1625, Charles I ascended the throne and quickly revealed Catholic sympathies. He affirmed the full ceremonialism of Anglican worship and sought to impose conformity on Puritan dissenters. To press his conformist campaign, Charles depended on a formidable figure, a man long remembered and reviled in New England colonial annals as the scourge of the region's religious founders. William Laud was appointed Bishop of London in 1628 and Archbishop of Canterbury in 1633. The dismissal of dissenting ministers, prosecution of laypeople in church courts, and censorship of Puritan literature all followed Laud's rise to power. Parliament offered no means of relief, since Charles had dismissed Parliament in 1629, launching more than a decade of autocratic rule. The Protestant Reformation seemed not only to grind to a halt; it appeared to have reversed course altogether.

During the 1620s and 1630s England's longstanding social and economic problems worsened, deepening a sense of gloom for Puritans. Much of the turmoil stemmed from England's ongoing shift from a manor-based to a market-oriented economy. The burgeoning of a "masterless class" in England and the decline of cloth manufacturing particularly troubled Puritans, who then set their sights on the New World. To boost agricultural productivity, market-oriented lords fenced in the fields and common land that formed their estates. Farm families and laborers were increasingly displaced at a time when England's population was surging. Unemployment, poverty, beggary, and crime afflicted the countryside. England's problems swelled the ranks of men and women who seemed to have lost control over their lives. Successive crop failures for three years beginning in 1628 added to the homeland's plight. In commercialized parts of England, such as Suffolk County in East Anglia, which sent large numbers of Puritan migrants to New England, the cloth industry suffered a major decline in the 1620s, one that aroused concerns for the homeland's future. In fact, one of the most heavily commercialized parts of England—an area that stretched from London northeast through Essex, Suffolk, and Norfolk counties and southeast to Sussex County—emerged as the heartland of Puritan migration.

Puritanism held great appeal to pious, literate, and enterprising middling men and women in England—property-owning families who inhabited commercialized towns or "urbanized" communities. The movement attracted artisans, merchants, clothiers, and propertied farmers, people who, with the assistance of Puritan religious values, had acquired some discipline and mastery over their lives, lives that now seemed threatened. It is difficult, then, to sort out the religious and economic impulses that provoked migration. The Puritans saw worldly activity and success as a way of worshiping God. They also viewed England's problems in the 1620s and 1630s as providential afflictions for the nation's failure to create a reformed Protestant church and nation. And some Puritan leaders believed that further providential judgments were about to descend on England. "The Lord hath admonished, threatened, corrected, and astonished us," John Winthrop confided to his wife in 1629, "yet we grow worse and worse, so as his spirit will not always strive with us, he must give way to his fury at last."[4] Migration offered a refuge from the homeland's distress. The Puritans' "New England" signaled a quest to fulfill the promise of the English Reformation. It also captured a longing to restore a prosperous and disciplined social order unlike what prevailed in England under Charles I.

## THE SIGNIFICANCE OF PLYMOUTH

The storied settlement at Plymouth preceded the Puritan colonization of New England. In 1620, thirteen years after the founding of Jamestown in Virginia, Plymouth marked the birth of the first permanent colony in New England. By the early nineteenth century, Plymouth, the Pilgrims, Thanksgiving, and the rock where the first settlers supposedly stepped ashore had been woven into a regional creation myth. After the bicentennial of 1820, the story of Plymouth became an epic narrative of American origins. But from a seventeenth-century perspective, and especially in comparison to Puritan colonization, Plymouth's significance falls well short of its mythologized standing in the American imagination.

The settlers of Plymouth were both too small in number and too divided between religious dissenters and worldly "strangers"—secular-minded individuals recruited for military or economic purposes—to engender intolerance or attract the notice of the world beyond their plantation in any meaningful way. Plymouth's pious leaders were known as Separatists, not Pilgrims. They had lost hope that the Church of England would alter its "Romish" hierarchy, sacramental ceremonialism, and sensual practices. Unlike the New England Puritans, Plymouth's religious founders distanced themselves from both the homeland and its established church; they were not part of a transatlantic reform movement.

Nor did the sectarian planters of Plymouth share John Smith's imperial vision. Separatists withdrew to the New World. As one of their leaders explained, "our dwelling is but a wandering, and our abiding is but a fleeting, and in a word our home is nowhere."[5] In contrast to their Puritan neighbors, early Plymouth settlers lacked the intellectual leadership, the commitment to literacy, and the support of education—cultural resources that were central to such developments as the fashioning of a regional identity. The Separatists did not have an ordained minister until

1629, and it would be decades before Plymouth claimed its first graduate of Harvard, the Puritan college founded in 1636.

The Separatists themselves comprised a minority of the population in early Plymouth. Of the 102 passengers on the May-flower, only 40 were Separatists. Others, including Miles Standish and John Alden—both became legendary figures in the nineteenth century—were strangers. Between 1621 and 1623 three more ships transported small groups of settlers to Plymouth in which strangers outnumbered "saints." Less than 400 people journeyed to Plymouth in its early years. Clearly, the peopling of the plantation constituted no "Great Migration."

Though the fabled rock is not even mentioned in Plymouth's annals until well over a century after the landing of the Separatists and strangers, the first Thanksgiving in 1621 is documented. The boisterous affair, however, hardly resembled what later generations imagined—a placid feast dominated by pious settlers. Native Americans placed their own stamp on an event that derived from England's annual harvest home festivals. More than ninety Wampanoag accompanied Massasoit to the three-day celebration. Devastated by the hardship of their first winter, only fifty English settlers participated in the feast. Plymouth's leading historical archaeologist has argued that the 1621 festivities were often disorderly, even raucous. Recreational activities such as marksmanship contests with guns and bows and arrows punctuated rounds of consuming abundant food and drink. The sounds of Natives and English struggling across language barriers certainly filled the air, as did the scent of roasting deer and fowl. Native people and strangers, not staid Separatists, probably dominated the merriment of the first Thanksgiving. In the following years, Plymouth developed as a colony of pious people and worldly strangers who inhabited small settlements stretching from Cape Cod to the Wampanoag homeland around Mount Hope Bay.

The mythologized story of its founding aside, what is Plymouth's significance for colonial New England history beyond its distinction as the region's original permanent English settlement? First, Plymouth's survival aided the founding of its much larger neighbor, Massachusetts Bay. Agricultural products and meat helped sustain the Puritan colony's early settlers. The Puritans' migration launched New England's first economic boom, as enterprises rushed to meet the needs of thousands of new colonists for provisions and services. Plymouth participated in this commercial expansion, bolstered by a major change in the colony's structure that occurred in the mid-1620s. In its first years Plymouth was a collectivist experiment. Colonists held land and farmed communally. But productivity lagged and food shortages emerged. Beginning in 1624, Governor William Bradford loosened the colony's socio-religious communal policies; he acceded to the distribution and sale of land. Massachusetts and other colonies in the region would follow suit, abandoning not the *idea* of communalism but modifying settlement plans on the ground. Thus, from Plymouth forward the expectation of an independent "freehold" would fuel the settlement and expansion of New England.

The change in Plymouth's structure encouraged agricultural productivity, which was also spurred by the market that resulted from the Great Migration. Plymouth's new land policy also dispersed the colony's population. Bradford even feared that Plymouth, the founding settlement by the harbor, would become a ghost town. John Winthrop would confront similar problems in Massachusetts Bay. Puritanism bequeathed a dual legacy of communalism and individualism. Winthrop would learn how to articulate and uphold communal religious ideals, exemplified by his "City upon a Hill" sermon, while acknowledging the individualism, ethos of improvement, and worldly enterprise that sprang from the Puritan faith.

## THE PURITAN MISSION AND WORK CULTURE

Both John F. Kennedy and Ronald Reagan quoted Winthrop's words describing the city upon a hill, and many others have used the phrase to explain how New England's Puritan founders forged the American sense of mission in the world. Yet the early settlers of New England were uprooted English men and women. Wrenched from their homeland, many migrants wrestled with doubts about their New World experiment. When Winthrop claimed that the "eyes of all people are upon us," he was not boldly announcing a sense of universal mission. Rather, he was referring to the audience of English Puritan critics who complained that the departure of devout people for a risky colonial venture would hurt the religious reform movement at home. "It will be a great worry to our church to take away the good people," Winthrop reported of critics' complaints, "and we shall lay it [England] more open to the [Providential] judgment feared."[6] Furthermore, during England's Protestant Reformation, leaders widely cited the biblical image of the city upon a hill (drawn from Matthew 5:14–15) to suggest how the homeland loomed as a "chosen" nation. Interestingly, Winthrop failed to invoke the "city upon a hill" trope after he settled in New England. (His original sermon was not even published until 1838.)

Winthrop believed that the "God of Israel" would be "among us." The Puritans named the first town in Massachusetts Salem, short for Jerusalem. But references to "New Israelites" and a "New Jerusalem" were not proclamations that New England's founders saw themselves as a chosen people destined to create an elect nation, a purely *American* city upon a hill. Puritans often employed "New Israelites" to identify the godly or spiritually reborn believers of a transatlantic English world. As the distinguished Puritan divine John Cotton told Winthrop's departing party in 1630, "be not unmindful of our Jerusalem at home, whether you leave us or stay at home with us."[7]

The Puritans did journey to their "new" England on a mission, though it was one not quite as grand as interpreters of their rhetoric have often claimed. New England offered a shelter, temporary in the minds of the many migrants who continued to own property at home in the hopes of one day returning to a reformed England or as a hedge against the failure of transatlantic settlement. In their New World sanctuary, Puritan migrants might escape the calamities about to descend on England, from which New England would provide a refuge for at least one remnant of God's people, who would develop and harbor purified forms of worship in anticipation of reexporting them to the homeland. The region also presented fertile land and commercial opportunities where industrious, enterprising improvers could recreate a stable, productive English social order. Puritans migrated in order to build a "new" England, not just to pursue purified religious worship.

In New England, an abundance of Native land, large supplies of fish and timber, and maritime trade with Europe and Caribbean slave societies reinforced Puritan industry and enterprise.

But if religious values and the New World setting promoted earthly success, they also created tensions within Puritanism. As historians have long observed, Puritans faced the dilemma of living *in* the world while not living *for* the world.

The productive religious-cultural values that large numbers of Puritans transported to New England constitute one of the distinctive aspects of the region's founding and development. Captain John Smith recognized that Puritanism cultivated personal discipline and industry among its adherents. Work was not simply drudgery required to sustain life. For Puritans it acquired the character of a vocation—a calling through which one improved the world, redeemed time, glorified God, and followed life's pilgrimage toward salvation. The stewardship of wealth defined another religious ideal that buttressed the Puritan dedication to self-discipline and work as a calling. Economic success, the fruit of human industry and God's blessing, did not justify material indulgence. Prosperous Puritans needed to consider themselves the stewards or caretakers of wealth. In both England and New England, Puritans were urged to be producers rather than consumers. Instead of spending most of their profits, for example, Puritanism encouraged successful merchants and farmers to reinvest money to create more jobs and more industrious citizens, who would in turn contribute to a productive society and a vital, expansive church. Puritanism also endorsed the quest for a worldly "competency" or "sufficiency." Competency defined a middling way of life, not an indulgent one. Puritans were to pursue sufficient comfort and economic self-reliance, not "luxuries" or material accumulation for their own sake.

Competency, industry, self-discipline, and stewardship were, of course, religious ideals; they did not automatically translate into pious practice. Whether within the entrepreneurial and literate regions of England that served as Puritan seedbeds or among the migrants who departed for New England, however, religious ideals shaped behavior. They also posed a dilemma for Puritans, especially in New England, with its commercial opportunities and abundant land. A year before he departed for New England, John Winthrop summed up the Puritan dilemma: "O Lord, crucify the world unto me that though I cannot avoid to live among the baits and snares of it, . . . I may not otherwise love, use, or delight in any [of] the most pleasant, profitable, etc.

earthly comforts of this life, than I do the air which I continually draw in."[8] We might enlarge Winthrop's description of the Puritan dilemma as follows: Religious ideals spurred worldly activity and success. But any such prosperity posed a threat to the productive ideals—competency, industry, and stewardship—that Puritanism cultivated in the first place. As ministers often put it, prosperity tempted people to redefine luxuries as "competencies."

Puritan religious ideals taught believers to live disciplined lives and thereby lead efforts to reform their local worlds. The English turmoil of the 1620s and 1630s challenged this aspiration. Puritans seemed to be losing mastery of their lives and control of local reform. New England offered a refuge where pious people would reassemble a work-centered, disciplined society committed to ordered liberty.

Religious migrants set out for the colonies, then, with far more than a purified church in mind. They thirsted for reform of "Merry Old England." Puritans yearned for the establishment of a strict holy Sabbath in the New World without the games and celebrations that undermined the sobriety of Sundays in the homeland. They wished to purge the calendar of holy days—including Christmas and Easter—and root out the custom of "Saint Monday," a medieval remnant of "undisciplined" workers. Through civil-religious regulations and self-discipline, Puritans strove to suppress unproductive English social behavior such as the drunkenness, rowdiness, and petty crime associated with the homeland's thriving alehouse world. In New England, Puritan authority contained but failed to eradicate the traditions of Merry Old England. Still, religious ideals inspired reforms that fostered a productive, work-centered way of life. One economic historian has estimated that sweeping alterations to England's ecclesiastical calendar eliminated numerous holy days and religious feasts and substantially boosted available work days in Massachusetts to more than 300 per year. In Puritanism's work-centered moral economy, able-bodied men who failed to achieve a competency had only themselves to blame.

## THE GREAT MIGRATION

The Puritans' religious ideals and reformist aspirations constituted one distinctive aspect of New England's colonization.

The demographic characteristics of the Puritan participants in the Great Migration were another. Of course, the approximately 21,000 saints and strangers who stepped ashore during those years were only a small portion of the tens of thousands who forsook the homeland in the seventeenth century and resettled in southern or Caribbean colonies. More than 100,000 migrants journeyed to England's southern outposts and over twice that number to its Caribbean colonies. In contrast to New England, thousands of impoverished and unfree young Englishmen perished in tropical and semitropical settlements.

The Puritans and strangers who sailed to New England during the Great Migration were overwhelmingly English. These founding settlers and their descendants shaped the region's population through the seventeenth century and beyond. From the end of the Great Migration to the close of the seventeenth century, more people left New England than settled in it. Aided by a healthy, temperate climate, New England's population expanded through natural increase. During the Great Migration the region received approximately five percent of the white migrants who came to the English colonies before 1700. Remarkably, despite the net loss of migrants in the decades after 1642, the descendants of New England's founders probably represented over 40 percent of the European population in colonial America in 1700. Diverse people always inhabited New England's colonies, as the migration of strangers and the continuing presence of thousands of Native people in the seventeenth century suggest. But compared to other English New World societies, the region emerged as the most Anglo corner of colonial America. New England's population surged through natural increase from the original English settlers, whereas ongoing infusions of new people—white and black, free and bound—transformed other English colonies.

Nevertheless, it was not so much the relative cultural homogeneity of the first settlers and their descendants that marked New England as a distinctive colonial society. Other demographic characteristics of the Great Migration underscored the region's difference. Middling families filled the ranks of the Puritan movement to New England. Neither the impoverished nor the wealthy migrated in significant numbers. Though they brought many bound servants to the region, Puritan families arrived as a free people who had paid for their own transportation across the Atlantic. As a result of the Great Migration, from its founding New England maintained an unusually balanced sex ratio for a colonial society. In England's early Chesapeake colonies, male settlers outnumbered females by six to one; in New England the ratio was three men for every two women. Early New England's social landscape encompassed impoverished people and indentured servants. Yet the dominant patterns of Puritan migration yielded a heavily free, family-centered, middle-class society of wide property ownership, a sharp contrast to the social reality of other New World colonies.

The Puritan participants in the Great Migration also represented the most literate and educated colonists to settle in the New World in the seventeenth century. They adhered to a religion of the word; Puritanism stressed the importance of print in the form of the Bible, sermons, and devotional tracts. Puritanism appealed to people in England's most modernized, commercial locations, where literacy—and numeracy—were central to economic activity. Though figures are not precise, at least 60 percent of males in New England around 1650 could read *and* write. The seventeenth century defined writing as more of a male skill that was important for commerce. Literacy for Puritan women centered on the ability to read for religious improvement, a skill widely possessed by pious females in early New England. Not surprisingly, the first two print shops in English-speaking America were established in Cambridge (1640) and Boston (1675).

In addition to a literate laity, the Great Migration transported a cadre of well over a hundred college-educated leaders to New England. Graduates of Cambridge and Oxford, the highly educated elite among the founders consisted primarily of ministers but also included lawyers such as John Winthrop. Harvard, America's oldest college, was founded in 1636 to sustain the Puritan commitment to an educated ministry. Colonial America's second college, William and Mary, would not be established in Virginia until 1693, two generations later.

Educated leaders, access to publication, literacy, and support of schooling reinforced New England's distinctive founding and early history. Over time, the region's print culture generated a powerful Puritan collective consciousness. The founders' pious offspring would recall the Great Migration as a heroic pilgrimage of saintly ancestors—though Native Americans experienced it as a deadly invasion, of course. For colonial historians, New England's settlement represents a "great" migration not because of its size, which was modest compared to the movement of people to other New World English settlements, but because of the Puritans' productive religious ideals and uncommon demographic characteristics for a colonial society.

## SETTLEMENT AND RESETTLEMENT:
## MASSACHUSETTS AND CONNECTICUT

The populating of Massachusetts and Connecticut is sometimes described as a "great reshuffling." After landfall and temporary residency, migrants often organized themselves, reconstituting groups based on place of origin, variations in Puritan belief or practice, and economic interests. By 1640, twenty towns dotted the Massachusetts and Connecticut landscape. Twenty years later, the two colonies boasted approximately seventy towns. In 1660, Massachusetts held nearly two-thirds of New England's estimated white population of almost 33,000, dwarfing its Connecticut neighbor (nearly 8,000). Together these Bible commonwealths held about 85 percent of the region's European inhabitants. (Of course, not all of these colonists were religious-minded Puritans.) New England originated and developed as a town-centered region with a landscape far different from England's Chesapeake colonies.

In 1630 Winthrop's fleet sailed for Salem, where a Puritan beachhead had been established a year earlier at a fishing plantation. Disappointed with conditions at Salem, Winthrop diverted his settlers southward toward Boston, where towns such as Cambridge, Charlestown, Dedham, Dorchester, Medford, Roxbury, and Watertown were launched. "That it might not be forgotten whence they came," observed William Hubbard, an early Puritan historian, the settlers imprinted "some remembrance of their former habitations in England upon their new dwellings in America."[9] The colonists' ties to England went beyond the transfer of town and county place names. Puritan migrants imposed cultural order on their new physical world by applying familiar geographic terms and classifications to the New England landscape. Through the use of English descriptive categories—brook, pond, marsh, orchard, and fen, for example—Puritans as-

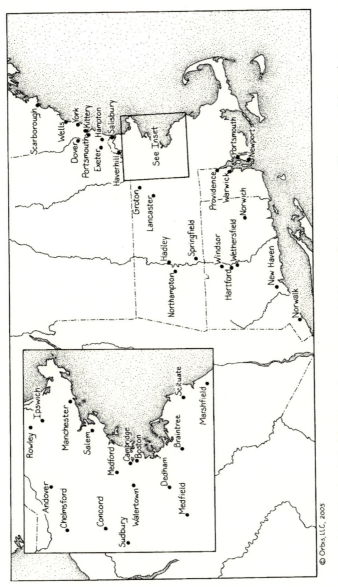

FIG. 5 New England Towns, ca. 1660. Courtesy of Worcester Art Museum, Worcester, Massachusetts.

© Orbis, LLC, 2005

sociated the regional landscape with the familiar physical world they had left behind. For all their dissatisfaction with the homeland, New England was to be a "transplanted English vine."

Town-founding accelerated until the Great Migration subsided in the early 1640s. During the years of heavy migration, towns were founded north of Boston, from Essex County to New Hampshire. Settlement also stretched to the fertile Connecticut River Valley, whose more than four-hundred-mile course from Canada to Long Island Sound led Reverend Cotton Mather to describe it as the "American Nile." In 1636, William Pynchon, a devout Puritan and ambitious entrepreneur, led a group of Roxbury residents to resettle in Springfield. Pynchon's movement is an indication of the kind of shuffling that was common in the 1630s. He arrived in New England with Winthrop's fleet and then moved from Dorchester to Roxbury to Springfield over six years. His early restlessness was a product of religious disagreements and his economic ambition. Pynchon and his family endured in Springfield. They controlled the fur trade down the Connecticut River, invested in land and shops, and built a commercial empire. His "company town" included tenant farming and social inequality on a scale that was unusual for seventeenth-century New England.

More equitable policies governed the founding of most early Massachusetts and Connecticut towns and regulated the distribution of "common" land. Towns were often founded by men who organized themselves into a proprietary group and acquired a land grant from a colonial government. These town proprietors assumed responsibility for surveying and allocating land, laying out roads, and providing a meetinghouse and minister. In the first generation, the vast majority of the adult male heads of families—if not all of them—received "proprietary" rights. That is, they acquired land as a freehold, often between ten and fifty acres in fields, pasturage, and woodlots. The size and status of the family and the household head's contribution to the town's founding determined how much land would be allocated. Most important, founding males held proprietary rights to the town's common lands, which were distributed over time. Some towns held town land for decades and distributed it in small amounts; other towns divided their land more rapidly in large chunks. With the original town grant and further allocations, founding families accumulated freeholds that typically ranged between 100 and 200 acres.

Piety and demographics fueled land hunger and the founding of Puritan towns. The Biblical injunction to multiply, subdue, and improve the land pervaded the Puritans' work-centered creed. One of the most famous migrants in the 1630s, Reverend Richard Mather, patriarch of the famous clerical clan, in 1638 even named his son Increase. Land undergirded the quest for a competency. A substantial freehold, moreover, was critical to patriarchal authority and to the perpetuation of a family economy. Puritan fathers headed large families; four to five sons were very common. Faced with abundant land and scarce labor, fathers in New England depended on their sons as workers. Land gave fathers some leverage over their male offspring. The easiest way for a son to establish his own "competency" was through inheriting part of his father's land. In other words, sons continued to work on a family freehold into early adulthood with the prospect of acquiring a deed to a father's land. Inherited land also served as a form of "social security" for elderly parents who made arrangements with sons for support and care.

The Chesapeake colonies developed a vastly different social and physical landscape from town-centered New England. In the South, huge tracts of land were granted to men of wealth and influence rather than to groups of middling settlers who shared proprietorship. Large counties with "plantations" defined the seventeenth-century South, not small towns. Chesapeake planters kept their large landholdings intact through primogeniture, the practice in which the eldest son inherits his father's property. Further, in contrast to New England's large freeholding population, the Chesapeake colonies depended heavily on the labor of tenant farmers, indentured servants, and black slaves.

The physical differences between the plantation South and town-centered New England should not summon familiar images of a tidy, compact Puritan landscape. No white-steepled meetinghouses or manicured greens graced seventeenth-century New England towns. Even during the first generation, New England settlements were not as compact as is often assumed, nor were they quite the "peaceable kingdoms" that later generations, including some historians, have imagined.

The Puritan founders of Massachusetts and Connecticut transferred to New England not only English town names and a familiar geographic lexicon; they also transplanted customary English settlement patterns, which included both open and enclosed field principles. Puritans from areas of England where the manor system had remained strong often adopted an open field town plan in the New World (see fig. 6). In open field towns, settlers acquired small house lots in a central village. Farmland, pas-

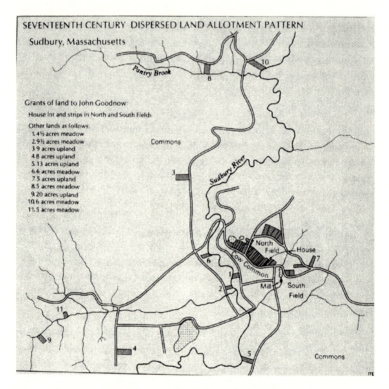

SEVENTEENTH CENTURY DISPERSED LAND ALLOTMENT PATTERN
Sudbury, Massachusetts

Pantry Brook

Grants of land to John Goodnow:
House lot and strips in North and South Fields

Other lands as follows:
1. 4½ acres meadow
2. 9½ acres meadow
3. 9 acres upland
4. 8 acres upland
5. 13 acres upland
6. 6 acres meadow
7. 5 acres upland
8. 5 acres meadow
9. 20 acres upland
10. 6 acres meadow
11. 5 acres meadow

Commons

Sudbury River

North Field — House
Low Common
Mill — South Field

Commons

FIG. 6 Sudbury, Mass., Open-Field Town. This shows the scattered grants of land to Sudbury inhabitant John Goodnow in the seventeenth century. Sudbury had a central village with open fields surrounding it. In more common closed-field towns, farmers consolidated their landholdings into outlying farmsteads, leaving sparsely settled town centers. Plate XV, "Grants of Land to John Goodnow, Sudbury" from Sumner Chilton Powell's *Puritan Village: The Formation of a New England Town* © 1963 by Wesleyan University, reprinted by permission of Wesleyan University Press.

turage, and woodlots held by the town in common were parceled out in strips, where neighbors held land next to each other in a series of open fields. Farmers walked from the central village to their outlying acreage, which was scattered in the open fields surrounding their house lots. Enclosed field towns established a more dispersed pattern of settlement. In these towns, Puritan settlers were able to consolidate house lots, planting fields, pasturage, and woodlots on enclosed farmsteads. Consequently, unlike open field towns, enclosed field settlements developed with spare village centers. The typically plain, unpainted, and steepleless New England meetinghouse and a few dwellings occupied the town center. Meetinghouse lots, which would not be transformed into beautiful commons or greens until the nineteenth century, remained treeless, grassless, unkempt places scarred by the crisscrossings of people, horses, and oxen in the Colonial Era.

An enclosed field system and a dispersed pattern of settlement emerged as the prevailing social arrangement in New England farming towns. As early as 1635 the Massachusetts General Court issued an order regulating the settlement of new towns in response to the dispersal of land-hungry migrants: "Hereafter no dwelling house shall be built above half a mile from the meetinghouse, in any new plantation, granted at this Court, or hereafter to be granted, without leave from the Court."[10] This regulation proved difficult to enforce, and in 1640 it was abandoned. In some towns farmers quickly began exchanging and purchasing lots in open fields, converting their scattered holdings into contiguous farms. In other towns, proprietors found it was easier to attract settlers with land policies that encouraged enclosed fields and a dispersed pattern of settlement. Even in the Connecticut Valley, where compact settlement persisted, the availability of land and the growth of the population eroded the open field system. Across seventeenth-century New England, large families with sons who required land to achieve their own competency strained the open field system and accelerated population dispersal. Of course, the region never approached the decentralized settlement landscape of the colonial South. New England remained a town-centered region. Coastal and river towns, positioned to engage in trade, preserved central cores. Many of the region's agricultural towns, however, did not resemble the compact, orderly white villages that bloomed in the nineteenth century. More often than not, the colonial New England town was a collection of dispersed villages and hamlets.

Nor were early Puritan towns free of conflict. Disagreements over the size and quality of land allocations stirred up acrimony. Townspeople argued over the location of the meetinghouse and the eligibility of voters in local affairs. They sometimes differed in doctrinal emphasis and religious practice. Puritanism, after all, was a faith of dissent, not a seamless, monolithic movement.

The early history of Connecticut reveals some of the religious and economic tensions within the Puritan settlement that colonists sought to resolve by remigration. The Puritan colonization of Connecticut originated in 1635 as part of the reshuffling of people that accompanied the Great Migration. The colony's founders left Cambridge, Dorchester, and Watertown in Massachusetts for the fertile Connecticut Valley. The largest group originated in Cambridge and was led by Reverend Thomas Hooker, one of early New England's most distinguished divines. In 1635, Hooker shepherded his congregation, along with 160 cattle and sizeable flocks of sheep and swine, as they undertook their own "great migration." They followed the Connecticut Path blazed by Native Americans and settled in Hartford, which joined with two other "river towns," Windsor and Wethersfield, to form the colony of Connecticut.

Connecticut's founders, like Springfield's William Pynchon, left eastern Massachusetts for a combination of economic and religious reasons. Hooker, for instance, complained to Massachusetts authorities that his people lacked "accommodation for their cattle" and were therefore unable to "receive any more of their friends" from England. Dissatisfied with the size and quality of their land in Cambridge, Hooker's followers were drawn by the "fruitfullness and commodiousness of Connecticut," as Governor Winthrop put it.[11] Hooker also questioned what he saw as the overly strict church admission requirements that were emerging in Massachusetts. Significantly, unlike Massachusetts, Connecticut did not require voters to be spiritually reborn full church members.

Remigrants from the Bay Colony and settlers from England planted other settlements in the 1630s and 1640s on Long Island Sound, at Saybrook, and on former Pequot land, later named

New London, on the Thames River. The colony at New Haven developed into the most important of these coastal settlements. Its founding suggests again the interplay within Puritanism of worldly and religious aspirations. New Haven also underscores the role of economic ambition in resettlement decisions.

Many of the original colonists of New Haven were members of the Reverend John Davenport's church in London; they had arrived in Boston in 1637. Davenport, like Hooker, was a powerful preacher, which was the key to gathering a large following and to securing a Puritan divine's reputation. In contrast to Hooker, though, Davenport and his followers fully accepted Massachusetts' policies on church membership and on restricted voting. Religious differences with the Massachusetts Bay Colony, then, did not create the friction that sparked the founding of New Haven. Rather, London merchants who had journeyed to Boston with their preacher sought a location of their own to pursue commercial activities. Instead of competing with already established Boston traders, the former London merchants founded a commercial port at Quinnipiac, a Native American site, in 1638. By 1640, when the settlement was renamed New Haven, a few hundred colonists, Londoners and others recruited from Massachusetts, made up the independent colony. Over the next two decades, New Haven and other coastal and river settlements would be absorbed by the original river towns, thereby creating the new Puritan colony of Connecticut.

In early New England, then, families sorted themselves in their pursuit of Puritan religious and economic aspirations. Generational persistence in new towns followed remigration, as settlers accumulated land or sought opportunities for trade to achieve and bequeath a competency. Civil and religious leaders often confronted local discord in their so-called peaceable kingdoms. Nevertheless, Puritan New England's family-centered, work-oriented communities of the seventeenth century achieved remarkable stability for a new colonial society—a social and political stability that derived not only from the widespread ownership of land but also from a distinctive civic culture.

## CIVIC CULTURE

Puritan New England was not a theocracy; the church did not rule the state. Rather, the Puritans established Bible commonwealths in which the church and the state allied to advance the reformed social order that could not be achieved at home. The Bible commonwealths of Massachusetts and Connecticut consisted of state-sponsored churches and colonial governments that included lay representatives. Within the two colonies, Puritan laymen dominated town meetings, approved local ordinances, and elected officials. Laymen also helped govern local congregations. Reflecting the Puritan commitment to lay literacy, schools filled out the region's civic landscape. From the first generation forward, New England's well-developed civic institutions and practices, combined with the Puritans' productive religious ideals and demographic characteristics, further distinguished the region from other English colonies.

The Puritans' belief that they were in a "covenant" with God framed civic life. The covenant described a contract, agreement, or special relationship with God. It is often assumed that this covenant demonstrates that New England's Puritan founders saw themselves as *the* chosen people, the New Israelites. But the Puritan reformers who remained in England were also part of the chosen people. Puritans on both sides of the Atlantic believed that England was a covenanted nation bound in a special relationship with God. In fact, many Puritans left England because the nation, with all of its misguided policies and resultant problems, had failed to live up to its godly covenantal responsibilities and would continue to feel divine wrath. New England offered Puritans an opportunity to erect a godly society and thereby fulfill their part of the covenant. In turn, providential blessings—prosperity, health, peace—would be conferred on their colonies. If they failed to live up to their covenantal obligations, New Englanders invited providential afflictions: drought, Indian attacks, famine, even witches.

As a *communal* agreement, the covenant explained *collective* blessings or afflictions. All New Englanders, from saintly Puritans to hardened strangers, lived under the communal covenant. Their behavior elicited either God's mercy or wrath. Cycles of success and hardship gave rise to thanksgiving and fast days. Such covenanted rituals fostered a collective consciousness; seventeenth-century New England outpaced other English colonies in forging a regional identity. Most important for the region's civic life, the covenant compelled the establishment of strong colony-wide and local governments. The Puritans erected Bible commonwealths in which political leaders and institutions supported a reformed moral order and admonished all New Englanders to honor their covenantal obligations.

In the 1630s Massachusetts Bay evolved from a commercial joint stock company to a colonial government with what were by seventeenth-century standards strong representative elements. As a joint stock company, Massachusetts was governed by its investors. According to the colony's royal charter, these "freemen" were to meet four times a year in a general court; during one of the meetings they were to elect an eight-member board of assistants or governing council, which would then choose the governor and deputy governor. During its first years, the colony was run by a small group of men, and few Puritan freemen participated in the general court election meetings that chose these leaders. In 1631, for instance, only 118 adult males appeared at the election meeting of the general court.

Winthrop carried the Massachusetts Bay Company's charter and records to the New World. Away from the scrutiny of English authorities, Puritans adapted their commercial charter and created a framework for a self-governing colony. In 1632, freemen won the right to elect the governor directly rather than through the assistants. Two years later, major political changes transformed the charter. Towns complained that they were being taxed by the general court despite not being represented at its meetings. The freemen in each town won the right to elect deputies to represent them at the general court. Deputies and assistants shared political authority and soon divided into a bicameral legislative body.

Except for three years when he was not elected, John Winthrop served as governor from 1630 to 1649. He often resisted the political changes that transformed a commercial charter into a representative government. Of course, in early Massachusetts colonial suffrage and office-holding were limited to free white adult men who were spiritually converted members of the church. The founding generation, however, included large numbers of these freemen, and it was they who provided the impetus for political change. Puritan laymen were not democrats, but, mindful of their experience in England, they could be prickly about their liberties. They created a republican type of government that was radical for its time. The lower house of deputies even impeached Winthrop in 1645.

The political evolution of Massachusetts in the 1630s shaped government in Connecticut as well. In 1639, the general court of the river towns approved the Fundamental Orders of Connecticut, which some historians consider the first colonial constitution. Freemen, who were not required to be spiritually reborn, elected the governor, his council, and representatives to the general court. In its Fundamental Agreement (1643), the New Haven Colony formalized a representative government that followed Massachusetts in limiting the rights to vote and hold office to converted church members. When New Haven and other independent settlements were incorporated into Connecticut in 1662, a new royal charter confirmed the self-governing policies that the river towns had devised shortly after their founding. Connecticut's charter survived as a governing document into the nineteenth century, evidence of the civic inventiveness of seventeenth-century New England.

The fabled New England town meeting served as the cornerstone of local self-government. Often celebrated as a distinctively American civic practice, the region's founders actually adapted to the New World elements of English local parish government. The Puritans were familiar with general parish meetings in England and with lay leaders, sometimes called "selectmen." New England towns never abandoned their English civic underpinnings, but familiar local customs did expand and evolve in new ways. In early Massachusetts, for instance, freemen were also town proprietors and church members. In effect, the town meeting functioned simultaneously as a civic body, a land company, and a church.

A board of selectmen (usually seven) was chosen to run local affairs between town meetings. Voters preferred church members distinguished by their standing, wealth, and willingness to listen to local sentiments. After their encounters in England with an intrusive royal government and state church, feisty colonial freemen often defended their liberty, as when they complained to the Massachusetts General Court about taxation without representation in 1632. But Puritan laymen were not democrats who believed in social equality. In most towns freemen repeatedly returned the same selectmen to office, and they elected new leaders who shared the social profile of their predecessors. Puritan civic thought recognized that some hierarchy was essential to the quest for ordered liberty.

Selectmen oversaw local finances; they apportioned taxes that were set by the town meeting, maintained the meetinghouse, ensured the collection of the minister's salary, and hired the local teacher. These "fathers of the town" also served as an arm of the Bible commonwealths. They advanced the Puritans' reformist agenda and worked to uphold covenant obligations. Selectmen monitored families. In 1642, the Massachusetts General Court directed them "to take account from time to time of all parents and masters, and of their children, . . . especially of their ability to read and understand the principles of religion and the capital laws of the country."[12] Connecticut and New Haven approved similar legislation in the 1650s. The Puritan family was considered "a little commonwealth," a civic institution where children first learned the importance of order, piety, and literacy.

Education in Puritan civic life extended from the family to the support of public schools. Learning began in the little commonwealth, where mothers were responsible for teaching their children to read. At first, such home schooling relied on imported English children's books. The *New England Primer,* which famously opened the study of the alphabet with the phrase "In Adam's fall we sinned all," later developed into a "little Bible" of piety and literacy. The Puritan regimen of moral and spiritual improvement depended on the laity's ability to read.

Publicly financed schools expanded the work of Puritan families. Boston hired a schoolmaster as early as 1635. By 1639, six other newly founded towns in Massachusetts followed suit. Hartford and New Haven established schools in 1642. Five years later Massachusetts passed the so-called Old Deluder Law, which is often cited as the first legislative mandate for a public school system. The law began with a description of how the "old deluder, Satan," thrived by keeping people in ignorance. It required towns with fifty households to appoint a teacher who would instruct children to read and write. When a town reached one hundred households, it would have to establish a grammar school to prepare boys for Harvard. Many towns were slow to comply with the law's provisions. School costs added to the local tax burden; townspeople were already supporting ministers and meetinghouses. Still, over time, local schools expanded across Puritan New England. The region's early support of education and the resultant rates of literacy enhanced New England's civic and religious life.

The Puritan church was woven into the fabric of local life. During the first generation most adult males were concurrently freemen, proprietors, and church members. The "church" referred not to a physical entity—a building—but rather to a spiritual body. It identified Puritans who were within the covenant grace, the reborn believers who were "elected" by God for salvation. Unconverted Puritans belonged to the congregation of worshippers. The church and the congregation formed the local religious "society."

Puritans worshiped in plain, unheated structures that were called meetinghouses rather than churches. They usually erected meetinghouses on hills or elevated sites to remind people of their priorities. A meetinghouse was not a sacred structure but rather a civic building where all town assemblies were also held. Puritans did not confine worship to a holy building (a church) where believers gathered on the Sabbath (and, in large towns, also on Thursdays). Church members glorified God through private devotions that included prayer and Bible-reading as well as through worldly activities. Though attendance at meetinghouse services was compulsory, Puritanism actually stressed the familial and individual practice of piety outside of formal worship.

Religious societies were self-governing. Their Congregationalism, which dictated a system of local control, represented another aspect of New England's town-centered civic culture. Local worshippers selected and ordained their ministers. They also admitted and disciplined members. Many New England Puritans reacted to the inclusive parishes of the Church of England. They preferred "pure" churches that restricted membership to individuals who had experienced spiritual rebirth. Candidates were commonly expected to give a public account of their conversion before the church. Women did so in private, often relating their experience to a minister and male elders. The church evaluated such testimony and in most cases admitted the new member; what was called a "judgment of charity" prevailed. Admission bestowed certain privileges on members. Access to communion, for instance, was usually limited to those who were within the covenant of grace. Some New England Puritans questioned the strict admission policies and the quest for "pure" churches containing only the reborn or "visible saints." Connecticut's Thomas Hooker believed that public accounts of conversion and tight restrictions on communion discouraged people from following the path to salvation and full church membership. The evangelical Hooker and other Connecticut ministers preferred to hear conversion accounts in private and to open communion to believers who affirmed Puritan doctrine and showed signs of spiritual awakening.

Massachusetts Bay advanced New England's pure church policies in the 1630s. They reflected how New World opportunities emboldened Puritan reform. Since so many first generation settlers were already converted, Puritan authorities seized the opportunity to purify their churches by using conversion accounts to identify new saints. The cleric-lay relationship is often summed up as a "speaking *Aristocracy* in the face of a silent *Democracy*."[13] But such passivity does not accurately describe the Puritan laity. Church admission policies as well as access to baptism and communion, the two sacraments Puritans preserved in church life, spawned continuing disagreement; disputes also arose over the appointment and support of ministers. Even converted women, though denied the right to vote in church matters, exercised informal influence over their menfolk and shaped their ministers' reputations.

Local self-governing congregations bolstered New England's civic culture. Yet Puritans did not behave like modern democrats in their religious societies. Seating arrangements in Congregational meetinghouses reflected deferential, hierarchical notions similar to those that shaped the choice of selectmen. A committee assigned seats based on wealth, age, and standing within the community. Seating in the meetinghouse mapped a town's social structure. Worship, then, was a kind of social drama in which Puritans continually reenacted their assigned ranking within the communal order. The politics of seating generated resentment and discontent. It was not always easy to weigh and reconcile the criteria that determined where one sat. Though a family's wealth and standing might grow, the progress toward more prominent seating could be slow; it often depended on the death of fellow members.

Thus, disputes did sometimes rankle congregations and town meetings. Protest, after all, was bound up in Puritanism's very origins. But town-centered New England developed a civic culture with stable institutions and prescribed practices. Once established by the region's founders, town meetings, local schools, and self-governing churches were reproduced in new settlements. These local institutions supported the Bible commonwealths and the communal covenant. Together they defined Puritan New England's distinctive civic landscape.

### GENDER RELATIONS

Women did not participate in Puritan civic life, though some girls gained limited access to local schools. Women could not vote in town or church meetings. Wives did not own property; under the English law of "coverture," a wife was incorporated into and sheltered under her husband's legal identity. Widows did own property, but in the case of remarriage it often came under the control of the new husband. Elements of Puritanism supported such traditional English patriarchy. Women were perceived as "weaker vessels" whose character, like Eve's, was flawed. They tended, Puritans reiterated, to be "passionate and uncontrolled, incapable of reason, supremely credulous, and, thus easily led astray."[14] From the Bible commonwealth to the little commonwealth, women fell under the governance of men.

Puritanism also tempered patriarchal authority and improved women's status in ways that distinguished early New England from the homeland and from the Chesapeake colonies. Preachers upheld the spiritual equality of men and women. Both sexes sought salvation on equal terms. Women, like men, were encouraged to cultivate a personal relationship with God that required prayer and Bible reading. Puritanism encouraged women's literacy. During the first generation, churches achieved a balanced membership of women and men. In subsequent decades, women came to dominate the ranks of the spiritually reborn, making up two-thirds of the membership in many New England churches. Puritans esteemed pious women who were godly wives. Marriage afforded women some protection against the abuses of patriarchal authority.

In Puritan New England marriage was a civil ceremony, not a sacramental rite. Puritans understood marriage as still another covenant or contract that imposed mutual obligations on men and women. Good wives accepted and obeyed their husbands' authority. But family patriarchs were bound by law and custom to respect and protect their wives. Civil and religious authorities monitored family life and intervened when the mutualism of the marriage covenant frayed. Watchful neighbors served as the marriage covenant's first line of defense, reporting evidence of verbal and physical abuse of spouses to church and town officials. Serious violators of the marriage covenant—men and women—often found themselves in court. Oversight of the marriage covenant and of family life in general was much stronger in Puritan New England than in other parts of seventeenth-century America, particularly the Chesapeake. For Puritans, the stability of the Bible commonwealth depended on the maintenance or restoration of family order.

One Puritan writer observed that "tho the Husband be the Head of the wife, yet she is the Head of the family."[15] The ideal good wife was also a godly mother who nurtured the moral and spiritual development of her children. The work of Anne Bradstreet (ca. 1612–1672) represents one of the few written sources that records a Puritan woman's perspective on marriage, motherhood, and the quest for salvation. A participant in the Great Migration, Bradstreet was Anglo-America's first published poet. Her brief spiritual autobiography, titled "To My Dear Children," offers insight into woman's role as "the head of the family." Seriously ill and facing the end of her life, Bradstreet penned a spiritual autobiography for the edification of her children. Her labor extended from children's physical birth to their spiritual rebirth. "I have brought you into the world, and with great pains, weaknesses, cares, and fears brought you to this," she observed. "I now travail in birth again of you till Christ be formed in you."[16] As family head, a Puritan woman's legacy to her children resided less in property than in the moral and spiritual estate that a godly mother bequeathed to her offspring.

Bradstreet's poetry also suggests that, contrary to the persistent view of repressed Puritans, love and passion pervaded the marriage covenant. Bradstreet's husband Simon held various positions in Massachusetts Bay Colony, including governor. He was frequently away from their homes in Ipswich and then Andover. Anne wrote passionate love poems to him. She spoke of her

FIG. 7 Mrs. Elizabeth Freake and Baby Mary, artist unknown, ca. 1671–74. The goodwife of a successful Boston merchant, Mrs. Freake is appropriately dressed in a stylish, though not ostentatious, fashion and also wears jewelry. She proudly holds her doll-like baby, who was later painted into the original portrait of Mrs. Freake. Courtesy of the Worcester Art Museum, Worcester, Massachusetts.

"glowing breast" waiting at home for her "dearest guest." She viewed her children as "those fruits which through thy heat I bore." She evoked the marriage bed, where Simon's "warmth such frigid colds did cause to melt."[17] Such poems are filled with images of passion and desire, which Puritans strove to confine to marriage rather than to repress.

Anne Bradstreet gave birth to eight children, near the average for women in seventeenth-century New England. Women's mean age of marriage was 22. Husbands were typically four years older; they often delayed marriage as they labored with fathers and waited to acquire sufficient family land to provide a competency. Premarital pregnancy in early Puritan New England fell well below rates that were common in England. In the seventeenth century, 5 to 10 percent of New England brides were pregnant on their wedding day, compared to 20 percent in the homeland. (By the middle of the eighteenth century, premarital pregnancy in New England would increase dramatically.)

New England women bore children from their early twenties to their late thirties. Births typically occurred about two years apart. For women who gave birth to more than the average of seven children, pregnancies might extend into the forties. Consider Anne Hutchinson: The famous religious dissenter challenged civil and religious patriarchal authority and was banished from Massachusetts in 1637, when she was forty-six years old and pregnant for the sixteenth time. That pregnancy resulted in a stillbirth. Hutchinson gave birth to fifteen children, all but two of whom survived infancy. In fact, infant mortality rates in early New England were low by seventeenth-century standards. Approximately 10 percent of newborns did not survive their first year. The high number of pregnancies contributed to a 20 percent death rate for mothers in childbirth.

Anne Bradstreet turned to poetry before giving birth; she strove to cultivate an acceptance of death and convey her love to Simon. She concluded "Before the Birth of One of Her Children" with these words for her husband: "And kiss this paper for thy love's dear sake, / Who with salt tears this last farewell did make." Men usually remarried after a wife's death in childbirth, and Bradstreet pleaded with Simon to protect their children "from step-dame's injury."[18]

With a relatively balanced sex ratio, marriage and family life brought more social stability to early New England than the male-dominated Chesapeake colonies experienced. New England families were larger and healthier than their southern counterparts. Women bore special burdens for the welfare of their large families. They faced three decades of bearing, rearing, and educating children. In addition, they made and mended clothes, cultivated vegetable and herb gardens, prepared and preserved food, and kept fires burning.

Yet New England women were not wholly confined to a separate sphere defined by domesticity. Women sometimes labored in family fields. Wives also served as "deputy husbands." When men were away on private or public business (Simon Bradstreet, for example) or when they were seriously ill, women temporarily assumed their spouses' duties. Some women established private "Dame schools," opening their homes a few hours a week to teach children to read. Wives ran taverns and shops with their husbands; widows often operated such enterprises on their own. Moreover, women possessed some informal influence and power in their villages and church societies. Midwives and their assistants presided over childbirths, comforting mothers and persuading unmarried women to identify unknown fathers. Midwives drew on their knowledge of herbs and served as healers. Networks of women neighbors exerted a moral "watchfulness" over family, village, and church life. Local reputations, including that of the minister, were often shaped by women's talk. (Some women were even summoned to court on charges of slander.) A Puritan goodwife's duties and influence clearly extended beyond her immediate family.

## OLD AND NEW ENGLAND

After she had arrived in New England, Anne Bradstreet recalled, her "heart rose" in silent rebellion against the "new world and new manners" she encountered.[19] Whatever the claims of Puritan promoters, the region was far from a "new" England. Bradstreet remained resolute in the face of disappointment and even warmed to her new homeland. But perhaps up to one-sixth of the participants in the Great Migration abandoned New England. Many returned to England; others sought a new start in different parts of colonial America. Remigration in the 1640s and 1650s provoked questions about New England's founding purpose.

The outbreak of the English civil war in 1642, which led to the beheading of King Charles I seven years later, brought an abrupt halt to the Great Migration. The triumph of Puritan and parliamentary forces over the royal and ecclesiastical authorities who had harassed the colonists in the homeland suggested to many New Englanders that the providential moment for England's reformation and for repatriation had arrived. Hundreds of New Englanders, including founding ministers, returned to England beginning in the 1640s. Some served in Parliament; others filled pulpits; still others fought in the army. Repatriated Puritans reported back to the colonies that it was "a matter of high account to have been a New English man" in revolutionary England.[20]

Of course, the vast majority of Puritan New Englanders, having invested money and labor in homes, fields, and livestock and having begun to raise American-born children, chose to stay in the region. They faced new challenges. New England suffered through its first recession. The economic boom of the 1630s eroded. The end of the Great Migration and the continuing remigration led to a significant decline in the sale of land and foodstuffs, for instance. Then, too, the seemingly epochal events in England raised questions for those who stayed behind about New England's role in transatlantic reform. The homeland once again emerged as the hothouse of Puritanism.

In the 1640s and 1650s, New England's Puritan leaders expressed cautious hope as they learned of the religious and political tumult in England. The region's Bible commonwealths regularly observed days of fast and prayer in support of the "blessed work of a public Reformation" in England.[21] Yet mounting discord and bloodshed muddled the providential meaning and outcome of the homeland's civil strife. New Englanders needed to persevere in their own mission, despite the economic problems, the promise of English reform, and the lure of remigration. Religious turmoil in Old England encouraged Massachusetts to affirm the "New England Way" of church government with the hope that it would influence ecclesiastical reform in the homeland. The *Cambridge Platform* (1648) codified the Congregational system of self-governing local churches and spiritual rebirth as the requirement for membership. Connecticut, New Haven, and Plymouth endorsed the document.

The *Cambridge Platform* and the commitment of the vast majority of colonists to remain in New England suggest a renewed investment in the Puritans' reformist experiment. In the 1640s and 1650s, some remigrants spread stories in England about the deficiencies of New England's climate and diet. The region's leaders were quick to defend their New World way of life against these slights. As one New England writer put it, "Did not some do so of the land of *Canaan* itself, yet *Canaan* was never worse and themselves smarted for doing so."[22] Thus did the stirrings of a truly *American* self-consciousness appear in the 1640s.

New England's Puritan founders formed a generation of English people living in colonial exile and attempting to reconstruct familiar ways. Though the very name "New England" proclaimed this quest for cultural continuity, the New World setting led the founding generation to adapt their English heritage. Their middling society of widespread landholding; their civic culture of extended suffrage, local self-rule, and representative colonial government; their Congregational way and Bible commonwealths—these and other early New England developments represented adaptations of or departures from the founders' English world.

Despite such alterations, the first generation remained very much a transplanted English people. In "A Dialogue between Old England and New," published at the outbreak of civil strife in the homeland, Anne Bradstreet underscored the transatlantic ties:

Dear Mother cease complaints and wipe your eyes,
Shake off your dust, cheer up, and now arise;
You are my Mother Nurse, and I your flesh. . . .[23]

Of course, the crises of the 1640s and 1650s also provoked defenses of New England's ongoing mission, which grew after the monarchy and the Anglican religious establishment were restored in 1660. The founders' passing, the coming of age of a new generation that had never known the homeland, and the collapse of the Puritan revolution in England promoted the growth of an Americanized regional identity after 1660. New England's founding would be recalled as an American epic of biblical dimensions.

THREE

# *Beyond Puritan New England*

## Profane, Maritime, and Dissenting Borderlands

Mɪᴅ-ꜱᴇᴠᴇɴᴛᴇᴇɴᴛʜ-ᴄᴇɴᴛᴜʀʏ New England was far from an exclusively Puritan world. Even within the Bible common-wealths of Massachusetts and Connecticut, pious authorities confronted "strangers" to their faith. In northern New England or what was known as the "eastern" frontier of coastal New Hampshire and Maine, non-Puritan investors and colonists launched worldly settlements. Impious New England produced its own forceful leaders. Consider Thomas Morton (1575–1646), the Puritans' earliest villain. His fate and significance have often been obscured by more famous incidents of seventeenth-century persecution: Roger Williams, Anne Hutchinson, Quakers, and witches. But Morton was the first prominent colonist who threatened and scandalized authorities in Plymouth and Massachusetts. Twice they shipped him back to England.

A lawyer and Anglican, Morton invested in Mount Wollaston, a commercial settlement north of Plymouth Harbor that later became part of the Puritan town of Braintree. In 1625, the fifty-year-old gentleman led the small plantation that had been established with indentured servants to pursue fishing, trade, and farming. Morton placated his servants with strong drink, English revelry, and promises of freedom. They danced around a Maypole, sometimes in the company of Native women. Mount Wollaston came to be known as Merrymount, a reminder of the popular customs of "Merry Old England." Morton and his servants, groused Governor William Bradford, slid into "great licentious-

ness [and] all profaneness."[1] Plymouth charged Morton with supplying alcohol and firearms to Natives. Miles Standish marched
on Merrymount in 1628, and Morton was seized and packed off
to England. He returned a year later. Massachusetts arrested Morton at Merrymount, burned his house, and sent him back to England again in 1630.

Nathaniel Hawthorne used the second assault on Morton's
settlement as the basis of his short story "The Maypole of Merry
Mount." In the tale, Hawthorne pitted the "grizzly saints" of
Massachusetts and their whipping post, the "Puritan Maypole,"
against the gaiety of Morton and his servants. Hawthorne preferred some middle way between the Puritans' moralistic work
culture and the Merrymounters' frolics. He depicted the encounter as a struggle for early New England's very soul. When
the Puritans chopped down the Maypole and routed Morton's
settlers, "the last day of mirth had passed from Merry Mount"—
and, presumably, from New England.[2]

Nevertheless, in 1643 Thomas Morton returned to the region
a third time. He visited Rhode Island and Maine and went back
to Massachusetts, where he was arrested and jailed for a year. He
spent the last two years of his life in Maine, whose coastal and island settlements harbored people similar to the Merrymounters.

Morton's career suggests how, despite their best efforts, authorities in Massachusetts and Connecticut were not able to ex-
punge "profane" settlers whose attitudes and behavior defied the
Puritans' reformist ways. The Puritans themselves contributed to
the rise of "strangers" in their midst; they brought servants to
the New World, recruited workers for their skill rather than their
piety, and attracted fishermen. Strangers to Puritanism dominated early settlements in northern New England. Fishermen
prevailed in Maine, and maritime entrepreneurs and workers
shaped the Piscataqua (Portsmouth) region of New Hampshire.

Rather than serving as a moat protecting New England from
outsiders, the Atlantic Ocean functioned as a maritime frontier.
Trade linked New England to Catholic Europe and to West Indian slave societies. The fishing, commerce, and maritime trades
lured worldly strangers. Rhode Island came to be known as the
"ocean colony"; a maritime orientation as well as liberty of conscience defined its character.

Between 1641 and 1643, Massachusetts annexed the settlements that formed New Hampshire. By 1658, the Bay Colony had extended its authority over Maine. Still, northern New England, with its worldly maritime elements, would not be fully incorporated into Puritan New England in the seventeenth century. Rhode Island avoided a Puritan takeover. In Puritan eyes it became the "sewer" of New England—a distressing reminder of the Bible commonwealths' geographical and cultural limits.

## SERVANTS AND OTHER STRANGERS

The human capital that built early New England was not solely Puritan. From the founding of Plymouth, indentured servants and free artisans joined pious colonists in settling the region. Plymouth leaders encountered defiant strangers from the colony's beginning. In 1620, settlers signed the famous Mayflower Compact. They united in a civic body and pledged to accept the laws and authority of the colony. The Compact was prompted, in part, by discontented strangers who threatened to strike out on their own because they had arrived in New England rather than northern Virginia, their official destination.

The Great Migration to Massachusetts Bay and Connecticut transported strangers to the emerging Puritan heartland. More than half of the families who settled in the Bay Colony in the 1630s were wealthy enough to bring servants. Male servants and maids labored for four to seven years in return for passage to New England and the prospect of acquiring skills and perhaps small parcels of land. Nearly 17 percent of the participants in the Great Migration stepped ashore as unfree colonists. In comparison to the Chesapeake colonies, the proportion of New England's bound workers appears modest. In Virginia and Maryland, indentured servants outnumbered free colonists by more than three to one. Though their ranks were comparatively small, servants shored up the family economy and commercial prosperity of early New England.

Servitude in the region was largely a family affair, with one or two bound workers attached to those Puritan households that could afford transportation and maintenance costs. Investors in commercial enterprises such as seventeenth-century New England's numerous ironworks also recruited servants for mining, smelting, and forging. In the 1650s, revolutionary authorities in the homeland shipped hundreds of non-English war captives to

New England as bound laborers. One ship sailed from London in 1651 with nearly 300 Scottish prisoners. Other vessels packed with young Irish servants followed. These bound commercial laborers represented a major element of the profane world that flouted Puritan piety and moral discipline.

Domestic and "company" servants—English and non-English alike—frequently fell afoul of the law. They appeared in court far more often than free colonists. Charged with crimes that ranged from drunkenness, assault, and lewdness to larceny, blasphemy, and slander, servants' attitudes and behavior reinforced the Puritan belief in the natural depravity of the human race, which could only be overcome by God's saving grace. Seldom offering much promise for conversion, profane servants often bore the brunt of Puritan discipline and punishment, usually in the form of fines, whippings, and confinement in stocks. In short, many servants belonged to a profane society that Puritan authorities continually struggled to regulate because it was less easily subdued than Hawthorne's Merrymounters. One Puritan founder fumed over the "multitudes of idle and profane young men, servants and others" who defaced his Bay Colony town of Ipswich.[3] This observer may have been exaggerating out of a desire to establish and preserve a pious moral order, but he still conveys the exasperation of officials forced to cope with the nettlesome white strangers who tarnished Puritan piety from colonial New England's birth.

Over the course of the seventeenth century, indentured servitude declined in New England. By the end of the century, servants made up less than five percent of the regional population. As servitude and slavery increased in the South and in the West Indies, New England evolved as a colonial society heavily dependent on family labor. Without a large staple crop such as tobacco or sugar, New England failed to generate the profits to maintain or expand a significant class of unfree workers. The region's large healthy families produced the sons and daughters whose labor took the place of bound servants. While debt peonage, a form of bound labor, developed among fishermen and Native Americans, the character of indentured servitude shifted in colonial New England toward a welfare institution. Town authorities or parents often indentured impoverished, orphaned, unskilled, and "unruly" youths.

The indentured servants who arrived in New England as part of the Great Migration and the prisoners who followed did not simply disappear once their terms of service ended. Some returned home or left New England for non-Puritan colonies. Others became wage laborers and small property owners. They married, raised children, and engendered a social element that often stood outside of the Puritan faith.

The Bible commonwealths not only recruited bound strangers; they also enticed skilled wage laborers who were often indifferent or even hostile to Puritan ways. Puritan New England rested on faith, but it was constructed in part by skilled secular hands. Colonial leaders depended on carpenters to build houses and millwrights to erect operations that produced boards and flour. Skilled, well-paid strangers labored at tanneries, salt works, shipyards, and ironworks. They often toiled side by side with disaffected company servants who did not receive wages.

Saints and strangers represented the horns of another Puritan dilemma. Religious ideals spurred commercial enterprise and the imperative to subdue and improve the earth. But strangers—free and bound—were needed to advance these religio-economic ambitions and to fashion a prosperous, pious society. In other words, the Puritans' economic needs and ambitions created subcommunities of strangers in their midst. Authorities in the Bible commonwealths hoped that, under a reformed moral order and disciplined work culture, profane strangers would become civil colonists, if not godly saints. That is, they would develop into sober, law-abiding citizens, what the Puritans called the "civil"— a moral class that resided between the profane and the godly.

Strangers often clung to profane ways, however, sometimes abetted by pragmatic Puritan authorities who sought to expand certain critical industries. In the mid-1640s, Massachusetts officials exempted ironworkers in Lynn from attending church or securing a minister. Puritan officials in New Haven put up with the profane behavior of ironworkers who were so crucial to the colony's commercial aspirations. The drinking habits of ironworkers and other strangers defined profane life and fueled outbursts of criminal behavior.

The Bible commonwealths aspired to reform the alehouse culture of "Merry Old England." The proliferation of licensed and unlicensed taverns, alehouses, and alcohol retailers in England created, in the words of one Puritan writing in 1635, a homeland overrun with "so many beastly, barbarous, belching drunkards."[4] To this observer, New England appeared far more sober than the mother country. The region also possessed fewer taverns per capita than Virginia; in Jamestown alone, it has been estimated, there may have been a tavern for every ten people. The English West Indies were awash in rum distilled from molasses; overseers sometimes emptied chamber pots into fermenting vats to discourage servants and slaves from imbibing the valuable, exportable brew.

New England Puritans regulated rather than prohibited the consumption of alcohol. They endorsed moderate drinking for its social and health benefits but repudiated the idleness, drunkenness, and profaneness that was disfiguring England. Most early New England towns possessed a "public house"—an establishment for travelers who needed lodging, food, and refreshment. Laws prohibited local residents from spending more than a half-hour in public houses. New England's larger coastal towns licensed multiple public houses as well as taverns, which did not provide lodging, and retail shops. Officials often awarded coveted liquor licenses to disabled and widowed residents so that they could support themselves and not become public charges. Women not only operated public houses; they ran and frequented less respectable taverns.

Under Puritan regulation, then, early New England emerged as a relatively sober region. Though some Puritans drank to excess, a regimen of self-discipline and public legislation reined in the abuse of alcohol. Yet laws were often difficult to enforce. Unlicensed taverns and retailers posed constant challenges to the authorities. Servants sought out taverns, mocking their masters' authority and ignoring laws that specified time limits for drinking establishments. Skilled, non-Puritan wage laborers and fishermen followed suit. Within and beyond the boundaries of Puritan New England, strangers fashioned pockets of a profane, alcohol-centered counterculture that clashed with more pious ways.

In port towns, at commercial operations like ironworks and shipyards, among fishing plantations that stretched to New Hampshire and Maine, taverns anchored the profane life of strangers. In northern New England "walking taverns"—ships filled with alcohol—tracked fishing fleets. By the middle of the seventeenth century, Boston supported more public houses than meetinghouses. With about three thousand residents, Boston contained thirteen licensed establishments that dispensed drink in 1648, and there were undoubtedly others not approved by the authorities. Alice Thomas, a seventeenth-century Bostonian, turned her unlicensed alehouse into a bordello and fencing operation. Court records describe her as a "common bawd" who provided her male and female patrons the "opportunity to commit carnal wickedness" on her premises. She was also convicted of buying goods that thieves stole from Boston ships and warehouses.[5]

Strangers often looked to the tavern over the meetinghouse. The significance of skilled wage laborers and indentured servants in early New England, however, extends well beyond the counterculture they represented that was indifferent to or openly defiant of Puritan ways. Strangers contributed to the building of the Bible commonwealths, and skilled workers in particular added to the region's human capital. Historians have suggested, for instance, that both Puritans and strangers shaped colonial New England's celebrated ingenuity. Some of the non-Puritan wage earning recruits, such as ironworkers and shipbuilders, were clever, inventive men. New England's maritime world offered an arena in which skilled strangers and resourceful Puritans confronted challenges that sharpened their worldly ingenuity.

THE SEA

Geography blessed coastal New England with physical features ripe for exploitation by all ambitious English people, whether pious or profane. New England did not claim fishing grounds comparable to Newfoundland's Grand Bank. But from Cape Cod to the Gulf of Maine, the region's coasts featured rich banks, a product of the retreat of the last glacier, over 15,000 years ago. Glacial deposits and a rising sea left behind relatively shallow water in places. At these banks light penetrated to the ocean floor, nurturing plankton—microscopic plant and animal life—on which fish thrived. The receding glacier sculpted New England's intricate coastline. From New Haven to Maine, the glacier also bequeathed coastal residents ready access to the open ocean from protected ports. Abundant supplies of timber represented a third natural feature of New England that proved crucial to the region's maritime expansion. Natives had cleared vast tracts of coastal land. Of course the size of their population and the limited demands Natives placed on the environment did not produce anything close to the kind of deforestation that seventeenth-century England saw. Particularly in northern New England, extensive first-growth forests supplied masts and lumber for shipbuilding and trade. Natural resources—timber, good harbors, and fishing banks—laid the foundation for New England's maritime development.

It would be hard to exaggerate the deep impression the sea made on early New Englanders. Glowing accounts of maritime opportunities—especially fishing and commerce—filled Puritan promotional tracts alongside testimonials of the availability of good land. Colonization originated with ocean voyages. For Puritans the physical-spiritual pilgrimage across the Atlantic remained a historic touchstone. The maritime world presented commercial prospects that incited the industry and enterprise of Puritans and strangers. New England merchants took commercial risks, which often yielded huge profits. The Puritan dilemma, with its tension between personal piety and worldly prosperity, most keenly marked life in commercial port towns, where the godly and the profane confronted each other most directly.

In those communities, the sea occupied a pivotal place in the Puritan imagination. The world, after all, was a "sea of sin." Early New England sermons and writings regularly invoked the sea in ways that resonated with both the moral bearings and the maritime activities of Puritan laity. Worldliness menaced the region like "violent winds and raging waves" assaulting a ship; sin threatened to expose New England as a "weak and ill-compacted vessel."[6] The oldest surviving oak-framed public building in New England, constructed in 1681, came to be called the "Old Ship" meetinghouse. Located in the coastal Massachusetts town of Hingham, the sturdy meetinghouse was probably built by local ship carpenters; its ceiling timbers resemble the inverted hull of a vessel, and a painted compass decorates the ceiling of its cupola.

Puritan ministers salted their sermons with stories of life's perils on the watery frontier. These sea deliverance tales—maritime versions of the more famous Indian captivity narratives—were aimed at Puritans and strangers alike. They told of captains

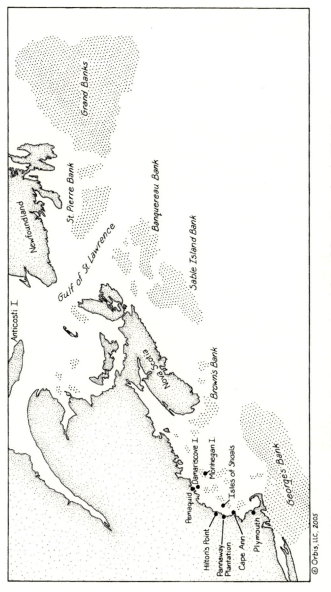

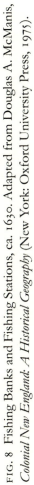

FIG. 8  Fishing Banks and Fishing Stations, ca. 1630. Adapted from Douglas A. McManis, *Colonial New England: A Historical Geography* (New York: Oxford University Press, 1975).

and crews whose ships were threatened by storms, lost in fog, and attacked by pirates. Providential deliverance from such "captivity" occurred only after mariners repented and placed their faith in God.

The sea enlarged and diversified the economic and moral boundaries of Puritan New England. When scores of ships deposited saints and strangers on the region's shores during the Great Migration, they also transported thousands of other newcomers to New England. These vessels were "conveyor belts" carrying all manner of plant and animal life from the Old to the New World. Attached below a ship's waterline, as one marine biologist has described it, "a wide variety of sea life," from "sponges, sea anemones . . . barnacles, mussels, sea squirts, [and] seaweeds," migrated to New England ports. At anchor, these marine "hitchhikers" jumped ship and colonized harbors, a process of ecological invasion that continues today with the dumping of ballast water from ocean vessels. From New Haven to Maine, settlement initiated ecological changes to shore waters, not just to coastal land. Indigenous organisms and European invaders bred harbor marine life, which became "cosmopolitan" over time.[7]

Marine biology suggests how the transatlantic movement of people and goods also affected the human ecology of seventeenth-century coastal New England. Itinerant fishermen, carried by the currents of trade or recruited by Puritan merchants, made their way to New England. Fisherfolk represented a significant segment of the region's profane class; it also included servants and skilled workers in major maritime trades like shipbuilding. The rich human capital that the Great Migration brought to New England did not include a wealth of maritime knowledge and skills. In large measure, the Puritans were a landed people drawn from eastern and southern England. Fishermen, sailors, and maritime workers typically originated in England's West Country, where Puritanism was far less entrenched. New England's maritime prosperity relied on the skills and labor of non-Puritans. Within the first decade of Puritan settlement, lucrative markets in the West Indies introduced slavery and Africans to New England. The region's seventeenth-century coastal ports were a far cry from the "cosmopolitanism" of nineteenth-century New Bedford, where South Sea Islanders sold shrunken human heads on street corners, as Herman Melville famously reported. Yet early maritime communities in New England did acquire elements of social and cultural diversity.

It is sometimes argued that cod rather than God created colonial New England. Massachusetts officials acknowledged cod's critical role in the region's past when they hung a model of the fish in the state's House of Representatives in the late eighteenth century. The New England cod fishery originated around 1600 as an extension of the longtime exploitation of Newfoundland's Grand Bank by English, French, Spanish, and Portuguese vessels. Crews established seasonal fishing stations, occupied from spring to fall, where cod was dried, salted, and shipped to Europe. In the early seventeenth century, expanding geographical knowledge and the quest for new fishing grounds led West Country investors to set up camps along coastal New England. These efforts began offshore such as on Maine's Monhegan Island and then spread to the mainland. By 1630, more than a dozen English fishing plantations dotted the coast from Cape Cod to Cape Ann and north to New Hampshire and Maine. Additional settlements, like Morton's Merrymount, were founded to pursue fishing along with the fur trade and farming. Growing numbers of fishermen became year-round coastal residents.

West Country fishermen were typically nominal Anglicans. The demands of fishery life fostered a work culture alien to Puritanism's more sober, disciplined habits. Their constant battle with nature and the competitive character of their trade hardened the fishermen. Seasonal cycles of intense labor followed by prolonged periods of relative inactivity defined fishermen's lives. Many fell into profane ways that embraced prolific cursing, heavy drinking, and Sabbath-breaking as well as violence against people and property. Fishermen were yet another class of valuable but troublesome strangers. And, like servants and many skilled tradesmen, fishermen forged a counterculture to Puritanism that blended a tepid Anglicanism and an attachment to English popular culture. More often than not, fisherfolk repudiated reformist Puritanism. One Marblehead fisherman, for instance, derided Puritan authorities by "vowing to have his dog baptized."[8] To develop the codfishery, Puritans had to recruit and tolerate English colonists who did not share their piety and values.

Promotional writers seized on the commercial prospects of the fisheries to encourage English people to invest their money (and their lives) in the colonization of New England. "Codfish hath been the enrichment of other nations," one promoter reminded his readers in 1634, "and is likely to prove no small commodity to the planters."[9] Puritan authorities attempted to draw their brethren into the fisheries. As they did in England, however, Puritan families preferred landed opportunities with regular cycles of work. Even as they profited from the New England fishery, Puritan merchants and investors maintained a moral distance from the work of fishermen, who often labored on the Sabbath. While Puritans fished for souls, itinerant and settled strangers hauled in great stores of cod.

Commercial fishing in New England entered a new era of expansion in the 1640s. England's maritime trade and the West Country's fishery were thrown into turmoil by the eruption of civil war. New Englanders expanded their trade to Catholic Europe, supplying increasing quantities of high-quality dried codfish to Spain and Portugal. Merchants also found a growing market for "refuse," or poor-quality, cod in the West Indies. Cheap New England cod nourished the surging African slave population of England's Caribbean colonies.

By the middle of the seventeenth century, then, a burgeoning fishing industry emerged as New England's most important commercial enterprise. It generated large profits, attracted broad-based investors who purchased shares in fishing/trading ventures, and employed hundreds of people along the coast. A booming market for cod drew Atlantic fisherfolk to New England. Some drifted through the region; others took up residence, married, raised families, and formed communities of secular-oriented fishing people in maritime towns. Moreover, the growth of fishing and trade sparked the development of related maritime trades, particularly New England's famed shipbuilding industry.

The region possessed natural advantages over the homeland that stimulated shipbuilding. New England contained mature forests of oak and pine, especially in New Hampshire and Maine. This abundance dramatically lowered the cost of shipbuilding materials—wood for masts and planks and also certain naval stores (pine tar and turpentine, for example). Readily available cheap material allowed entrepreneurs to pay good wages to recruit skilled shipwrights, sawyers, iron workers, and sail makers from the West Country and other parts of England. Shipbuilding required a range of artisans. By 1650, thriving operations in Boston, Salem, and the Piscataqua River region of New Hampshire and Maine became major employers of coastal residents. Well over one hundred workers were needed to build a good-sized vessel. Growing numbers of woodsmen felled the hundreds of trees—perhaps two thousand for a large vessel—that went into a single ship. Sawyers erected mills along the rivers that connected forests and the coast to satisfy the shipbuilding industry's demand for lumber. Responding to the needs of the region's fishery and maritime commerce, New England entrepreneurs dominated colonial shipbuilding. At the end of the seventeenth century, Boston claimed fifteen shipyards. It was colonial America's shipbuilding capital, and, after London, the second largest source of sea vessels in England's colonial empire.

New England's bounty of lumber not only supported shipbuilding; it served as a major item of trade. Fish was the region's most profitable commodity, but it did not rank as a staple product comparable to Chesapeake tobacco or West Indian sugar. These colonies invested heavily in single marketable crops with bound labor expanding their cultivation. Such "monocultures," particularly in the Caribbean, stood in sharp contrast to New England's commercial diversity. New England's merchants shipped fish and forest products around the Atlantic world; they also exported grains, beef, pork, and mutton. Maritime trade offered opportunities for some New England farm families to produce a surplus of agricultural products and livestock for the marketplace. Without a single staple crop, Puritan and non-Puritan merchants aggressively sought both an array of regional commodities and markets in the South, the Caribbean, and Europe.

Indeed, New Englanders' far-flung and diverse commerce extended the moral boundaries of the Puritan work ethic and cultivated behavioral traits that would later be deemed "Yankee." Willing to accept commercial risks and to reinvest profits, the region's merchants pursued maritime trade with shrewdness and ingenuity. They financed voyages by selling shares to wealthy and middle-class local investors. They learned to dicker with producers at home and with consumers in Atlantic markets. They resold tobacco and sugar acquired in trade and accumulated credit and money to purchase manufactured goods in England. By the middle of the seventeenth century, New Englanders were known at home and abroad for commercial skill and craftiness. "Tho' they wear in their faces the Innocence of Doves," an English critic bitterly complained of New Englanders, "you will find them in their Dealings as *Subtle* as *Serpents*. *Interest* is their *Faith, Money* their *God*, and *Large Possessions* the only *Heaven* they covet."[10] Such a sweeping moral indictment, of course, is too one-dimensional. Nevertheless, it suggests how some maritime New Englanders lived and worked—namely, with an acute case of the Puritan dilemma.

Beginning in the 1640s, the sugar colonies of the West Indies emerged as a major market for New England fish, lumber, meat, and farm produce. At mid-century, Barbados had a larger population than New England. In 1660, the profitable sugar colony had well over forty thousand people, nearly ten thousand more than New England. Within a decade blacks comprised 60 percent of the island's people. The wealthy white planters of Barbados concentrated on cultivating sugar for the market; the basic necessities of life could be imported. New England meat and agricultural products sustained white planter life while the slaves got by on refuse cod. Planters built homes, sugar distilleries, and slave shacks with New England lumber. They paid merchants with sugar, molasses, money, and bills of credit that New Englanders deployed to enlarge their inventive transatlantic traffic in wide-ranging commodities and markets. In the second half of the seventeenth century, merchants increasingly carried West Indian molasses to New England. Distilleries multiplied in coastal communities. New England rum became another item of trade; abundantly available, it began to replace beer and ale as the drink of choice, with a resulting increase in drunkenness among port dwellers.

New England trade with the West Indies supported colonial slave societies. Commercial contact in the sugar colonies also taught New Englanders about the system of slave labor and introduced the first bound Africans to the region. New England's earliest slaves were Native people sometimes forced into penal bondage. Fifteen boys and two women, captives from the Pequot War of 1637, were sold into slavery at Providence Island in the West Indies. Official records describe the Pequots as "Cannibal Negroes brought from New England."[11] On the return voyage in 1638, the ship, which had sailed from Salem, transported West Indian slaves to the Bay Colony. Their arrival marked the modest beginnings of the New England slave trade and the probable birth of black bondage in the region.

New Englanders, like other English colonists, justified the enslavement of Africans and Natives on principles that were codified in Massachusetts in 1641. The colony's Body of Liberties legalized slavery for "lawfull Captives taken in just wars, and such strangers as willingly sell themselves or are sold to us."[12] Black slaves from the West Indies were presumably the captives of "just wars" in Africa. In addition, colonials viewed Africans and Indians as "un-English" heathen—"savage" strangers to Christianity whose condition made them fit subjects for enslavement. Though some early court decisions condemned white criminals to lifelong penal servitude, by the early 1640s enslavement was restricted to Africans and Indians.

Neither slavery nor the slave trade flourished in seventeenth-century New England. But some colonial leaders did see West Indian slaves as the region's solution to the turnover of indentured servants. In 1645, John Winthrop's brother-in-law, an enterprising Salem merchant, urged warfare against the Narragansett so that Native captives could be exchanged for badly needed West Indian slaves. The Bay Colony would not "thrive," he claimed, without "a stock of slaves sufficient to do all our business."[13] West Indian slaves, like Tituba of Salem witchcraft fame, served out their bondage in coastal towns. But the absence of a staple crop and the availability of family labor in the New England hinterland limited the need for slave labor and confined most Africans to commercial ports. From less than six hundred at mid-century, the number of blacks in New England grew about three-fold by 1700; they comprised approximately two percent of the region's population. In New York, the Chesapeake, and South Carolina, by contrast, blacks represented, respectively, 9, 22, and 43 percent of the population in 1700.

New Englanders' participation in the seventeenth-century slave trade was also limited. As early as 1644, Boston merchants sent ships directly to Africa for slaves, who were exchanged for sugar, tobacco, and other goods in Barbados. Portugal, France, and England, however, dominated the seventeenth-century transatlantic slave trade. For New Englanders, traffic in slaves remained one relatively small part of commerce with the West Indies. Nevertheless, the region's early encounter with African slaves and the transfer of bound human cargo bore fruit in the eighteenth century. New Englanders would rise to the leadership of a new *American* slave trade, and the longtime black population of ports such as Boston and Newport would swell to impressive percentages.

New England's seventeenth-century coastal communities remained staunchly English. Still, by midcentury burgeoning transatlantic trade, shipbuilding, and fishing injected social and cultural diversity into New England. The presence of religious and racial strangers amid the Puritans derived from commercial enterprise. The Bible commonwealths' commitment to maritime growth brought with it distinctive religious and social challenges to Puritan piety and civic life. Puritans recruited or bought strangers and then strove, not always successfully, to impose sober ways on them.

## THE LIMITS OF PURITAN IMPERIALISM: NEW HAMPSHIRE AND MAINE

In the 1640s and 1650s, at the same time that the colony was confronting growing numbers of strangers in its midst, Massachusetts annexed New Hampshire and Maine. These colonies did not spring from communal origins or a covenanted identity. Anglicans, the religiously indifferent, and profane English people inhabited northern New England's first plantations launched in the 1620s. Maine hosted New England's first Anglican chapel, built in 1635 at a settlement that Massachusetts later renamed York. The Bay Colony extended its authority over New Hampshire between 1641 and 1643; it took six years (1652–58) to gain political control over Maine. And yet, given the worldly origins of the two colonies, neither New Hampshire nor Maine would be fully incorporated into Puritan New England in the seventeenth century—or, for that matter, beyond.

Northern New England's early plantations were strongly tied to the sea. Farmers grew crops and raised livestock for survival. But limited high-quality soil and a much shorter growing season than in southern New England restricted agricultural production. New Hampshire and Maine possessed New England's most abundant fishing grounds, its thickest beaver pelts, and its richest stands of forest. Traders, transients, and then permanent settlers exploited these natural advantages. They shifted from island to mainland settlements, scattering small plantations in the 1620s and 1630s along drainage basins from the Piscataqua River between New Hampshire and Maine north to the York, Saco, and Kennebec river systems. Northern New Englanders lived and worked on or near water; they built tidal-powered sawmills and gristmills; and they traveled by boat and dugout canoe along the coast and up the rivers. Fishing, the fur trade, lumbering, and, after 1650, shipbuilding linked northern New England to the Bay Colony, the West Indies, and the larger Atlantic world.

Through the Council of New England early New Hampshire and Maine forged important connections to England's coastal ports in the West Country and south along the English Channel. Founded in 1620, the council was authorized by the Crown to oversee the colonization and development of New England. Two years later, Ferdinando Gorges, the council's president, and John Mason, its secretary, gained proprietary control of all the territory between the Merrimack and Kennebec Rivers. They called their dominion the Province of Maine. In 1629, Gorges and Mason divided their realm. Gorges secured complete control of Maine north of the Piscataqua River, and Mason became the sole proprietor of "Piscataqua plantations," which he renamed New Hampshire. The Mason family seat was located in Portsmouth, on England's south coast, in Hampshire County.

Mason had served as the governor of Newfoundland for six years. The accounts of fishermen who had visited New England shores stirred his colonial imagination and commercial ambitions. It was not faith but fish and fur that would be the building blocks of Mason's New World fiefdom. The proprietor failed to reap his earthly reward, however. Before they divided their domain, Mason and Gorges had gathered investors and launched a fishing/trading plantation on the Piscataqua River in 1623. They had also granted land drained by the river to English merchants and investors, who also initiated settlements, some of which failed. When Mason died in 1635, he left behind a colony made up of plantations with a total population of only several hundred. Most of New Hampshire's Anglican-oriented fisherfolk, traders, and farmers had arrived directly from England.

Though modest, New Hampshire's non-Puritan commercial beginnings reverberated through the colony's development after Mason's death. New Hampshire consisted of four settlements when it was annexed by Massachusetts in the early 1640s. Two of these plantations became the towns of Dover and Portsmouth; they originated under the Mason-Gorges proprietorship. Two other communities, Exeter and Hampton, were founded by Massachusetts Puritans in the late 1630s. Early New Hampshire, then, sheltered a mixed multitude of Anglican, profane, and pious Puritan people, some recruited directly from England, others re-migrants from Massachusetts.

Dover, four miles up the Piscataqua River, had been established in 1623 as a commercial fishing plantation. Ten years later, English Puritan investors acquired the settlement, a development that was followed by migration from the Bay Colony. Some of these new arrivals were Puritan radicals. One leading migrant, a follower of Anne Hutchinson, claimed to have "found the spirit of God in a pipe of tobacco."[14] Dover's Puritans fought among themselves and jousted with Anglican rivals. By 1639, annexation by Massachusetts emerged as one solution to the religious conflict and social turmoil that prevailed in Dover.

Portsmouth grew from pre-1630 commercial plantations on the south bank near the mouth of the Piscataqua River. Mason transported at least one hundred servants and wage laborers to "Strawbery Banke," the most successful plantation. The settlement did not prove to be profitable, but it did survive through a combination of fishing, lumbering, and farming. Strawbery Banke merchants oversaw fisheries on the Isles of Shoals, the seven glacial outcroppings four miles off the coast of New Hampshire and Maine. Established by West Country fishermen in the early seventeenth century, the Isles developed into a permanent settlement under Mason and Gorges. After midcentury, the Isles grew into one of New England's most populous and important fishing plantations, with five hundred permanent inhabitants and three times that number at the peak of the fishing season. Both the Isles of Shoals and Strawbery Banke, dominated by the material interests of Anglicans and the unchurched, offered the strongest resistance to the Puritan cultural makeover of New Hampshire.

Massachusetts migrants founded two towns in New Hampshire prior to the Puritan annexation of 1641–43. The Reverend John Wheelwright, brother-in-law of Anne Hutchinson, led about twenty families to the Piscataqua region in 1638 and established the town of Exeter. John Winthrop had banished Wheelwright from the Bay Colony a year earlier for espousing Hutchinsonian views, which included the accusation that Massachusetts ministers and magistrates were unconverted and, therefore, spiritually corrupt. The incorporation of an "orthodox" Puritan town at Hampton in 1639 followed the settlement of the dissenting community in Exeter. Massachusetts authorized the founding of Hampton, a coastal town that lay between Piscataqua and the Bay Colony. Hampton extended the northern border of Massachusetts and gave the Puritans access to tracts of valuable salt marsh. Another important early New England marine resource, saltwater hay sustained cattle herds that were often driven to market, providing meat for local consumption and trade.

When the Puritan state extended its authority over New Hampshire, the province's four distinctive towns held a combined population of about a thousand residents, perhaps half from Massachusetts. Bay Colony Puritans sought to secure their "eastern" frontier, enlarge commercial opportunities, and expand the civic-religious culture of their Bible commonwealth. Yet annexation fell short of a bold, imperial land grab. The dissolution of the Council of New England after 1629 and John Mason's death six years later had thrown land claims into chaos. Merchants, fishermen, and workers at Strawbery Banke, for example, worried about losing title to their land. In addition, controversy strained life in Dover. Some New Hampshire colonists sought the aid of Massachusetts in securing titles to their land; while they welcomed the prospect of improved social order, they often resisted Puritanism's pious ways. Other inhabitants, such as the Bay Colony migrants at Hampton, strongly embraced annexation. Still other colonists, including religious dissenters in Exeter, resisted merging with Massachusetts.

As they would in Maine, Puritan authorities negotiated with Anglican leaders in the Piscataqua plantations and made concessions in response to local concerns. In New Hampshire the Bay Colony compromised one of the pillars of the Bible Commonwealth: in Dover and Portsmouth freemen were not required to be members of Puritan churches in order to vote and hold office. With Hampton already a Massachusetts town and the Piscataqua settlements annexed in 1641, the dissenters in Exeter finally accepted governance from the south in 1643.

Over the next three decades New Hampshire's population increased modestly. In 1670, the colony held approximately eighteen hundred inhabitants, including sixty-five Africans. Expanding maritime opportunities underpinned New Hampshire's economy: fishing, the trade in lumber-related products like masts and naval stores, and shipbuilding. One report in 1665 described more than twenty sawmills on the Piscataqua River alone. Boards, naval stores, and ship masts were exported to Boston, the West Indies, and London. New Hampshire not only supplied large quantities of lumber to Boston's busy boat yards; it also developed its own shipbuilding industry in the second half of the seventeenth century. A Boston visitor to the colony in 1687 watched in amazement as a gigantic pine tree began its transformation into a ship mast. It required seventy-two oxen to drag the massive pine to a sawmill. In Portsmouth, merchant-entrepreneurs coalesced into a local elite that organized capital; recruited fishermen, lumbermen, and shipbuilders; and marketed commodities of the sea and forest.

Annexation by Massachusetts contributed to the commercial growth of New Hampshire by relieving the political, legal, and social instability that the province experienced in the 1630s. But not all the new settlers after 1643 were pious Puritans; the expanding fishing and lumbering industries continued to attract strangers. Migration from Massachusetts Bay after annexation did diffuse Puritan civic culture. Resistance and indifference to pious ways persisted in New Hampshire nevertheless. A Congregational church was not created in Portsmouth until 1671, a generation after the town's incorporation into Massachusetts. On the Isles of Shoals, fishermen welcomed the action of the Crown in 1679 that changed New Hampshire into a royal province separate from Massachusetts.

Puritanism was more frail in midcentury Maine than in New Hampshire. Massachusetts needed six years to absorb Gorges's province. As late as 1673, Maine had only one settled Congregational minister. Several years earlier, a royal commission claimed that in parts of Maine "as many men share a woman as they do a boat."[15] As they were drawing on secondhand reports, the commissioners may have been exaggerating. Even so, Maine was further estranged from pious Puritan ways than New Hampshire.

From the early 1620s to the Massachusetts takeover thirty years later, Maine's island and mainland fishing camps evolved from seasonal to permanent plantations. Some resembled the western mining camps of a much later era. Dominated by men, troubled by rowdy transients, and filled with hard drinkers, fishing plantations were also ramshackle, foul-smelling places. Temporary shacks and huts slowly gave way to more substantial plank dwellings, though many fishermen kept crude fish houses where they stored their gear. The commercial fishery required an elaborate infrastructure that shaped Maine's coastal landscape: platforms for cutting fish, wooden stages for drying the catch, and storehouses for packed barrels and salt. Coastal Maine was defined by more than the salty scent of the sea. The fishery gave the air an added tang. The reek of rotting and drying fish and of processed cod liver oil wafted near all of the inhabitants of fishing plantations.

Of course, not all fishermen were "slaves of the bottle," as Reverend Cotton Mather claimed, or led the lives of vice that descriptions of shared women suggested.[16] Resident fishermen brought families to Maine and pursued worldly lives that were not completely bound to profane ways. Other fisherfolk were more than nominal Anglicans. In a few island and mainland fishing plantations, investors recruited Anglican clergy and built chapels. Despite an Anglican presence, religious piety, churchly practices, and civic institutions did not shape early Maine. The province stood out as the most secular corner of New England. Maine's scattered coastal settlements devoted to fishing, lumbering, trade, and farming attracted individuals and families who trusted more in their own labor and skill for survival than God's providence. Merrymount's Thomas Morton even gained an economic foothold in tolerant, worldly Maine, acquiring substantial tracts of land along the Kennebec River. Fur, timber, and especially cod were commercial gods in early Maine.

Ferdinando Gorges (1565–1647) fashioned a proprietary vision to develop Maine beyond its frontier outposts. His family hailed from the important English port of Bristol, on the border of the West Country. Gorges is occasionally singled out as the "father of New England," though Pilgrim- and Puritan-centered narratives of the region's origin obscure his role in colonization. Gorges never set foot in New England. He spent half of his eighty-two years vigorously promoting and participating in efforts to colonize the region. He was one of the leaders of an early attempt to establish a permanent colony in New England. Sagadahoc, founded at the mouth of the Kennebec River in 1607, collapsed within a year. Gorges's Council of New England supported Plymouth Colony. He encouraged merchants in England's West Country and port cities to advance the council's colonizing mission. Under his leadership, the council granted settlement patents in the 1620s to groups such as the Merrymounters who antagonized Plymouth and Massachusetts officials.

In the 1630s Gorges devised an ambitious, fanciful plan to organize the straggling settlements that made up his Province of Maine. On paper, Gorges, as the governor-proprietor, divided Maine into units based on English county government: "bailiwicks," "hundreds," and "parishes." Gorges established the Church of England as the province's official faith. He chose "Gorgeana," a renamed fishing, lumbering, and trading settlement of less than a hundred people along the Agamenticus (York) River, as the provincial capital, from which the governor-proprietor intended to gain control over the independent plantations of his kingdom. The aristocratic Gorges envisioned a semifeudal system of landholding, with tenants paying rents to and providing services for the proprietor. Such a plan faced better prospects in other parts of colonial America than Maine and New England. It challenged the individualism and commercial opportunism of early Maine; it also countered New England's dominant freeholding practices.

In 1640, Deputy Governor Thomas Gorges, the aged proprietor's twenty-two-year-old nephew, arrived in Maine to oversee the province. He took the reins of Gorgeana, where recruited settlers were already laboring for the proprietor. But the Gorgeses failed to attract the immigrants who were so crucial to their plan for Maine. England's Civil War undermined their efforts before the realities of frontier Maine could accomplish the same end. As in other parts of New England, the disruption of immigration reduced the demand for Maine products like timber and even drove some settlers back to England. In 1643, Thomas

Gorges abandoned Gorgeana for the homeland. When his uncle died four years later, Maine slipped free from the never exactly tight grip of the Gorgeses only to fall into the hands of Puritan Massachusetts.

The turmoil of civil war and the temporary ascendancy of the Puritan cause in the homeland impelled Bay Colony authorities to expand their jurisdiction beyond New Hampshire. They encountered more resistance in Maine. In 1652, Massachusetts annexed Gorgeana and two nearby settlements in Wells and Kittery. Associating their imperialism with the progress of the Civil War, Massachusetts leaders changed the name of Gorgeana to York, in honor of an important Royalist city in England where Puritan forces had triumphed. The New England Puritans prevailed over opposition from some settlers in Sir Ferdinando's capital. As Bay Colony authorities moved up the Maine coast, stiffer resistance emerged, particularly among settlements on and near Casco Bay (present-day Portland) that held out until 1658. All along the coast, Massachusetts absorbed settlements by negotiating with local non-Puritan leaders and incorporating them into a new county government. Maine became bound to but not completely part of the Bible Commonwealth.

The Puritan annexation did promote the development of Massachusetts civic institutions and practices in Maine. After 1658, new migrants from Massachusetts Bay and New Hampshire arrived in the province. By 1671, Maine's more than three thousand people were still scattered along the coast and still had strong ties to the sea. But over the next forty years the Abenaki, who often favored the French, offered their own resistance to Puritan imperialism. Native raids and protracted warfare forced settlers to abandon towns; many fled to the safety of Essex County, Massachusetts, north of Boston.

Thus, even after the Puritan takeover, Maine did not become a pious province of the Bay Colony. York, the former seat of Ferdinando Gorges's paper empire, was transformed into a Puritan town, but few other settlements in the seventeenth century followed suit. Toleration and religious indifference continued to characterize Maine. Ten years after the Puritan conquest, Massachusetts reported that Quakers controlled Kittery. Cotton Mather later related the story of a Massachusetts minister who made a missionary visit to Maine. He gathered a small audience and urged his listeners to embrace pious ways and not "contradict the main end of planting this [New England] wilderness." An assertive fisherman interrupted the sermon. "Sir, you are mistaken: you think you are preaching to the people at the Bay; our *main* end was to *catch Fish*."[17]

## THE OCEAN COLONY: RELIGIOUS DISSENT
## AND MARITIME OPPORTUNITY

Although it was founded by religious refugees from Massachusetts, early Rhode Island resembled the settlements of northern New England more than its neighboring Bible commonwealths. During the 1630s, radical religious dissenters from the Puritan beliefs and practices of Massachusetts established four towns that formed Rhode Island: Providence and Warwick on the mainland and Portsmouth and Newport on Aquidneck Island in Narragansett Bay. In their quest for religious perfection and "soul liberty," many of Rhode Island's early settlers were more Puritan than the rank and file of Massachusetts and Connecticut. Rhode Island's founders continued the tradition of dissent within a Puritan movement that itself had been born out of protest. The protesters in Rhode Island, however, found little agreement about religion—or about much else, for that matter. In response they removed religion from the public realm. Rhode Islanders separated church and state, privatized religion, and planted a scrawny civic culture. Freedom of conscience and release from state or church regulation promoted economic liberty. The privatization of religion enabled individuals to pursue worldly interests with conscience as their primary guide.

Early Rhode Island had much in common with northern New England. The colony did not spring from a communal vision. The settlement of individual towns preceded the formation of a colony-wide government. As in New Hampshire, the towns defended their status as independent settlements. Rhode Island's weak civic culture, religious toleration, and commercial individualism all had parallels in northern New England. In addition, Rhode Island's ties to the sea were every bit as strong as Maine's. New England's smallest colony claimed one of the region's largest accessible coastlines. From its founding through the Colonial Era, Rhode Islanders located the bulk of their towns on Narragansett Bay. Geography provided a physical setting for extensive maritime commerce, and Rhode Island came to be known as New England's "ocean colony."

Leaders of the Bible commonwealths also viewed the Narragansett Bay area as a "latrina," the repository of New England's moral misfits. Puritan moral geography located Rhode Island "between the devil and the deep blue sea."[18] Both Massachusetts and Connecticut pressed territorial claims against Rhode Island. Recalcitrant settlers and the labors of Roger Williams precluded the kind of Puritan annexation of New England's smallest colony that took place in northern New England.

Williams established Providence, Rhode Island's first town, in 1636 as a haven for fellow religious dissenters. A devout Puritan and recent graduate of Cambridge, Williams (1603–83) had arrived in Boston five years before he fled to Providence. The young minister's piety incited controversy wherever he preached—first in Boston, then in Plymouth, and finally in Salem. Williams advocated Separatism; he attacked Puritan churches for not withdrawing completely from the Church of England. He repudiated the authority of Puritan civil magistrates to enforce public worship on the Sabbath. Williams was a religious perfectionist. His evolving acceptance of religious tolerance and conscience-based soul liberty derived from his fear that the state would corrupt spiritual life. Later proponents of the separation of church and state have usually feared the opposite: that religion would corrupt the state. Beyond his pietistic individualism and religious perfectionism, Williams also antagonized Puritan authorities because he attacked their land acquisition policies. He charged that Massachusetts falsely claimed territory based on a patent issued by the king instead of negotiating with Native people and paying them for their land. The Massachusetts General Court banished Williams to England in 1635. Before he could be deported, Williams fled toward Narragansett Bay. By the spring of 1636, Williams and perhaps a half-dozen families from Salem founded Providence on land granted by the Narragansett.

The settlement's name commemorated Williams's belief that divine intervention had guided his escape from Massachusetts. He designated Providence as a refuge for religious dissenters who suffered, as he had, for conscience's sake. Religious toleration failed to produce the harmonious haven that he envisioned.

Providence attracted small groups of religious dissenters and individualists, people whose commitment to soul liberty and antiauthoritarianism infected civil affairs. "Sometimes," Williams remarked, "every meeting we were all on fire and had a terrible burning fit ready to come to blows."[19] Williams's hand was weakened by the fact that he had no official authorization—no charter, land patent, or covenant—for his settlement. Providence was torn by land disputes, as strong-willed individualists aggressively pursued their worldly interests. The settlement's reputation for acrimony contributed to its slow growth. Approximately 250 people inhabited the town in 1645.

During Providence's early years, Williams's religious perfectionism compelled him to forsake affiliation with any church. A Separatist-Congregationalist, Williams endorsed local self-government by church members when he founded Providence. By 1639, he became convinced that infant baptism was unscriptural; the sacrament needed to be restricted to people who could testify to their spiritual rebirth. In keeping with that belief, Williams and some of his followers rebaptized themselves. They formed the first Baptist church in colonial America. But within months Williams began to question Baptist practice. He abandoned the church and never again joined a religious body. He became a "Seeker" of truth, a pietist who realized that his quest for religious perfection would never be fulfilled in this world. Other seekers found refuge *and* religious truth in Rhode Island during its first decades. They launched three more independent towns, which Williams, in the face of determined foes, labored to unite into a functioning colony.

Samuel Gorton proved to be one of the most querulous radicals drawn to Williams's "lively experiment" in religious liberty. Though he was not a minister, like Williams Gorton ignited disputes wherever he settled. Gorton was banished from Massachusetts and Plymouth within two years of his arrival in New England in 1637. He found his way to Providence by 1640, where he agreed with Williams on the separation of church and state but not much else. Gorton's belief in an indwelling spirit anticipated the Quaker doctrine of the inner light. Such a conviction extended the Protestant notion of the priesthood of all believers, the idea that the individual had direct access to God without churchly mediators. Gorton attacked ministers, endorsed lay preaching, and opposed baptism and communion. Along with some of his followers, Gorton purchased land from the Narragansett in 1643 and formed his own settlement, Warwick, on the western shore of Narragansett Bay less than ten miles south of Providence. The Gortonites, as they called themselves, pitted Warwick against the already divided dissenters of Providence.

Religious and political factionalism also characterized the towns on the eastern side of Narragansett Bay. Anne Hutchinson (1591–1643) was the second major religious radical expelled from Massachusetts in 1637. The Hutchinson family had settled in Boston three years earlier. William, Anne's husband, was a prominent London merchant. They joined the Boston church, a congregation packed with pious, commerce-oriented members. By then in her early forties, Anne's intellectual ability and skills as a midwife and healer thrust her into a position of authority among the women of the Boston church. She led popular religious meetings for women at her house. The sessions, in which she explained Calvinist dogma, were then opened to men. John Winthrop condemned Hutchinson for reversing gender roles; her "public" speaking, for example, was considered appropriate for a minister or magistrate, not for a Puritan goodwife. Anne's behavior challenged the Bible Commonwealth's hierarchy and social order. She was recast as New England's "Jezebel," the evil, shameless wife out of the Old Testament. Rhode Island, with its freedom from government restraints on religious and commercial matters, would provide fertile ground for this Jezebel's followers.

Gender shaped the Hutchinson controversy. Yet Anne was a radical Puritan like Roger Williams, not a proto-feminist. She presented a doctrinal challenge to the Massachusetts authorities. Hutchinson accused most ministers of overemphasizing the role of external morality as preparation for spiritual rebirth. She criticized them for preaching a "covenant of works," the idea that morality would lead to salvation. For Hutchinson, conversion had little to do with good behavior. Rebirth resulted from the sudden infusion of God's grace; it was an internal ravishment of the soul that created a mystical union with the Holy Spirit. Such converts, she suggested, were no longer bound by ordinary moral law. Opponents accused Hutchinson of "antinomianism," that is, of standing "against law," a theological perspective that stressed the internal life of Christians over the external one. The Hutchinsonians' antinomianism reinforced the soul liberty that Williams had initiated in Rhode Island; it interiorized personal piety and diminished the spiritual significance of conventional morality. In the ocean colony, the Hutchinsonians found the freedom to pursue, as well as to disagree over, their religious piety and to exploit aggressively the maritime commercial opportunities that Rhode Island offered.

Hutchinson and some of her most ardent supporters, many of whom had also been banished, arrived on an island in Narragansett Bay in the spring of 1638. With the assistance of Roger Williams, they acquired Aquidneck from the Narragansett sachem Miantonomi and established the town of Portsmouth. The dissenters elected William Coddington, one of Boston's wealthiest merchants, as their leader. The Hutchinsonians carried with them a written agreement of cooperation signed by Coddington and eighteen other household heads. The promise of accord dissolved quickly. The refugees became embroiled in religious and worldly quarrels. They chafed under the authority that Coddington asserted, they fought over the distribution of land based on wealth and social standing, and they failed to agree on religious matters. Unable to organize a church or attract a minister, the Hutchinsonians reluctantly pushed religion to the private sphere. By 1639, local government on Aquidneck Island was essentially a civil polity based on English law, a far cry from the commonwealth inspired by Biblical injunction. Soul liberty now surfaced on the eastern shore of Narragansett Bay.

Dissatisfaction with Portsmouth led to the founding of Newport at the southern tip of Aquidneck Island. In 1639, Coddington and a small group of Portsmouth leaders established their own plantation. Many of the Hutchinsonians sought a commercial as well as a religious haven. For ambitious maritime traders such as Coddington, Newport offered a protected harbor far superior to Portsmouth's. With their antinomian individualism and commercial backgrounds, Newport's merchant-planters set the seaport's course of development. No established church shaped Newport's civic life; no communal vision restrained the individual pursuit of maritime opportunities. From less than a few hundred settlers in the 1640s, Newport would grow over the second half of the seventeenth century into a major New England mercantile town—the most populous and prosperous seaport in Rhode Island.

Not surprisingly, some Newporters, led by Coddington, resisted Roger Williams's efforts to unite the independent towns along Narragansett Bay into a colony. In 1644, Williams secured a patent from Parliament to organize civil government in Rhode Island. The patent excluded the church from civic life. Property ownership and not church membership determined freemanship. The dissenting founders' localism and distrust of authority defined the new political order—a weak federation in which towns retained power. The General Assembly, the colony-wide body of elected representatives, needed the consent of the towns to pass legislation. More than any other English colonists, Rhode Islanders preferred to keep power close to the people. This localism combined with soul liberty and individualism to foster in the ocean colony the strongest democratic spirit and practice in Anglo-America.

Even after the patent of 1644, Rhode Island's "democratical" elements generated factionalism. Coddington and others in Newport refused to acknowledge the new political arrangement, for instance. The colony's Puritan neighbors coined the term "Rhode Islandism" to describe the state of affairs in the Narragansett region and to warn the inhabitants of the Bible commonwealths. Rhode Islandism referred to a polity that lacked the Puritans' commitment to ordered liberty and stable civic/religious institutions. It identified the factionalism, libertarianism, and disorder that seemed to prevail in "Rogue Island."

Vivid Puritan images of "sluttish" Rhode Island clung to the colony well beyond its founding, perhaps obscuring how the Narragansett Bay settlements changed. Charles II granted Rhode Island a charter in 1663 that strengthened the power of the colonial government in its dealings with towns. The charter buoyed prospects for new political stability in the colony. In fact, because of its liberal provisions, the charter effectively served as Rhode Island's constitution until 1843. It endorsed the right of freemen to elect the governor, assistants, and deputies and legalized the separation of church and state. Nonetheless, even under the new colonial government, jealous localism and other elements of

Rhode Islandism persisted. Free market individualism in religious and economic life retarded the development of a strong civic culture.

Greater Newport's domination of the ocean colony accelerated in the decades following the charter of 1663. Merchant-planters plowed the sea for profits. They relied less on fish than on farm products and livestock to expand trade along the coast and to the West Indies. Merchants like Coddington laid out extensive estates on Aquidneck Island, hired tenant farmers, and constructed wharves on Newport Harbor. They shipped produce, horses, cattle, and sheep to other colonies. Sheep became so central that it usurped the place of codfish in Newport. The image of a sheep adorned the town's official seal, testimony to the animal's role in local maritime prosperity. Newport merchants also traded Indian and black slaves, though Rhode Island's ascendancy over the American phase of the traffic in Africans would not arrive until the eighteenth century. Far-flung trade stimulated local shipbuilding. Maritime prosperity attracted new settlers. Newport's population grew to approximately 2,000 by 1690, with maritime trades and related labor employing the bulk of the town's workers.

The thriving seaport served as Rhode Island's capital. It also became the hub of New England Quakerism. The Society of Friends burst into England's religious life during the tumult of the 1640s and 1650s, a tumult that inspired expressions of Protestant sectarianism. English Quaker missionaries made their way to Massachusetts and converted small groups of believers dissatisfied with Bay Colony orthodoxy, just as Hutchinson, Gorton, and Williams had been. Officials in Massachusetts mobilized state power against the Quakers, fining and banishing them. If the Friends returned, as some did, they faced severe punishment: whipping, ear cropping, even hanging. Four Quakers were hanged in Massachusetts before officials relaxed the persecution, which had only seemed to embolden the dissenters.

Some Quakers sought refuge in more tolerant Maine, but the Society flourished in Rhode Island. Friends advocated the separation of church and state; more importantly, their mystical spirituality resembled the views of the Hutchinsonians and Gortonists—an interiorized faith that stressed the priesthood of all believers. The Quaker faith rested on the doctrine of the "inner light," the divine spirit that all people possessed, rather than on the Calvinist notion of natural depravity. Quakers radically reduced the role of ministers in religious life and encouraged spiritual egalitarianism. Through their inner light, believers had direct access to God. Religious quietism, which derived from an intimate individual relation with the divine, characterized Quaker spirituality. Many of Anne Hutchinson's followers on Aquidneck Island, including Coddington, joined the Friends. Quaker spiritual equality may have been particularly appealing to women. Empowered by the doctrine of inner light, Quaker women spoke in meetings and sought converts by testifying to their faith in public.

The rise of the Quakers bolstered the practice of soul liberty in Rhode Island. In heavily Quaker Newport, religious faith also reinforced the industry, individualism, and self-discipline that often led to commercial prosperity. Certainly, connections with Quaker merchants in other colonies facilitated the Newporters' maritime trade.

The seal of Rhode Island's charter of 1663 displayed an anchor with the word "Hope." The anchor was a familiar Christian symbol that seamen later had tattooed on their bodies. But the anchor also suggests the importance of maritime trade, as opposed to religious dissent alone, in Rhode Island's development.

Seventeenth-century New England evolved both as a haven for religious reformers and dissenters and as the home of people estranged from Protestant piety. Maritime enterprise imbued life in much of the region. In northern New England, coastal settlements originated in worldly calculations. In the Bible commonwealths and Rhode Island, different religious cultures underpinned commercial pursuits. Colonial New Englanders have been called "the Dutch of England's empire."[20] Midcentury commercial and geographical expansion launched New England's rapid rise into a maritime region. By the late seventeenth century, it also provoked Puritan concerns that the region was in moral and spiritual decline, threatened by a creeping Rhode Islandism.

# FOUR

# New England Besieged, 1660–1700

IN EUROPEAN AND Native warfare, the human body often furnished trophies of triumph. Scalps are the best-known example, but not the only one. In the decades after 1676, thousands of travelers to Plymouth, both pious and profane, visited the town's first historical landmark: the shrunken head of King Philip resting atop a watchtower. Metacomet, as his Wampanoag people knew him, endures as the most notable foe colonial New England ever confronted. He sparked the Native uprising called King Philip's War in 1675. The intercolonial rebellion led to the destruction of English and Native villages across New England. Even after the Wampanoag sachem was killed and dismembered in August of 1676, the war continued in New Hampshire and Maine well into 1678.

Other intercolonial crises threatened second-generation New Englanders. After its restoration in the homeland in 1660, the royal government aggressively sought to tighten its control of the New England colonies in the 1680s. It recalled charters and reorganized the separate colonies into one supra-dominion under royal authority. The turmoil of Native warfare and the Crown's sweeping political intervention contributed to colonial New England's most infamous event: the Salem witchcraft hysteria of 1692. This complex episode, frequently seen as representative of the Puritans' blind faith and bigotry, was an exceptional outburst. The decades before the witchcraft crisis saw no precedent for the events of 1692.

Puritan leaders interpreted the major public upheavals of war, royal intervention, and mass witchcraft accusations as providential "afflictions" for a backsliding people. Indeed, second-generation Puritan preachers and writers perfected the American jeremiad, a sermon that took its name from Jeremiah, the Old Testament prophet of doom. Jeremiads rebuked the second generation for failing to live up to the religious ideals of New England's founders. From weather problems to warfare, jeremiads attributed the numerous regional crises of the late seventeenth century to divine wrath. God raised his disciplining rod and regularly smited a covenanted people who had overseen New England's moral and spiritual decline.

Jeremiads recorded official responses to a changing colonial world and to ongoing tensions within Puritanism and between saints and strangers. Shaped by the rhetorical weight of the jeremiads, the history of seventeenth-century New England has too often been told as an overdrawn story of Puritan declension from the piety and supposed worldly restraint of the founding generation. Second-generation Puritans made their own contributions to the perpetuation of a pious New England. They did not simply shed their Puritan skin to reveal Yankee souls.

RESTORATION AND AFFLICTION

Puritan reform perished in the homeland after 1660. The failed revolution ended with the restoration of the Stuart monarchy; Charles II occupied the throne from 1660 to 1685. The Restoration reestablished Anglican worship. Some Puritan leaders fled the homeland; others were beheaded for regicide. The Puritan movement in England disintegrated.

Among New England Puritans, the demise of their English brethren dissolved any hope that purified Protestantism would succeed in the ancestral land the way it had in the New World. This turn of events provoked clerical concern for New England's future as the standard-bearer of reform. The Restoration also encouraged Puritan preachers to put new emphasis on New England's moral standing in a spiritual wilderness—one that now appeared to include England. Unlike the region's English-born founders, second-generation Puritans acquired more of an *American* collective consciousness.

Despite expanding transatlantic trade, the demographic realities of late seventeenth-century New England reinforced a regional sense of distance from the homeland. Death increasingly silenced the region's English-born founders: John Winthrop (1649), John Davenport (1670), Anne Bradstreet (1672), Roger Williams (1683). The New England Congregational ministry became filled with native-born graduates of Harvard College rather than English products of Cambridge University. New immigrants were not arriving in significant numbers to replace the region's founding settlers. Puritan refugees from Restoration England did seek haven in New England. Josiah Franklin was one. A religious dissenter and a dyer by trade, the father of Benjamin arrived in Boston around 1682. Merchants from the homeland, often Anglican in faith, also made their way to New England in pursuit of commercial opportunities. But the region's population swelled in the second half of the seventeenth century by natural increase, not by immigration. In fact, beginning in the turbulent 1680s and 1690s, New England experienced more out- than immigration. Yet its population stood at an impressive 93,000 by 1700. Second-generation New Englanders constituted an overwhelmingly American-born population, pious and profane descendants of the region's founders—with increasingly slender personal and cultural ties to England.

Of course population growth, land hunger, and expanding trade over two generations altered the texture of New England life from what it had been in the 1630s and 1640s. Such change excited late seventeenth-century Puritan preaching about the region's moral and spiritual decline. Then, too, the slow-paced, even halting incorporation of Maine and New Hampshire into an "orthodox" New England troubled authorities who feared the "Indianization" of settlers in the region's outback. In addition, Rhode Island continued to be plagued by contention and was mockingly called the "Isle of Errors." Throughout New England, distilled rum—a by-product of trade with the West Indies—presented a growing challenge in the late seventeenth century to the enforcement of sober ways, especially within the profane communities of Boston and other port towns.

Unlike the region's founders, second-generation New Englanders faced a series of major crises, which were widely viewed as divine afflictions for moral and spiritual declension. Except for hardened profane folk, seventeenth-century New Englanders had long understood worldly "mercies" or calamities as divine rewards or punishments for individual or collective behavior. Indeed, fears of divine retribution on corrupt England helped propel the Puritan migration. In New England, personal catastrophes such as the fire that destroyed Anne Bradstreet's house in 1666 were usually interpreted as the consequence of God's disciplining rod. Bradstreet wrote a poem in which she explained the affliction as the consequence of her investment in domestic comfort interfering with her focus on her heavenly home. God also rewarded or punished collective behavior. Sometimes divine moral law operated through nature to bless or chastise a backsliding society. Diarists documented, for instance, how New England's weather turned sharply colder in the 1680s and 1690s. John Calvin taught many New Englanders that the "intemperature of the air, ice, thunder, unreasonable rains, drought, hails, and whatsoever is extraordinary in the world, are the fruits of sin."[1]

In many respects, the decades from 1660 to 1690 were a season of affliction in New England. Drought, crop blights, cold, and catastrophes like the fire that ravaged the center of Boston in 1676 seemed to replace the abundant mercies bestowed on New England's pious founders. Most important, unparalleled intercolonial crises—King Philip's War and the royal seizure of the region in the 1680s—underscored God's seeming quarrel with New England.

Providential readings of late seventeenth-century crises that invoked God's moral law were not confined to Puritans. Quakers in Rhode Island, for instance, saw King Philip's War as divine punishment for Puritan persecution of the Society of Friends. Yet through their prolific preaching and their control of New England's printing presses in Boston and Cambridge, Puritan authorities created a powerful colonial story of a region in decline from its pious origins and the obligations of the communal covenant. The jeremiad took many forms: election and fast-day sermons; histories of the region's founding; Indian captivity narratives; and poetry. It spoke to American-born descendants of New England's founders, especially pious people, who were further from the homeland, culturally speaking, than their English-born parents. The jeremiad encouraged an American regional self-consciousness by warning that New England's distinctive moral identity, created by the founding generation, was being threatened by the corrosive forces of impiety and economic ambition. But the jeremiad has also distorted our understanding of seventeenth-century New England's historical development. It mythologized a heroic founding generation's achievements and faulted or ignored the accomplishments of its post-heroic sons and daughters. Jeremiads wove a narrative of declension that was more inspirational than historical.

## THE JEREMIAD

The famous Halfway Covenant of 1662 has been frequently cited as early evidence of Puritan New England's decline. During the first generation, ministers baptized the children of converted full church members. Puritans assumed that these children of visible saints would follow through on baptismal promises, experience spiritual rebirth, and become full church members. Many did not, and therefore their offspring—the grandchildren of the first generation—were not eligible for baptism. The Halfway Covenant made the sacrament available to the children of moral and Sabbath-worshiping but unconverted adults. Halfway membership, like other Puritan church policies, encountered dissenters. By the end of the century, however, the Covenant had become widely accepted practice.

The Halfway Covenant was hardly an unequivocal sign of generational spiritual decay. The new policy had little effect in much of Connecticut, where access to the sacrament was more open than in Massachusetts. Connecticut ministers such as Thomas Hooker had feared the consequences of strict pure churches, which required a public relation of conversion as a requirement for communion. Indeed, many pious descendants of the founders failed to advance to conversion because of their own scruples and hesitancy over recounting their spiritual experience. The Halfway Covenant brought pious families into the church to encourage conversions and full membership. Too often, the rhetoric of the jeremiad has shaped understanding of the Covenant as the opening chapter in the history of Puritan New England's decline.

Though New England preachers relied on the jeremiad to forge an epic American account of the region's founding, this mode of sermonizing actually originated in England. A ritualized chastisement summoning a covenanted people to reform their ways and appease divine wrath, the jeremiad was a staple of English Reformed Protestantism. England had been conceived as a covenanted nation—a chosen people—with its own heroic age of Protestant reformers and martyrs. For early seventeenth-century Puritans, including those who settled New England, the homeland had retreated from the initial promise of sweeping Protestant reform. Its declension provoked divine wrath and spurred New England colonization.

Second-generation Puritans adapted the English jeremiad to tell a story of New England's heroic origins and subsequent decline. The region's early history replaced the homeland's sixteenth-century progress toward reformation as the "golden age" of piety—"Protestantism's finest hour."[2] The jeremiad transformed New England's founding into an American epic of biblical proportions; the recently deceased leaders of the Puritan exodus to the New World were recalled as American types of Old Testament figures—Aaron, Moses, and Nehemiah. By mythologizing early New England history, Puritan jeremiads sought to inspire the second generation. In the process a tidal wave of printed and spoken words overwhelmed Puritan descendants with a chronicle of their shortcomings.

Jeremiads addressed the communal covenant: the idea that New Englanders were part of God's chosen people and would be rewarded or punished based on the collective behavior of the godly, the civil, and the profane. Jeremiads represented "civic preaching," sermons reserved for ritualized occasions: election, fast, and thanksgiving days. At the start of a legislative session elected officials met with ministers for moral instruction. Beginning in the 1660s election sermons expanded into detailed written texts that were usually printed, distributed, and discussed from meetinghouse pulpits. Fast days, when New Englanders gathered to pray for relief from an affliction such as a drought, multiplied during the second half of the seventeenth century. Connecticut adopted weekly fast days for most of King Philip's War. Thanksgiving days, which acknowledged God's mercies, added to the late seventeenth-century bumper crop of public religious rituals inspired by afflictions. Civic preaching and publications institutionalized the jeremiad's interpretive conventions of a heroic settlement followed by generational decline and providential chastisement. From Nathaniel Morton's *New England's Memorial* (1669) to Cotton Mather's magisterial seven-volume *Magnalia Christi Americana* (1702), the second generation produced numerous regional histories that were shaped by the jeremiad.

The jeremiad's pervasive laments about a backsliding people may have stirred the founders' descendants. They have also convinced some modern historians that seventeenth-century New England followed a trajectory of moral and spiritual decline. The jeremiad should neither be dismissed as clerical propaganda nor accepted as informative history, even as it embraced elements of both. The New England jeremiad deployed history for civic, religious, even tribal ends. Its providential explanation of the second generation's crises reasserted New England's moral identity as a place in a special relationship with God. The jeremiad thereby reaffirmed obligations of the communal covenant. In other words, for all of the rhetoric about decline, Jeremiahs and their receptive audiences reveal the generational continuity of Puritan ideals.

Still, in the service of didactic, inspirational Puritan goals, the jeremiads created a selective, imagined New England past. Late seventeenth-century preachers and writers eliminated how the founders themselves often felt like uncertain, bewildered refugees who sometimes reemigrated. They became religious figures, shorn of their mortal dimensions as English folk engaged in the daily tasks—and disputes—of building a life in exile and of warding off disillusionment with the New World or with their own religious and political authorities.

Consider, for instance, the jeremiads' indictment of the second generation's land hunger and worldliness. One apostle of doom claimed that land had become an idol. "Whereas the first planters . . . were satisfied with one acre for each person, and after that with twenty acres for a family," he thundered, "how have men since coveted after the earth."[3] This misleading historical perspective slighted the land hunger and population dispersal of the founding generation. Most early colonists, with multiple sons to settle, could not be content with twenty acres. Legislation failed to keep farmhouses within a half mile of a meetinghouse. Dissenters seeking good land scattered to Connecticut in the

1630s. Plymouth colonists dispersed in the same decade that the Great Migration created new commercial opportunities for farmers.

To be sure, population growth accelerated land acquisition and speculation in the late seventeenth century, and new towns "hived off" from older settlements. By the mid-1670s, Connecticut contained twenty-five towns and Massachusetts had more than twice that number. Far from evidence of decline, the scattering of people and the incorporation of new towns advanced Puritan piety and civic culture. Townspeople built new meetinghouses and schools, appointed ministers and teachers, and organized representative governments. In short, worldly ambition and success produced the material resources that sustained Puritan New England's expansion. The second generation accepted the principle enunciated by one founding minister as early as 1628: "Christ cannot be had for money, yet sometimes without expense of money he cannot be had."[4]

This minister described one way that Puritan piety and worldly prosperity intersected. The founders conceived of New England as a place of religious reform and commercial enterprise. Late seventeenth-century jeremiads typically represented New England as a region established almost exclusively for pious purposes. Salem minister John Higginson warned merchants in 1664 that "it was not for worldly wealth or a better livelihood here for the outward man" that early settlers journeyed to the New World. He admonished his "Brethren" to remember that "New England is originally a plantation of Religion, not a plantation of trade."[5] Higginson and other Jeremiahs reacted to the late seventeenth-century expansion of commerce in ports like Salem. Certainly one function of the jeremiad was to patrol the shifting boundaries of competency and worldliness in the second generation. But the Puritan dilemma became a blunt historical instrument in the hands of New England's Jeremiahs. They purged the founding generation of commercial ambitions and worldly taint. John Winthrop would not have recognized the imagined New England of the jeremiads. In 1639, Massachusetts fined Robert Keayne, a devout Puritan and Boston import merchant, for price gouging; then the First Church censured him. Keayne was singled out for punishment, but Winthrop believed that excessive pricing was rampant in early New England. In other words, despite the rhetoric of Jeremiahs like Higginson, early New England was a plantation of religion *and* trade.

Puritanism was a faith lived in the world and not a religion fulfilled in a monastery or reserved for the Sabbath. Yet the verbal flogging of the second generation diminished their worldly accomplishments while it exalted the otherworldliness of the founders. The jeremiads laid the foundation for the claim that New England's development is a story of declension from Puritan to Yankee. This line of interpretation obscures how piety and worldly engagement interpenetrated in Puritanism. Many New Englanders were both Puritans and Yankees almost from the start. The early history of the Bible commonwealths was so much more than a parade of piety with single-minded saints marching in unison toward a celestial city.

Jeremiads fashioned an influential but selective and exclusionary Puritan-centered narrative of New England's past. Native people were relegated to the margins of early New England. Colonial promotional literature had described the openness of coastal terrain that Natives cultivated. Second-generation jeremiads and histories depicted the presettlement landscape as nothing but a "howling wilderness." New England had been not only a spiritually barren place, preachers asserted, but a thick forested land unimproved by Native hands. In the 1660s and 1670s, jeremiads began famously referring to New England's Puritan settlement as an "errand into the wilderness."[6] This phrase distilled the essence of the region's early history: heroic, saintly founders transformed New England spiritually *and* physically in one generation.

In many ways, of course, New England's Puritan founders did represent a "great" generation of thinkers and doers. The region's Puritan settlers were certainly an exceptional colonial population, and they created a distinctive civic culture. The jeremiad, however, mythologized them and the character of early New England. It imposed a moral burden on the second generation and propagated a sacred account of the region's colonial past that obscured the role of merchants, dissenters, servants, the profane, and Indians in creating New England.

Beyond decidedly shaping how we have often viewed seventeenth-century New England, second-generation jeremiads left another legacy. They endowed New England with the most well-developed, if selective, collective historical identity in colonial Anglo-America. The second generation gave birth to a distinctive regional historical consciousness that, over time, propelled New Englanders to the forefront of the study of America's past. Moreover, for Puritan descendants who stood culturally and morally distant from the English homeland, the jeremiads encouraged an Americanization of collective identity. The jeremiads reimagined the region's founding as an *American* epic. The apex of heroic Reformed piety took place on *American*, not English, soil. Devout New Englanders became an increasingly important part of the New Israel—the transatlantic community of saints. New Englanders stood out as a "peculiar people." As one Jeremiah put it, speaking for God, they were a "People that . . . I have known above the families of the Earth."[7] God afflicted America's New Israel because he expected so much from it.

Repentance and reform brought temporary deliverance from God's judgments, until backsliding provoked his wrath once more in an ongoing cycle. In the outpouring of verbal assaults cataloguing the second generation's moral frailties, jeremiads ironically fathered a powerfully historicized New England regional identity. Such an accomplishment more than matched the heroic deeds of the founders.

## NATIVE AMERICANS AND COLONISTS: THE SECOND GENERATION

For Jeremiahs the ongoing encounter and cultural exchange between Natives and colonists revealed both the menace and the reality of "Indianization." In 1675 New England's aboriginal population stood at about 18,000; the colonial population numbered approximately 60,000. Perhaps all colonial societies confront the prospect of "going native." By abandoning a "civilized" European homeland, New World settlers faced adaptations that were often seen, especially in the homeland, as cultural degeneration. With the encouragement of their Indian allies, for example, colonial forces battling King Philip's warriors adjusted their tactics to accommodate a skulking way of war.

Several decades of close interaction between Natives and colonials induced Jeremiahs to accuse the second generation of a corrupting Indianization. Despite their dependence on aboriginal people, New England's founders had "heroically" resisted cultural degeneration. Their American descendants proved less resolute, jeremiads scolded. Some land-hungry settlers lived like "heathen," without villages and churches. Indolence and lax child-rearing, behavior imputed to Indians, increasingly infected Anglo households, religious and civil authorities complained. New England's bloodiest Native war appeared as an appropriate affliction to reverse the course of cultural degeneration. Colonists fought like Indians while redeeming New England from Indianization.

One way, short of war, for a colonial people to reaffirm cultural superiority and dominance is through conversion of the aboriginal population. In the three decades leading up to what resulted in a debacle for New England's Natives, Puritans launched serious efforts to Anglicize and Christianize tribal members. Communities of "praying Indian" towns stretched from Massachusetts to Plymouth, Martha's Vineyard, and Nantucket. More than 2,300 Natives inhabited these settlements at their high point in 1674. Interestingly, praying towns did not appear in Rhode Island, where large concentrations of Narragansett lived. Roger Williams pursued peaceful coexistence, and he knew the Narragansett intimately. In 1643 he published a pioneering text, *A Key into the Language of America,* in which he translated Algonquian words and phrases in an attempt to improve communication between Natives and colonists. The conversion of Indians was another matter. Williams lacked missionary conviction; he did not believe a true faith existed on earth. Furthermore, the still-powerful Narragansett, like other large tribes, welcomed English goods but not the Anglos' God. Under New England's famous "Indian Apostle," John Eliot, Puritan missions made significant progress among depleted tribes such as the Massachusett and Nipmuck. By the eve of King Philip's War, nearly half of all praying Indians (1,100) resided in communities organized by Eliot in eastern and central Massachusetts.

The seal of the Massachusetts Bay Colony indicated that the Puritans viewed the conversion of Native people as a major reason for New England's founding. The devastation of the Pequot in 1637 inaugurated nearly four decades of relative peace between the Natives and colonials in southern New England. In 1646 Eliot began preaching to the Massachusett tribe in their own language. Five years later he established his first praying town in Natick. Congregational ecclesiastical structure seriously hampered the Puritan missionary impulse. Ministers were attached to individual congregations; Eliot spent his life serving the white church in Roxbury. New England's settled ministers were unable to travel through the countryside seeking converts among the scattered bands of Indians who moved seasonally. Praying towns, reservation-like sedentary settlements, provided easier access to potential converts. Eliot persuaded weakened remnant tribal bands to gather in self-governing missionary communities that were modeled on the New England town. Natives had their own reasons to resettle in praying towns; they sought to protect land ownership in the face of a steadily encroaching colonial population, for example.

As the praying towns grew, Eliot translated Christian texts into the Massachusett language, creating an impressive "Indian Library" that included the entire Bible by 1663. Eliot also trained Christian Native leaders in the gathered communities; individuals with advanced knowledge of English and the Puritan faith became Indian preachers. In 1655, Harvard erected a building called the Indian College for the instruction of promising Native youth. Only four managed to attend Harvard, suggesting the limits of Eliot's missionary experiment before King Philip's War undermined the praying towns.

The missionizing of Eliot and other Puritans far surpassed what other colonies, especially outside New England, attempted in the seventeenth century. But for all his labor to convert, protect, and defend Indians, it is easy, perhaps even requisite, now to see Eliot as a cultural imperialist. Like seventeenth-century colonists in general, including Roger Williams, Eliot viewed Indians as savages. They had to be remade into English people before they were fit subjects for the Gospel. He conceived the praying town as a permanent, "civilizing" settlement where Natives followed Anglo agricultural practices and raised cattle, horses, and hogs. Indians were pressured to cut their long hair, adopt Puritan work habits, embrace Anglo gender roles, adhere to Christian morals, and abandon linguistic and cultural traditions. In other words, along with Puritan Christianity, Eliot advocated a kind of cultural hygiene, what would later be called the missionary "gospel of soap."[8]

Yet cultural blinders aside, the Christianizing efforts of Eliot and other Puritans were limited by the very nature of the religion they propagated. The failure of powwows to arrest the decline of Native people encouraged praying Indians' interest in Christianity. Puritanism was a doctrinal, literate faith, however. It lacked the ceremony and sacramentalism that, in some parts of the New World, allowed Spanish Franciscans and French Jesuits to oversee the emergence of a syncretic Catholicism. Calvinist beliefs like the doctrine of depravity were alien to Algonquian spirituality. Puritan churches also required a religious conversion and a relation of that experience for full membership. This hurdle stymied many English-speaking believers; it presented that much more of an obstacle to praying Indians. Eliot did record Native conversion narratives. Nevertheless, in 1674, of all the praying Indians in New England only approximately 350 had qualified for baptism. Not surprisingly, Puritans ridiculed the French for the "hollow" practice of baptizing untutored savages.

New England's praying Indians never fully recovered from King Philip's War. They fought on both sides and suffered through the hardship of internment on Deer Island in Boston Harbor. Bloodshed eroded support for the Indian missionary cause during and after the conflict.

The war erupted in 1675 after colonial development seriously weakened the English-Native interdependence that marked New England's founding decades. Commercial cooperation was built mainly around wampum, fur, and land. Treated as official currency, wampum enabled Indians in southern coastal New England to acquire furs from tribes in the interior. Natives then exchanged furs and land for European goods. With iron tools obtained in trade, Natives speeded up the production of wampum. By the 1660s, expanding transatlantic commerce significantly increased the supply of coined money in the colonies, crippling wampum's value as currency. Badly depreciated wampum flooded the market, hindering Indian trade, especially the acquisition of furs. Land survived as the principal asset of southern New England tribes. Natives used it to pay off English debts incurred under the wampum economy. They also sold land for goods that could no longer be acquired with wampum or fur pelts. After Philip became Wampanoag sachem in 1662, he exchanged land for money so he could purchase material goods.

From surviving records we get glimpses of King Philip: not the "savage devil" who emerged during the war and long endured in the regional imagination but the Native man straddling two cultures. On one of his prewar trips to Boston, Philip appeared "with a coat on and buckskins set thick with ... [wampum] beads" (see fig. 9).[9] Philip, like many Natives, despised praying Indians, especially after Eliot made inroads among the Wampanoag in the 1670s. That hatred did not stop the sachem from adopting some of the praying Indians' Anglo ways. Philip raised swine for market. He also acquired some knowledge of English; he took lessons under John Sassamon, a praying Indian who had attended Harvard.

If Philip was far more assimilated than we have often assumed, he still boiled with resentment against the colonists and their governments. The collapse of longstanding cooperative trade patterns left Philip more economically dependent on the English. Wampanoag land was a finite asset, already drastically reduced in size. By the 1670s Philip found himself pressed against Mount Hope Bay in Plymouth Colony, where his home village lay. Some Wampanoag people sought security in praying towns; others resented Philip for his failure to protect them from aggressive colonists. War loomed not only as an expression of Wampanoag discontent and hostility but also as an alternative to the tribe's seeming extinction.

The murder of John Sassamon hastened the start of bloodshed. Sassamon served as Philip's secretary and teacher and also as an informant for colonial authorities. He was found murdered in February 1675. Three Wampanoag men, loyal to Philip, were tried and hanged for Sassamon's death in early June. Suspicion now focused on Philip's complicity. Before authorities could act, his Wampanoag braves attacked the town of Swansea near the Indian village at Mount Hope. Over the next six months, Natives assaulted more than half of New England's ninety towns. Thirty had to be abandoned; at least twelve were almost completely destroyed. Indians torched churches and dwellings, killed families, seized captives, tore down fences, and slaughtered cattle. Armed with flintlock muskets, acquired illegally from traders, Natives unleashed their fury against the artifacts of English civilization that had spread to praying towns. No wonder warriors did not spare Eliot's villages from the onslaught.

PHILIP. *KING* of Mount Hope.

P.Revere sc

FIG. 9 Paul Revere, "King Philip" (1772). This engraving of Metacomet with a hatchet at his feet captures his image in New England memory as a "savage" warrior rather than as the Native leader who was partially assimilated into seventeenth-century Anglo life. © American Antiquarian Society.

Initial Native successes attracted extensive Algonquian support for Philip's cause. Although the Wampanoag sachem displayed military skill and leadership, the war that carries his name was not a campaign he coordinated. News of early victories encouraged Natives throughout New England to turn against the colonists. From southern New England to the upper Connecticut Valley and beyond to New Hampshire and Maine, the region came under siege. Nothing close to a pan-Algonquian alliance emerged, but the war won the support of Natives from many tribes in southern New England. Connecticut's Mohegan, Pequot, and Niantic people, however, sided with the colonists. Vulnerable to attack from both sides, praying Indians exhibited a more divided loyalty. Many praying Indians joined Philip, while others fought for the colonists. With parts of the region in ashes, neutral praying Indians faced the suspicion and hostility of whites. In the fall of 1675, Massachusetts ordered the evacuation of some praying towns, whose remaining Christian Indians, poorly clothed and fed, endured the war or died in confinement on Deer Island.

Amid days of fasting and praying, with the mangled corpses of colonists and Indians strewn across the landscape, the Massachusetts General Court invoked the jeremiad to explain the meaning of the war. Legislation approved on November 3, 1675, proclaimed that God "had given commission to the barbarous heathen to rise up against us . . . hereby speaking aloud to us to search and try our ways, and turn again unto the Lord our God, from which we have departed with a great backsliding."[10] The experience of the most famous white captive of the war dramatized the official explanation of the bloodshed.

In February 1676, Philip's fighters attacked Lancaster, Massachusetts. They captured thirty-year-old Mary Rowlandson and twenty-two of her neighbors. Wife of the town minister and mother of three, Rowlandson spent three months with the constantly moving enemy. After her release, she wrote an enormously popular and repeatedly reprinted account of her experience. *The Sovereignty and Goodness of God* (1682) was the first free-standing Indian captivity narrative published in Anglo-America. It became the colonial equivalent of a "bestseller," the most widely read and influential publication generated by the war. Probably on the advice of her husband and perhaps other ministers, Rowlandson crafted her frontier adventure story into a didactic Puritan inspirational account with strong ties to the jeremiad.

In the narrative, Rowlandson functions as a stand-in for the larger Puritan community that needed to accept the war as an instrument of God's wrath. Early in her ordeal, she comes to see captivity as just punishment for her moral deficiencies and spiritual complacency. In close combat with despair, the heroine relies on her Bible, renews her faith, and waits for deliverance from her captives. She quotes the Bible to reaffirm the communal covenant and to point the way toward military triumph: "Oh, that my people had harkened to Me, and Israel had walked in My ways, I should have subdued their enemies, and turned My hand against their adversaries."[11]

A second-generation New Englander, Rowlandson resists Indianization during her captivity. Far from threatening her, Philip treats his captive humanely. He welcomes Rowlandson to his wigwam and offers her a pipe of tobacco. The need to survive tempts her to adopt Native ways. She is forced to eat boiled horse feet and broth thickened with bark. She consumes only partially roasted horse liver that leaves "blood about my mouth."[12] But she does not succumb to cultural degeneration. She returns to white society in May with her chastity preserved, for example. Her "restoration" combines religious rebirth and cultural deliverance.

By the time Rowlandson was ransomed in the spring of 1676, the fortunes of war had decidedly turned in favor of the United Colonies. A military confederation formed in 1643 to intimidate southern New England's most powerful tribe, the Narragansett, the United Colonies mobilized forces from Massachusetts, Connecticut, and Plymouth. Fearful of Puritan designs on the small colony, Rhode Island decided not to join. Even after Natives burned houses in Providence and Roger Williams was forced to find refuge back in Massachusetts, Rhode Island maintained its official neutrality. In probably the bloodiest battle of the war, which recalled the Pequot Massacre, the United Colonies marched on a fortified Narragansett encampment in the midst of a great swamp. They burned the village and killed at least 400 men, women, and children.

The "Great Swamp Fight," like the war as a whole, did not

simply pit Natives against colonists. One-third of Connecticut's approximately 450 troops at the Rhode Island battle were Mohegans and Pequots. Other campaigns organized under the United Colonies combined similar proportions of Natives and colonists fighting side by side to suppress King Philip's rebellion. As one close student of the war has suggested, it is possible that, in proportion to their population, Natives contributed more fighters to the United Colonies cause than whites did. The colonists benefited significantly from historic Indian rivalries, such as the Mohegan-Narragansett hatred, and from the tribal political-economic calculations of sachems like Uncas.

Precolonial Iroquois-Algonquian hostility presented another obstacle to Philip's crusade. When the sachem and his warriors retreated to New York during the winter of 1676, they were attacked by Mohawks. Malnutrition and disease also exacted a toll. Raids against the colonists continued into the spring, but by June, one year from the start of the war, Philip's revolt was nearing exhaustion. Surrendering Indians were required to fight for the United Colonies. Despite John Eliot's objections, the colonists and even some praying Indians sold many of the Natives who surrendered or were captured into slavery. Philip's wife, Wootonekanuske, and their nine-year-old son were seized in early August of 1676. At Mount Hope on August 12, Philip was shot by an Indian and his body hacked to pieces. The proud sachem's wife and son endured perhaps a worse fate: sold into slavery, they were never heard from again.

Philip's death effectively ended the war in southern New England. Accounts of the conflict typically conclude with Philip's demise. But bloodshed continued on the northern frontier, especially Maine, into 1678. This frontier provoked the greatest Puritan concern over the Indianization of New England people. From Penobscot Bay northeastward, groups of French settlers lived intimately with the Abenaki. One feared French leader on the Bay, the Baron de Castine, married the daughter of the Penobscots' chief sachem. French-Indian settlements posed not only religious and military threats to New England; the interbreeding of different people and cultures also embodied the menace of colonial degeneration. Overall, thinly settled northern New England held a more balanced Native/European ratio than the colonies to the south.

War engulfed Abenaki country because northern and southern New England were linked. The collapse of the wampum economy disrupted trade in furs and European goods in New Hampshire and Maine. Warring Algonquians in southern New England sought shelter and assistance from the Abenaki. Furthermore, the outbreak of war in Plymouth Colony inflamed white fear and distrust of Natives throughout New England. In September 1675, Abenaki attacked Falmouth on Casco Bay, which announced the arrival of King Philip's War on the northern frontier.

Over the course of the war, Abenaki bands raided coastal settlements from the northernmost Anglo-American fishing-trading village at Pemaquid, Maine, to towns in the Piscataqua region of New Hampshire. Most Maine towns were abandoned, with refugees fleeing to Essex County in Massachusetts for shelter. At one point in the war fishermen bore the brunt of attacks. Abenaki captured at least twenty fishing ships and their crews. In July 1677, one crew regained control of their ship and sailed for Marblehead with Abenaki captives in tow. The Natives met a gruesome end. A mob of women, fishermen's wives and frontier refugees armed with stones and pieces of wood, pounced on the Abenaki captives. They were beaten to death and left "with their heads off and gone, and their flesh in a manner pulled from their bones."[13] Both sides in King Philip's war committed acts of brutality, of course. For the colonists, however, incidents such as the Marblehead riot raised the problem of whether Anglo-American settlers had themselves become "savages."

In the north the war finally ground to a halt by the spring of 1678, twenty months after King Philip's death. Much of the northern frontier faced resettlement and rebuilding. Throughout New England death, enslavement in the West Indies, and migration during the war reduced the region's Native population by more than half, from over 20 percent of its inhabitants to probably less than 10 percent. The rebellious and decimated Wampanoag, Nipmuck, and Narragansett tribes no longer posed a military threat. The war did not mark the death notice for praying towns, but Christian Indians suffered a decline similar to other Algonquians. Eliot was left with 567 Natives, and the number of missionizing towns diminished to four. In the wake of war, entrenched hatred of Indians undermined interest in saving their souls. Harvard authorities eventually demolished the Indian College and put the salvaged bricks to better use in a new building for other purposes.

Contemporary estimates of the number of colonists killed in the war ranged anywhere from 400 to about 900. After the conflict, New England's Anglo-American population continued to surge, further reducing the percentage of Native inhabitants in the region. For postwar colonists, a deluge of print replaced the tide of fear. Triumphant accounts of the war rehearsed, jeremiad-like, an American frontier story of God's affliction and deliverance of the New Israelites. Philip was preserved in history and memory as colonial New England's most fierce foe. How colonial-era Native lore recalled his life has not been recovered.

## ROYALIZING NEW ENGLAND, 1680–1692

Particularly in southern New England, victory pacified the countryside. Yet it did not lead the colonists out of their moral wilderness, according to the Jeremiahs. Afflictions ensued; a new intercolonial crisis again threatened New England's civil and religious foundations. Royal authorities attempted to transform New England's distinctive political landscape and tighten control of its independent colonies.

Seventeenth-century New England was a region of charter governments. Colonists ruled themselves under independent charters issued by the crown. Freemen elected officeholders, including governors. For most of the seventeenth century, Virginia was the sole royal colony with governors appointed by the Crown. Beyond New England and Virginia, proprietary colonies prevailed. Group or individual proprietors—Lord Baltimore, the Duke of York, William Penn, for example—held rights to land and in most cases appointed governors. In New England, the proprietary colonies attempted by John Mason and Ferdinando Gorges failed. Thus late seventeenth-century New England stood out as Anglo-America's most independent and self-governing colonial region. Restoration-era imperial authorities set out to curb its republican and Puritan character and reverse two generations of New England political development.

A new determination to regulate trade within an emerging English empire paralleled Restoration assertions of royal political power. Navigation Acts passed in 1660 and 1663 restricted all trade within the empire to ships built in England or its colonies. Highly valued commodities that generated significant custom revenue—principally tobacco and sugar—were "enumerated" —that is, they had to be shipped to England. In addition, non-English European goods had to be imported from the homeland; they could not be carried to the colonies directly from countries like France, Spain, or Holland. These trade policies implemented the political-economic concept of mercantilism, namely, the imperial European idea that colonies existed to support the fiscal, commercial, and military needs of the home government. The promotion of trade and shipbuilding within the empire aided New England merchants, tradesmen, and sailors. But the Navigation Acts were followed by political overreaching in New England, which fomented resistance and rebellion.

Imperial authorities delivered the first political blow in 1679. They separated New Hampshire from Massachusetts and turned the towns that had been annexed more than a generation earlier into a royal colony with an appointed governor. This imperial "reform" was intended to diminish the power of the Bay Colony, the locus of New England independence and Puritanism. Royal control would also enable imperial appointees to enforce the collection of customs duties on Portsmouth's expanding trade. Clearly, change in New Hampshire signaled more sweeping assertions of royal authority, which soon threw New England into disarray.

The short-lived Dominion of New England (1685–89) proclaimed the growing English determination to subordinate the American colonies to royal authority. In 1684, the home government revoked the Massachusetts charter. Royal authorities soon annulled the charters of Connecticut and Rhode Island as well. All of the region's colonies were reorganized under the Dominion of New England, which later included New York and New Jersey, to be overseen by a single royal governor. The Dominion was to be the first of probably two supra-colonies stretching from Maine to Carolina.

In 1686, Sir Edmund Andros, the permanent royal governor of the Dominion and a former military officer, arrived in Boston. He brought with him two companies of soldiers fitted out in red coats, a menacing invasion to most New Englanders, who had only recently subdued a Native revolt. Armed with broad executive, legislative, and judicial power, Andros mounted his assault on the Puritans' New Israel, with emphasis on customary practices throughout New England. He used Congregational meeting-houses for Church of England services. He elaborately celebrated Christmas in Boston and allowed the erection of a Maypole. Most important, he challenged New England's longstanding freehold system. He claimed the power to revoke land grants under the old charters and to assess rents on new distributions, which he now controlled.

Though the Dominion attracted pockets of support, Andros's policies stirred up piety and resistance. Puritan preachers stressed the urgency of renewed personal piety and moral reform to preserve New England's communal covenant. Some churches experienced religious revivals. In New Haven and Milford, Connecticut, church admissions reached their peak between 1685 and 1690. Resistance to Andros's authority was a more common reaction. Connecticut avoided surrendering its old charter, hiding it at one point in a hollow oak tree, according to legend. Towns ignored Andros's land policies and his restrictions on meetings.

Nonetheless, fear, confusion, and political disorder vexed New England even after Andros was overthrown in 1689. While Dominion officials struggled to gain control of Massachusetts, New Hampshire was left in turmoil. The authority of the provincial government all but collapsed. Power reverted to the towns, raising questions about whether New Hampshire continued to exist as a province. Townspeople assailed local leaders who cooperated with the Dominion. When Andros was jailed and shipped back to England, the people of New Hampshire split over rejoining Massachusetts.

During and after the Dominion, Rhode Island, always politically brittle, nearly descended into anarchy. The small colony became a county within the Dominion. Representative government under the charter of 1663 dissolved. Towns again focused on their own interests. The Dominion was unable to create a new effective government or enforce its policies. Intended to affirm royal authority, the Dominion actually reinvigorated Rhode Island's political fragmentation and antiauthoritarian individualism. After the Dominion was overthrown, many Rhode Islanders still resisted or ignored the restored colonial government. Records suggest that for four years in the early 1690s, the General Assembly met only once.

By then, the other New England colonies were recovering from the impact of the Dominion and its demise. England's Glorious or "Bloodless" Revolution of 1688–89 spelled the end of the Dominion. It also proved to be a constitutional turning point in England that shaped American colonial politics right up to independence. The Glorious Revolution overthrew the Catholic, autocratically predisposed James II, who had ascended to the throne in 1685. The Stuart monarch strongly supported the Dominion and the royalization of the American colonies. William of Orange, who had been invited by Protestant parliamentary representatives to depose James, assumed the throne with his wife Mary, James's daughter. The Glorious Revolution restored Protestant succession in England. It also imposed new constitutional limits on the monarchy. As a condition of their assumption of the throne, William and Mary were required to acknowledge the rights of Parliament. The revolutionary settlement continued with the passage of an act of religious toleration in 1689 and a bill of rights in 1692. The Glorious Revolution thus became an Anglo-American constitutional landmark. It limited the power of the Crown, bolstered Parliament's governing role, and protected the civil and religious rights of English people on both sides of the Atlantic.

In New England, the Glorious Revolution legitimized the bloodless overthrow of Andros and the Dominion. A new set of political arrangements, nevertheless, testified to English officials' continual resolve to implement royal supervision of New England. In 1691 imperial authorities approved a new charter that transformed Massachusetts into a royal colony with a Crown-appointed governor. A property requirement replaced church membership as the basis of voting rights. The charter extended religious toleration to Massachusetts, except for Catholics. Plymouth's towns were incorporated into the Bay Colony. The land of the "Pilgrims," which would enter American mythology in the nineteenth century, came to be known as the "Old Colony" after 1691. The new charter confirmed Massachusetts's jurisdiction over Maine. New Hampshire was reestablished as a separate royal colony. More than two-thirds of New England's population—

the residents of Massachusetts, Maine, and New Hampshire—now lived under royal government. Only Connecticut and Rhode Island retained their independent charters, which would be scrutinized and threatened in the decades to come.

The charter of 1691 dismantled major elements of the Bible commonwealth of Massachusetts. With new provisions for voting and religious toleration, for instance, the exclusive elements of the Puritan state vanished, never to reappear. Some critics heaped scorn on the new document as a pale substitute for the charter that John Winthrop transported to New England in 1630. The charter did not confer the last rites on the Puritan Era, as is sometimes assumed. The Bible commonwealths were never theocracies. Puritan authorities had long responded to worldliness, dissent, and profane defiance with a blend of coercion *and* moral suasion. Exhortation acquired a new importance in the decades after 1691. Election sermons, jeremiads, and historical works continued to uphold the communal covenant and to commemorate a history of divine blessings (and scourges) for a peculiar people.

THE DEVIL'S INVASION

Sir William Phips, a poorly educated native of Maine, was knighted and appointed governor of Massachusetts as a reward for military service. When the new governor and the royal charter arrived in May 1692, the colony was already in the throes of another affliction. Accused witches crammed Massachusetts jails. Phips quickly created a special court to hear their cases. Nineteen people were hanged, and Giles Corey, who refused to testify, was famously crushed to death. Four adults and several children died while in custody. Nearly two hundred people fell under accusation; many languished in jail; others fled from New England.

The turmoil surrounding the Dominion and the uncertainty over the new charter have often been cited as explanations for an emotional climate that fostered the witchcraft outbreak. In Salem, fear and doubt inflamed smoldering strife between the town's commercial port and its interior village that went back at least two decades. Then, too, a new Abenaki uprising in northern New England, starting in 1688, further unnerved the inhabitants of Essex County. Settlers from Maine and New Hampshire once again sought refuge across the Massachusetts border. Frontier bloodshed reanimated memories of King Philip's War. The Carib Indian slave Tituba, the first accused witch, described her role in a devilish Salem conspiracy. Often associated with Satanic Indians and their co-conspirators, witchcraft was also closely identified with the "shape of a woman." Among the accused and executed, women far outnumbered men, as they did in European witchcraft crazes.

Though we know much about the witchcraft hysteria of 1692, it remains a complex event that, in many respects, has resisted satisfactory explanation. The episode did not have enduring historical consequences for colonial New England, as King Philip's War or the Glorious Revolution did. Yet it became the most infamous colonial drama and was later used to tar Puritans and to stigmatize New England for its distinctive blend of superstition and intolerance. Massachusetts and Connecticut were the only New England colonies to execute convicted witches in the seventeenth century. But belief in and accusations of witchcraft appeared throughout the region and beyond. The unusual eruption of 1692 not only illuminates the place of witchcraft in colonial life; it also broadens our understanding of late seventeenth-century New England.

The often recounted key events that exploded into a hysteria unfolded over roughly the first ten months of 1692. Trouble first appeared in Salem Village (what is now Danvers), the heavily agricultural part of the settlement five miles west of commercial Salem Town. Several young girls who had experimented with fortune-telling began to behave as if they were tormented. They fell into fits and complained that they were being choked, pinched, and pricked. The odd behavior originated in the home of Samuel Parris, minister of Salem Village. His nine-year-old daughter Betty and her eleven-year-old cousin were the first to be afflicted. The local doctor concluded that the girls were suffering from bewitchment. Parris consulted with neighboring ministers, who agreed that the girls were not directly possessed by Satan, but victims of his agents—human witches. Parris relied on traditional Puritan remedies: prayer and fasting. He and other authorities also pressed the girls to identify their tormenters. In February, the girls named three women, including

Parris's slave Tituba. By then, several other girls, aged twelve to nineteen, exhibited the symptoms Parris saw in his own family.

At this point the hysteria was not inevitable, even under the stressful conditions of the time. Small outbursts of witchcraft were common in New England. Typically, authorities responded with caution and skepticism about Satan's ways. In Salem, fellow ministers urged Parris to "sit still and wait upon the Providence of God, to see what time might discover."[14] Unlike the contentious Parris, some pastors used the crises of the 1680s and 1690s to channel lay anxiety into revivalism. Physical manifestations similar to bewitchment often accompanied spiritual conversions.

Witchcraft and "white magic" joined the litany of second-generation moral offenses against the communal covenant that required reformation. Through the use of charms and spells, "cunning people" claimed the power to counteract witchcraft and heal its victims. Common people in New England and beyond lived in an enchanted world replete with belief in white magic and witchcraft folklore. New Englanders still say of frigid weather that it is "as cold as a witch's tit," a saying derived from the seventeenth-century folk belief that the devil used a "familiar," or animal go-between, to suck blood from his human agents. The familiar left behind disfigured cold flesh where blood had been drained, evidence of witchcraft that could be found through physical examination. To benefit pastoral work and reform occult folk belief and practice, Increase Mather published an *Essay for the Recording of Illustrious Providences* (1684), which discussed both black and white magic in New England.

Reverend Parris, a former businessman in Barbados, was a divisive figure rather than a skilled pastor. Neither religious revivalism nor skepticism reined in witchcraft accusations in Salem. At a preliminary inquiry in March, the Salem Village meetinghouse provided a stage for the young girls to display their much-discussed behavior. Two of the accused witches professed their innocence. In contrast, Tituba's explosive testimony persuaded a credulous audience, living through perilous times in their strife-ridden town, that the devil was loose in the land. One of two Indian slaves owned by Parris, Tituba was beaten by the minister for her involvement in the occult activities that had occurred in his home. Fearful of Parris, Tituba confessed. She led an en-thralled audience through the byways of New England's diabol-ical underground. Numerous witches and familiars linked Salem to the invisible world. Clandestine meetings and dark rituals flourished side by side with pious worship. Strange apparitions threatened to harm Tituba if she did not serve as Satan's agent or reward her if she did. She confirmed that her codefendants (Sarah Osbourne, age 49, and Sarah Good, age 38) were practic-ing witches and claimed that the circle of black magic extended well beyond them.

The initial inquiry, which at other times marked the end of witchcraft accusations, launched a hunt for Satan's vassals in Salem. Confession turned into dramatic exposé, suggesting that Salem and Massachusetts were facing a demonic conspiracy. Tituba's testimony and the girls' behavior at the hearing helped legitimize spectral evidence: under affliction, witchcraft victims identified the image of their tormenters. Ministers had always cautioned that, to sow havoc, the devil could use the specter of an innocent person. After the dramatic meetinghouse events in a troubled town within a seemingly besieged colony, caution was the first casualty. Tituba and the other two witches were packed off to jail in Boston.

Still, a widening ring of girls continued to be afflicted. Accu-sations and arrests surged throughout the spring. Hysteria took hold of Salem. The first three witches were social outsiders—a querulous neighbor, a profane beggar, and a West Indian slave. Accusations soon climbed the social ladder. Respectable church-going women were hauled before magistrates. The net of accu-sation snared men, including George Burroughs, a former Salem Village minister living in Maine. Indictments spread from Salem Village to Salem Town and beyond. Ultimately, Governor Phip's wife would be identified as a witch.

Until Phips arrived with the new charter, Massachusetts au-thorities were unable to proceed against jailed witches because the colony did not have a legal government. So the trials and ex-ecutions finally began in June and extended into September. By the middle of July, six women had been hanged on what came to be called Witch's Hill in Salem. Sarah Good was the only one of the three original witches who was executed, in July. Sarah Os-bourne had died in jail, and Tituba escaped the hangman's noose by confessing. Other accused witches confessed, thereby avoiding the gallows and buttressing popular belief in a Satanic conspiracy. Those hanged declared their innocence, sometimes defiantly, until the end. Five more convicted witches were hanged in August; authorities reprieved a sixth because of her pregnancy. The final and largest group of executions occurred in September, when eight witches were put to death. The witchcraft hangings, like colonial executions in general, were public events. Afflicted girls observed the September executions and continued to hurl accusations as the condemned stared into eternity.

Jails remained full of accused witches. Significant clusters of accusations erupted in the nearby Essex County towns of Andover and Gloucester. Afflicted Salem girls visited Andover in July to assist in the detection of witches. Forty accusations emerged from Andover alone. The traditional focus on Salem may obscure how the hysteria soon acquired the dimensions of an "Essex County witchcraft crisis."[15]

The crescendo of accusations that reached into the ranks of merchants and ministers, the reliance on spectral evidence, the empowerment of young girls, the death of pious people—all of these aspects of the hysteria stirred doubts as summer shaded into fall. One judge quit the court after the first hanging. In October, Increase Mather preached a sermon that attacked the court's use of spectral evidence. "It were better that ten suspected witches should escape," he admonished, "than that one innocent person should be condemned."[16] (Fourteen ministers signed their names to Mather's sermon when it was later published.) Governor Phips then halted further arrests and dissolved the court.

A new, more cautious court convened in January. Forty-nine accused witches were acquitted. The jury convicted only three women, but the governor reprieved them. The hysteria had imploded well before April, when Phips released the last of the accused from jail. Though belief in witchcraft persisted, no one was ever again executed for the crime in New England.

The Salem, or Essex County, hysteria far surpassed earlier episodes of New England witchcraft. Prior to the events of 1692–93, records document less than one hundred New England cases directly related to witchcraft. They typically involved one or two accused who were often brought to trial; most were acquitted. Before the hysteria in Essex County, the most significant outbreak of witchcraft in New England took place in Hartford, Connecticut, between 1662 and 1663. Thirteen people (9 women and 4 men) were accused of "entertaining Satan." Five people faced trial; three women and one man were convicted and hanged. For the next twenty-five years, authorities did not execute a single suspected witch. From 1638, when the first New Englander was put to death for witchcraft, to 1692, Puritans executed a total of sixteen witches (11 in Connecticut and 5 in Massachusetts). The events in Salem and its neighboring towns far exceeded this earlier record of limited capital punishment for witchcraft.

Cumulatively, witch crazes in sixteenth- and seventeenth-century Europe produced thousands of executions. Considering the size of New England's population, the witchcraft hysteria of 1692 may have been proportionate to most isolated witch frenzies in England. After the Restoration of 1660, witchcraft mania faded in England. As witch hunts receded in most of Europe, they took on new life in New England and parts of Scotland.

The hysteria of 1692, then, arrived at a late moment in the history of witchcraft in the West. The events in Essex County, however, adhered to one characteristic of witch outbursts that remained consistent across time and place. Numerically and imaginatively, women occupied the center of witchcraft controversies. In seventeenth-century New England, women represented four out of five accused witches. Men charged with witchcraft were often married to accused women or connected to them by kinship. Women were more likely to be tried, convicted, and executed than men. Salem's encounter with Satan reflected historic gender patterns. Of 185 accused witches, more than three quarters were women. Close to half of the forty-four accused men were husbands and relatives of these women. Courts tried more than seven females for every male. The gender gap among the executed (14 women and 5 men) would have been wider if accused and convicted women had not confessed to avoid the hangman, died in custody, or been reprieved.

The familiar stereotype of the quarrelsome, profane hag fit some of the accused and executed women in Essex County. Witchcraft charges had long been deployed to stigmatize marginal women and to warn against occult practices. Yet Puritan belief in witchcraft rested on an understanding of female nature that left all women susceptible to Satan's intrigues. Women were "weak vessels." They became goodwives by subordinating themselves to a patriarchal God and to their husbands' authority. Puritans also associated women's weak nature with emotion, evil, temptation, Satanic seduction, Jezebel, and Eve. As Reverend Parris put it, women carried "a seed of the Serpent."[17] Healers and midwives often aroused suspicions of female occult power. Anne Hutchinson's reputation persisted in the seventeenth-century not only for her antinomianism but also because she was suspected of being a witch who had presided over "monstrous" births. As a midwife she had delivered a stillborn and secretly buried it. Later, Puritan authorities exhumed the decayed, deformed fetus and concluded that it was a child of the devil. In sum, assertive public females like Hutchinson, Quaker women inspired by an inner light, and disruptive accused witches in Salem reinforced an ingrained Christian-Puritan view of the "weak" and vulnerable constitution of females.

A failure to fulfill the requirements of a goodwife connected many women who were accused of witchcraft before and during the Salem hysteria. Some quarreled with neighbors; others fought with husbands. Both groups included profane women who transgressed sexual norms or dabbled in the occult. Other accused witches were single women—widows, for example, who owned property but had no male heirs. Nonconformity in various forms significantly enhanced women's exposure to witchcraft accusations and prosecution.

In seventeenth-century New England, females also dominated the ranks of possessed victims who identified witches. In Salem, afflicted girls and young women initiated the hysteria by accusing older females. As "weaker vessels," women were directly vulnerable to Satan's power. They were also more likely to be victims of the devil's agents. Salem's young females were doubly weak and defenseless vessels by reason of their gender *and* their age.

Local disputes and a heavily gendered web of village gossip were often at the core of New England witchcraft accusations. A conflict between neighbors might be followed by a personal misfortune that befell one party: a bout of sickness, the death of a hog, the disappearance of a hoe. Suspicions and rumors enlivened the network of gossip so central to village life. Accused witches frequently acquired public reputations forged in local conflict. A new clash or rising village tensions often thrust suspected women before civil authorities.

Salem claimed more than its share of common local strife. The town had also long harbored a large profane community, which reinforced a division between Salem's commercial port and its agricultural hinterland. Within Salem, accusations followed an east-west geography that suggests the contours of distress in the community. Many accusers clustered around Salem Village in the west. Alleged witches often resided to the east, within Salem Town and especially in the section of Salem Village closest to it. Such divisions characterized many New England port towns as initial coastal settlement spread into the backcountry. Local authorities often preempted prolonged conflict between sections of a town through a hiving-off process. New England towns were created in two ways. Groups that received land grants in uninhabited areas founded new settlements, or they were spun off from older towns. Before the witchcraft upheaval, four towns had already split off from Salem. But Salem Village would not be incorporated as the independent town of Danvers until 1752.

In the late seventeenth century, Salem's east-west tension only aggravated the kind of low-grade local strife that many New England towns experienced. Within Salem Village, farmers in the west felt overly dependent on and disconnected from Salem Town; residents in the east possessed stronger economic and kinship ties to the commercial port. A divided village foreclosed the prospect of hiving off from Salem Town.

In 1672, the villagers did win what were called "parish privileges." As New England towns expanded and settlers dispersed to outlying farmsteads, attendance at meetinghouse services often became a hardship. Snow and ice blocked roads in winter; heavy rains washed out and gullied them in spring. To accommodate outlivers and to avoid acrimony, town authorities frequently formed a new parish and allowed its residents to use tax money for their own minister and meetinghouse. Worship privileges commonly led to another stage of independence: new parishes were eventually incorporated as separate towns.

Not only did Salem Village fail to follow this path; the new parish created a public arena where village factions skirmished unrelentingly, especially over the appointment of ministers. When Samuel Parris arrived in 1688, he was the fourth minister of the Village church in only sixteen years. He witnessed the hanging of a predecessor, convicted witch George Burroughs, in 1692.

Years of village dissension turned Salem into a combustible place. Conflicts that in other towns would be resolved were left to fester in Salem. Then the rise and fall of the Dominion added another layer of confusion and uncertainty, which helps explain the timing of the witch mania. Once ignited in Salem, accusations spread to other towns, abetted by hysterical or fraudulent testimony.

Moreover, another long-ignored dimension to the witchcraft hysteria helps account for its timing and expansion to neighboring Essex County communities: frontier warfare and refugees fleeing from "diabolical" Indians. In the 1680s, colonists resettled the Maine and New Hampshire towns that had been abandoned during King Philip's War. By 1688, an expanding population in northern New England challenged Native land and fishing rights, which had been negotiated a decade earlier to end frontier bloodshed. As the Dominion of New England collapsed and a political vacuum in the region emerged, Natives and their French allies once again raided Maine and New Hampshire settlements from Pemaquid to Piscataqua. These developments resurrected memories of King Philip's War and fueled fears of a French-Indian conspiracy against New England. Essex County was directly in the line of the assault from the north.

In late January 1692, less than two weeks before the first three Salem witches were identified, one of the bloodiest raids of the frontier war devastated the southern Maine town of York. Fire consumed much of the settlement, fifty people perished, and the raiders marched one hundred captives through the snow. In already overwrought Salem and in other Essex County communities, frontier warfare heightened the already rampant uncertainty and conspiratorial fear. Links between Indian warfare and witchcraft recur in the records of the hysteria beyond general references to Satanic Indians. Both King Philip's War and the second Native uprising created refugees, including orphans, who resettled in Salem and other Essex County towns. As the witch hysteria expanded in 1692, several young female war refugees suffered afflictions and became accusers. Interrogations and trials were spiced with charges that Satan's agents were conspiring with the Indians and French in a campaign of terror against New England. One young accuser lashed out at a Salem defendant: "He sells Powder and Shot to the Indians and French, and lies with Indian Squaws, and has Indian Papooses."[18] During the Salem frenzy some witches were accused of Indianization. After all, Natives and their powwows were New England's original devil worshippers.

The Salem witchcraft episode sheds light on many aspects of late seventeenth-century New England life: village conflict, new parish and town formation, colonial political instability, frontier violence, folk belief, and gender, to name several. The hysteria stands as a distinctive upheaval of the Colonial Era. It will continue to attract attention and new interpretations because the frenzy was so exceptional and complex.

For many Puritans, at least, Satan's onslaught, like Native warfare, was far less complicated than historians have documented. In the midst of the demonic crisis, the denizens of Salem Village held fast days, as New Englanders had for other afflictions. Prominent ministers such as Cotton Mather wove jeremiads connecting Satan's deceits of 1692 to other providential judgments on a backsliding people, some of whom practiced the occult. Crop blasts, Indian uprisings, the Dominion's assault on liberty, and the eruption of 1692 all spoke to the need for reform in New England. In this Jeremiah's explication, the devil reserved his greatest mischief for those summoned to be a covenanted people. As in Salem witchcraft, the profusion of jeremiads and the ritualized fast and thanksgiving days that accompanied the second generation's crises combined to create a new, historicized identity for Puritan New Englanders. This accomplishment alone calls into question narratives of pious New England's decline.

FIVE

# Saints and Strangers
# in the Eighteenth Century

WAR WITH FRANCE embroiled New England from the late 1680s through 1713. In 1689, newly crowned King William declared war against the French for the Bourbon monarchy's aid to supporters of the deposed James II. The Abenaki-French frontier raids in New England, which seemed to catalyze the Salem witchcraft hysteria, were one theater of this essentially European imperial warfare. A treaty signed in 1697 did not usher in an era of peace.

Within five years new hostilities erupted when France's Louis XIV attempted to place his grandson on the vacant Spanish throne, thereby uniting two imperial powers and their colonies against England and its New World possessions. In colonial America the conflict came to be called Queen Anne's War (1702–13). Joined by Native allies, colonial New Englanders fought not only to protect their lives and homes; they were defending their English Protestant civil and religious liberty, secured by the Glorious Revolution, against the menace of French political and ecclesiastical tyranny.

The French and Indian raids of Queen Anne's War devastated frontier communities from Maine to the Connecticut River Valley. Settlers in New Hampshire and Maine again fled to populous coastal towns; others were captured and marched off to Canada. In the Connecticut Valley town of Deerfield, Massachusetts, Abenaki, Huron, and Mohawk allies of the French executed the war's most famous assault, in March 1704. They attacked the

131

frontier town, killed nearly fifty settlers, and carried off to Canada more than a hundred captives, including Deerfield's minister, John Williams. Upon his release after three years in New France, Williams published *The Redeemed Captive, Returning to Zion* (1707), a popular account of his congregation's captivity. Williams's daughter, like at least fifty young, predominantly female Indian captives of various New England wars, chose to stay in Canada. Seven-year-old Eunice Williams committed a double apostasy: she converted to Catholicism and later married a Mohawk. More typically, for the several hundred New Englanders who fell into French-Indian hands, captivity reinforced loyalty to English Protestant ways.

Eighteenth-century New Englanders, then, faced periods of open warfare and the perilous French-Indian presence on the region's expanding borders. Such realities underscored New England's membership in a transatlantic realm of English civil and religious liberty. All the colonies supplied soldiers for military campaigns. Colonial assemblies appropriated money to prosecute wars against the French and their Indian allies. In many respects, Queen Anne's War was a dress rehearsal for the mid-century imperial confrontation that culminated in England's expulsion of France from the North American mainland in 1763.

Between Queen Anne's War and the final contest for empire, New England experienced three comparatively peaceful decades. Refugees and land-hungry migrants rushed toward the frontier. New towns extended the region's settled borders to the west and north. Massachusetts authorities and migrants incorporated parts of New Hampshire and Maine into a "Greater Puritan New England." Rhode Island finally achieved a stable civic order under the dominance of a prosperous and powerful Newport.

During the eighteenth century New England's population doubled every generation. From 93,000 in 1700, the region's population soared to 359,000 inhabitants fifty years later. Other regions of colonial America, particularly the Middle Colonies, received tens of thousands of Scots-Irish and German settlers in the eighteenth century. Once again, natural increase rather than immigration fueled New England's demographic expansion. Eighteenth-century New England remained the most heavily English colonial region. A common English heritage even more than the expanded Puritan religious-civic order consolidated eighteenth-century New England as a cultural region.

Still, Native people did not vanish from the region's landscape in the eighteenth century. Moreover, colonial New England's African-American population reached its height by the middle of the eighteenth century. Though New England's black population remained the smallest in colonial America, it was mostly concentrated in cities, where slaves formed highly visible communities of domestic workers and productive laborers in maritime trades. The slave trade extended eighteenth-century New England's involvement in black bondage. Yankee merchants and ship captains dominated the modest but profitable American phase of the Atlantic slave trade.

## PEOPLE ON THE MOVE

Demographic growth and temporary peace set eighteenth-century New Englanders in motion. Half of Connecticut's sixty towns in 1740 were founded in the eighteenth century. These new towns extended into the northwest corner of Connecticut (Litchfield County), where the colony's largest unsettled territory lured migrants. In eighteenth-century Connecticut and Massachusetts, New England's most populous colonies, young men increasingly moved farther from their hometowns to secure an independent freehold. Fathers in the first generation accumulated land in their hometowns or in nearby communities for their sons. Over three generations, fathers in the older towns of Connecticut and Massachusetts subdivided land until the parcels were no longer large enough to settle their sons. Eighteenth-century New Englanders from older, crowded towns pushed west across the Connecticut River and north into central New Hampshire and Maine through a process of chain migration. Pioneering families informed relatives and former neighbors of their new towns' prospects and progress. Additional migrants—a human chain—imprinted the local culture of the old towns, especially religious orientation, on new settlements.

Migrating families and neighbors, then, made new communities the offspring of "mother" towns. Frontier migrants, for example, gradually replicated the fundamental institutions and practices of their places of origin. Eighteenth-century resettle-

1660

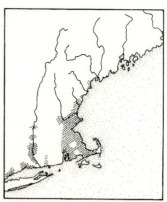

1677

1713

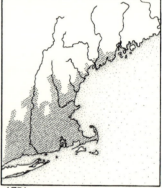

1754

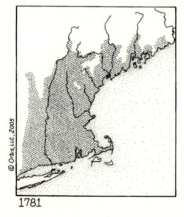

1781

© Orbis, LLC, 2005

Settled Areas

ment enlarged the boundaries of New England's distinctive local civic-religious culture. Land-hungry migrants helped advance what the seizure of New Hampshire and Maine in the middle of the seventeenth century had not achieved: a civic order that bore the Bay Colony's imprint.

The peace that followed Queen Anne's War launched the most prolific period of town founding in New Hampshire's history. Thousands of migrants followed the course of the Merrimack and Connecticut rivers into the region's interior, much of which remained a contested borderland between New England and New France. Defense needs, jurisdictional disputes, and land speculation accelerated the laying out of townships. Massachusetts claimed the Merrimack River as its northern boundary, a dispute that was not decided until 1741, in New Hampshire's favor. New Hampshire asserted its authority over land west of the Connecticut River, land that was also claimed by New York—this eventually became Vermont. Townships proliferated in eighteenth-century New Hampshire not only in response to heavy migration but also as part of intercolonial legal struggles over disputed territory. New towns were charted with great care on maps and surveys as well as carved out on the ground.

In a new stroke of imperialism, Massachusetts established a clear majority (21) of New Hampshire towns founded during the twenty-five years that followed the end of Queen Anne's War. The Bay Colony sought to secure its claim to the Merrimack Valley and erect a string of towns as a buffer against French-Indian assaults. Even after Massachusetts lost these towns, their inhabitants, welcomed by New Hampshire authorities, continued to flock northward. Of course, these migrants were looking to better their lives; many seem to have been pious, if not deeply devout Puritans. Religious revivalism would not sweep through New Hampshire at midcentury the way it did in much of southern New England. The colony also continued to be inhabited by descendants of non-Puritan and profane early settlers. Nevertheless, Massachusetts and Connecticut migrants transported

FIG. 10 The Expansion of New England Settlement. Adapted from Douglas R. McManis, *Colonial New England: A Historical Geography* (New York: Oxford University Press, 1975).

more than axes, plows, and firearms northward. They spread the Puritan colonies' civic and religious culture.

The arrival of peace in 1713 also renewed another dimension of Puritan imperialism: official efforts to integrate Maine into Massachusetts. To relieve its towns of war refugees and to strengthen frontier defenses, Bay Colony leaders asserted their authority over Maine in unprecedented ways. They approved land claims and closely regulated plans for resettlement. They required returning refugees to build more clustered, fortified houses. Massachusetts even provided towns with subsidies to erect meetinghouses and hire permanent ministers.

When the repeopling and expansion of Maine settlements provoked Abenaki raids, supported by the French, in the early 1720s, Massachusetts waged war. A three-year military campaign (1722–25) restored peace, which would last for two more decades. During those years chain migration and the founding of new towns strengthened Maine's ties to Massachusetts. Yet Maine's profane, worldly heritage did not simply become a relic in the eighteenth century. In some respects it was extended by those new migrants who came north not with an eye trained on both heaven and earth but with an exclusive vision of the opportunities offered by land, timber, and the sea. Despite increasing institutional stability and the growth of Congregational churches along the coast, *Puritan* Massachusetts never achieved hegemony over Maine.

Migrants from Rhode Island settled in northern New England after Queen Anne's War. But the principal movement in the small colony was toward the new towns away from the coast and to bustling Newport. Under the seaport's influence the ocean colony evolved from the near-anarchy that followed the collapse of the Dominion of New England to a new era of civic development. Rhode Island began to solidify its political institutions in ways that approximated the practices of its colonial neighbors.

Rhode Island's new civic stability was born of necessity. As one of New England's two remaining independent colonies, it fell under continual royal scrutiny. Rhode Islanders had to prove themselves capable of self-government and demonstrate their support of imperial policy by, for instance, contributing soldiers to military campaigns. Failure to do so invited a royal takeover.

In 1708, 30 percent of Rhode Island's population resided in Newport, the colony's capital. Only one governor from outside the seaport was elected in the first half of the eighteenth century. Newporter Samuel Cranston, a former ship captain who became a merchant, served as governor for nearly three decades (1698–1727). Under his leadership Rhode Island finally established a stable civil polity, if not a land of steady habits. Dominated by Newport interests, the General Assembly began to function as an assertive legislative body for a colony characterized by aggressive maritime enterprise. Most important, Cranston standardized the operation of town government, thereby affirming colonial authority and reining in, rather than erasing, Rhode Island's tenacious localism. Thus the colony made strides toward eighteenth-century New England's civic mainstream of strong elective assemblies and clearly defined, functioning town governments.

At the same time Rhode Island developed more cultural (and religious) diversity than other New England colonies. The region's smallest colony came to hold the highest percentage of Africans and a cluster of surviving Native people. Its commercial life revolved around cosmopolitan Newport, whose merchants were drawn from all over the Atlantic world. On the whole, however, eighteenth-century New England did not receive a mass infusion of non-English newcomers—free or bound, white or black—in the way that the Middle and Southern colonies did.

The eighteenth-century growth of commerce widened the transatlantic shipment of people as well as goods. Some colonies appointed agents to recruit immigrants, especially to help secure control of backcountry borderlands. Emigration shifted away from England to Scotland, Ireland, and Germany. Scotland and England formed the union of "Great Britain" in 1707; by the middle decades of the century, growing numbers of Scots took up their British citizenship in colonial America. The Scots-Irish were the largest group of eighteenth-century immigrants, numbering approximately 150,000. These new colonists, driven by crop failures, were Scottish Presbyterians who had been transported to northern Ireland in the seventeenth century to assist England's subjugation of the Catholic country. To encourage emigration and the peopling of the New World empire, Parliament passed legislation in 1740 offering British citizenship to foreign colonists. Furthermore, over 100,000 Germans settled in eighteenth-century colonial America.

The bulk of this new movement of people across the Atlantic bypassed New England. Most Scots-Irish and Germans disembarked in Philadelphia. They migrated toward Pennsylvania's frontier and then down the Shenandoah into Virginia and the Carolinas. As a populous, heavily Puritan region without an abundance of available land, New England did not beckon eighteenth-century immigrants. Yet because of their record of colonial hardiness, forged in the crucible of Ireland, the Scots-Irish did make some inroads in the region.

In 1719 a Presbyterian congregation of twenty-eight families settled in the Merrimack Valley with New Hampshire's approval. Other church members from Ulster joined them, and they named their town Londonderry. Through additional immigration and natural increase, Londonderry grew into a Scots-Irish mother town that spawned new frontier settlements to the west. More than a thousand Scots-Irish lived in New Hampshire within a decade or so of Londonderry's founding. One eighteenth-century estimate claimed that the Scots-Irish made up 10 percent of the colony's population.

Massachusetts, too, saw advantages in directing to the colony's edges immigrants who had been toughened by decades of intractable ethnic and religious hostilities in Ireland. In 1713 a group of Scots-Irish newcomers settled in Worcester, considered a frontier town at the time. Other Scots-Irish immigrants pushed westward or moved up Maine's Kennebec River Valley. At midcentury, Scots, Scots-Irish, and scatterings of Irish and Huguenots (French Protestants) may have comprised 10 percent of the *white* population of New England's largest colony. Other colonies, most notably Rhode Island, had more non-English white inhabitants.

But New England persisted as British America's most English region. A comparison with the Middle Colonies is striking. Less than half of New York's colonial population in the middle of the eighteenth century and only a third of Pennsylvania's inhabitants were of English origin. J. Hector St. John de Crévecoeur, the most famous midcentury traveler through the colonies, described how New England society differed from the diversity of people to its south. New Englanders, he observed, were "the unmixed descendants of Englishmen."[1] The region's contrast with the Middle Colonies may have led Crévecoeur to overlook the real, if limited, growth of non-English white people in eighteenth-century New England.

## THE POOR AND SOCIAL WELFARE

Scots-Irish immigrants encountered considerable hostility and resistance in 1720s Boston. When one boatload sailed into Boston Harbor in 1729, a mob blocked the immigrants' landing. Bostonians feared that, as impoverished "strangers," the "confounded Irish will eat us all up."[2] The city had long supported relief for war refugees. Peace did not shrink the poor rolls, however. The middle decades of the eighteenth century actually saw an increase in New England poverty. The growth of landlessness, transience, unskilled or semi-skilled maritime work, and premarital pregnancy enlarged the number of people who lived on New England's social margins.

Eighteenth-century New England remained a region filled with the "middling sort," moderately successful independent farm families and tradesmen. Tenant farming, indentured servitude, or plantation slavery, common in other colonies, did not define New England's social order. For many young men, landlessness and poverty proved to be a temporary stage of life. Through hard labor and frequently with family assistance, they would acquire and improve a freehold or develop a trade to achieve a competency. Of course, some young men and families found themselves unable to accumulate the resources needed to become self-sufficient. They belonged to the working poor, people who often led transient lives as they pursued temporary employment. As seasonal farm workers, they cleared fields, mended fences, tended livestock, and aided harvests throughout the countryside. Others traveled to large towns or cities in search of unskilled jobs: dock work, the merchant service, carting goods, chopping wood. The rise of an impoverished, landless, wandering working class in the eighteenth century prompted communities to strengthen poor laws, expand almshouses, and erect new workhouses.

Settlement policies and poor laws codified the treatment of New England's indigent. Towns provided poor relief to their own legal "inhabitants." Birth in the town, the purchase of property, or the completion of an apprenticeship conferred legal residency. Towns required strangers or "transients" to report to local authorities; if these newcomers were not "warned out" during their first year of residency, they would become inhabitants entitled to poor relief. Colonial warning-out practices derived from English laws that established local responsibility for care of the indigent, disabled, ill, and aged. Town officials warned out migrant individuals and families who were likely to become public charges. So-called transients, who provided cheap labor, were often allowed to remain in a town, though not as legal inhabitants. As long as they had been officially warned out, marginal people could be legally removed from a community, even after years and decades of residency, if they became unable to support themselves. One aged, infirm, and poor man, Obadiah Brown, who had worked for more than fifty years in Providence during the eighteenth century, was sent to Cumberland, the town where he had been born. Cumberland provided Brown with poor relief for the last two years of his life.

Overseers of the poor managed relief. They looked to families as the first source of support. Churches also offered limited assistance to their indigent members. As Boston's First Church put it, "the poor being [the] poor of the Town so under their care, and only as church members to have some addition."[3] "Outdoor" relief prevailed in the seventeenth century. People impoverished by illness, infirmity, widowhood or old age were not institutionalized; they received help at home or from family members and neighbors. Towns frequently "boarded-out" dependent people to nonrelatives. Overseers of the poor paid these families, usually stintingly, to care for the unfortunate. With the major exception of Native Americans, by the eighteenth century indentured servitude had evolved into more of a social welfare practice than a labor system. Towns arranged indentures for orphans and neglected or abandoned children until they were twenty-one.

Poor relief was one of the largest public expenses in eighteenth-century New England port towns. The maritime working class represented a mix of the skilled and the unskilled, the pious and the profane, legal inhabitants and warned-out strangers. Commercial development and population growth urbanized port towns and required new ways of dealing with poverty. New England claimed two of eighteenth-century colonial America's largest cities. With approximately 16,000 people in 1740, Boston was the most populous colonial port. In part because of the city's unreceptiveness to immigrants, Boston would soon drop to third place behind Philadelphia and New York. During the 1740s Bostonians maintained forty wharves, more than 160 warehouses, the most productive shipyards in the colonies, an array of maritime enterprises like ropewalks, and, as one newspaper reported, "swarms of rum-sellers . . . in every remote corner and by-alley in the town" (see fig. 11).[4]

Other New England ports possessed well-developed, if modest, maritime infrastructures. With a population of 6,500 in 1748, Newport stood as colonial America's fifth-largest city, just behind Charleston, South Carolina. Newport's long wharf extended more than 2,000 feet into the harbor. Smaller New England ports from New London, Connecticut, to Portsmouth, New Hampshire, and Falmouth, Maine, prospered in the eighteenth century and attracted their own mix of people, including paupers. Portsmouth, with a population of 4,500 in 1740, had been operating an almshouse for twenty-five years.

"Indoor" relief in almshouses and workhouses became common in populous ports and towns in the eighteenth century. These institutions were designed to control the rising costs of poor relief and, in the case of the workhouse, to sharpen the distinction between the "worthy" poor who were impoverished by age, illness, or disability and the indigent who were able-bodied. Boston constructed an almshouse in 1660 and rebuilt it in 1685 after a fire. By the 1730s, selectmen approved new measures to control expenses for the growing number of poor. They not only adopted a law that bypassed the requirement of a court warrant for warning-out, thereby expediting the procedure; the selectmen also authorized the construction of a brick workhouse on Boston Common. The publicly supported almshouse continued to serve the worthy poor. The self-supporting workhouse was reserved for the able-bodied but unemployed, at least some of whom were perceived as "shiftless." Put to work picking oakum (used in ship caulking), producing shoes, or weaving cloth, workhouse residents labored to support themselves while they improved or acquired industrious habits.

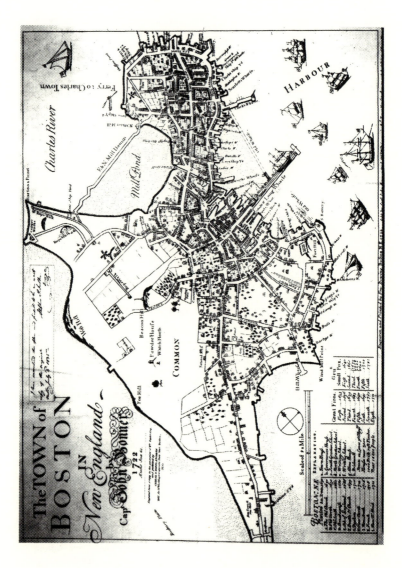

Institutional responses to poverty expanded in eighteenth-century New England as local officials strove to make relief more efficient in the face of growing need and costs. Newport constructed its first almshouse in 1723. By midcentury Newporters had opened a workhouse that demonstrated the punitive side of the institution. Workhouses sometimes functioned like jails. In Newport, troublesome, warned-out strangers who refused to leave were held in the workhouse. At the same time, the Connecticut General Assembly directed all of its counties to plan workhouses for petty thieves, "idlers," and "vagabonds." Some workhouses contained "cages" to discipline troublesome "inmates."

The penal aspects of eighteenth-century workhouses discouraged poor people from seeking such institutional relief. Men, in particular, appear to have resisted the workhouse. Records indicate that women and children dominated outdoor and indoor relief in commercial ports by the middle of the century. Two years after Boston's workhouse opened in 1739, there were only ten adult males among its fifty-five residents. A decade later Boston created an early textile mill, the "manufactory," to provide work for poor widows and their children. In eighteenth-century Newport, women (115) were the major recipients of relief, followed by children (62) and men (52). In addition, Newport officials bound out more than a hundred other children as indentured apprentices.

Families confronted special challenges in New England's port towns. Wives often struggled while mariner heads of households toiled at sea. Some combined their households while their husbands were away, a survival practice that became common among whaling families as the voyages lengthened into years. Providence officials investigated three transient wives of seafarers who established a household with their eleven children in 1757. Beyond women who temporarily fended for themselves, the perils of

FIG. 11 John Bonner, Map of Boston (1722). The map depicts a busy harbor and the numerous wharfs that extended from the shore. A variety of consumer goods were sold from warehouses on Long Wharf, which connected with King Street and the commercial core of the seaport. The map is an 1835 facsimile of the original. Courtesy of the Massachusetts Historical Society.

maritime work—especially shipwreck and disease—left many widows on shore. Fishermen also perished at sea, and eighteenth-century military campaigns produced their own share of widows.

Nevertheless, the increase in widows does not fully explain the growth of poverty among eighteenth-century women. Other factors included a rise in premarital sex and births to single women. The rising transient and profane populations in commercial ports contributed to the growth of single motherhood. Poor, unmarried pregnant women were important targets of warning-out laws. Removal spared a town the expenses of childbirth; it also blocked the legal inhabitant rights of a newborn. Premarital sex extended well beyond the profane. More than 30 percent of brides in some midcentury New England towns were pregnant on their wedding days. Courtship came to include more sexual activity and bundling, in which the betrothed slept together fully clothed. Ministers railed against the "frolics" of youth and the titillating use of graphic midwife manuals. Confessions of youthful sexual transgressions became common in the conversion narratives of the time.

Such changing mores in the region may have been part of a larger "sexual revolution" in late colonial America that would be reversed in the early nineteenth century. In New England, the shrinkage of transferable family landholdings loosened parental authority. Fathers found it more difficult to shape their sons' decisions about work, migration, and marriage. With the expansion of trade, the region's courts became preoccupied with oversight of commercial activities and less interested in control of sexual behavior. Though premarital pregnancy did not destine colonial women to a life on the margins, it did consign some mothers to dependence on relatives or public relief.

## WOMEN AND RELIGION

In the eighteenth century New England women were not only major recipients of poor relief. They were also the principal beneficiaries of saving grace. New England's founding generation consisted of large numbers of migrants who had already experienced spiritual conversion. They formed Congregational churches that achieved a gender balance of reborn full members. By the late seventeenth century, many men remained halfway members; women converts far outnumbered them. As early as

1692 Cotton Mather noted, "There are far more *Godly Women* in the world than there are *Godly Men*." Drawing on his observations in Boston, Mather claimed that "in a church of between *Three* and *Four* Hundred *Communicants,* there are but few more than *One* Hundred *Men;* all the rest women."[5]

A decrease in male conversions encouraged late seventeenth-century Jeremiah-patriarchs to lament New England's spiritual declension. Gender shaped fears of spiritual decline. Whether or not male piety diminished, the *number* of men who became full members by recounting their conversions dropped. No comparable decline in conversions occurred among women, who increasingly vitalized churches from the second generation through the eighteenth century. As "Daughters of Zion," pious women often became full church members a decade before men of the same age followed their path. Women led their spouses into the church. Still, despite the example and urgency of wives, many husbands never completed the journey to full church membership in the eighteenth century. In one southern Maine church, for instance, 155 women were admitted to full membership in the first half of the eighteenth century, but only 39 of their husbands became visible saints.

During that period, women made up between 60 and 70 percent of Congregational church members throughout New England. The most thorough studies on this subject have looked at Connecticut. After the 1670s, church admissions never again achieved gender balance in New Haven's First Church, to cite one example. Females constituted approximately two-thirds of converts admitted to the church from 1700 to 1750. Similar gender imbalances characterized most Connecticut churches, particularly the colony's older, well-established ones. Religious revivals brought more men into churches but did not significantly alter gender imbalance in most towns. Indeed, the balance of men and women converts among New England's first generation of Congregationalists appears exceptional. Women prevailed in colonial Congregational churches (as they have in most Christian denominations throughout American history).

While they dominated the spiritual core of Congregational societies and exercised informal influence, Puritan women held no formal ecclesiastical power. They could not vote to hire or dismiss ministers, set their salaries, or admit and discipline members.

Women often strongly supported the creation of new parishes in towns. Pregnant and nursing mothers in outlying villages faced the hardships of distance and weather that prevented attendance at Sabbath services. Women often encouraged the creation of new parish churches, but Zion's Daughters were excluded from signing the covenant. Only a small group of men, the "pillars of the church," authorized the covenant that created new religious societies. Congregational policy restricted the office of deacon and lay leader to men.

Given the discrepancy between women's numerical-spiritual ascendancy in eighteenth-century Congregational churches and their lack of official power, historians have often turned to Cotton Mather's claim that the perils of childbirth explain female religiosity. But the impressive female dominance of church membership rolls has no single explanation. Puritan patriarchy—social and religious—may have facilitated women's conversion and stymied men's. A reigning marital metaphor represented converts as "Brides of Christ." For many women, emotional submission to a patriarchal God was more of a progression than an alteration of their subordination to husbands and magistrates, as feminist historians have suggested. Men's surrender to God's patriarchal authority entailed a role reversal. Moreover, in much of New England men were usually required to make a public confession of their saving faith. Women did not face this sometimes daunting requirement. They provided testimony in private that ministers or male elders later reported to the church.

Other aspects of Congregational development help explain women's prominence. The founding of new churches required "manly" public tasks ranging from gaining legal authorization to raising money. The role of laymen was especially important in the early history of churches. Men signed the covenant, called the minister, supervised the construction of the meetinghouse, determined seating arrangements, and, in other ways, oversaw the progress of the church into a stable religious-civic institution. Once the institutional life of the church was secured, often within two decades, ecclesiastical matters demanded less of laymen. Women increasingly sustained the spiritual life of established churches.

Women's spiritual impact on Congregationalism exceeded the informal institutional influence that stemmed from their numerical dominance of churches. Religion offered women opportunities to meet with other women for edification outside of formal worship. Prayer groups were the most common gatherings. New England Puritans had regularly met in prayer groups for men and women during their decades of persecution in England. Anne Hutchinson extended this tradition in controversial ways. Yet gatherings for private prayer, especially among women, remained part of the Puritan practice of piety. In the eighteenth century, local religious revivals breathed new life into prayer groups.

Sarah Osborn emerged as perhaps the most impressive and successful midcentury leader of a prayer group. Widowed at 19 with an infant son, Osborn was a devout member of the First Congregational Church in Newport. To support her family before she remarried, Osborn began running a private school in the 1730s, which thrived under her direction. In 1741, when she was twenty-seven years old, a group of young women asked her to help them form a praying society. Osborn opened her home to the women, became their spiritual leader, and watched the praying society grow to sixty members. The society established its own rules, which included confidentiality. Osborn informed a minister, "All things are carried on in an orderly secret way[;] we have none that divulges to the world what passes amongst us . . . [so] that we enjoy the sweetest freedom with each other."[6] Osborn and the prayer group later mobilized to help win the appointment of a controversial Calvinist minister who faced strong opposition from halfway members. Of the seventy full church members, fifty were females. Their activities document how eighteenth-century Congregational women exerted influence in the church and promoted spirituality outside of formal worship.

Women's prominence in the eighteenth century was not confined to Congregational churches. Baptist women achieved their own visibility. In the decades after the enactment of religious toleration in 1689, the Baptist church slowly expanded beyond its base in Rhode Island. The first organized Baptist church in Connecticut did not seek legal recognition until 1704. By 1740 there were twenty-five Baptist churches in the region: fourteen in Rhode Island but only eleven in Connecticut and Massachusetts combined. Baptist churches did not get organized in northern New England until after 1750.

In the middle of the eighteenth century, Baptist women possessed more ecclesiastical authority than their Congregational counterparts. Surviving church records indicate that women in Baptist churches participated in the selection of ministers and in the discipline of members, especially in Rhode Island. By a show of hands, women actually took part in the votes to admit new members and the elections of deacons in the large Baptist churches of Providence and Newport.

Quaker women attained even more power in the eighteenth century. By then, the center of New England Quakerism stretched from Rhode Island to southeastern Massachusetts (including Nantucket), where the Friends were in the forefront of an emerging whaling industry. Men and women missionary preachers helped spread the Quaker faith. One highly successful English woman missionary, Mary Weston, drew large crowds in southeastern New England on a preaching tour in 1750. Weston estimated that she spoke to 4,000 at Newport; 3,000 in Dartmouth, Massachusetts; and 1,500 on Nantucket.

Women's major roles in the Society of Friends extended well beyond public preaching. During the late seventeenth century, Quakers organized into a series of monthly, quarterly, and yearly meetings in which local, colony-wide, and regional members participated. These meetings conducted church business, resolved disputes, and enforced discipline. In the eighteenth century separate men's and women's meetings were established, sometimes in meetinghouses divided by a partition. Religious gatherings created networks of Quaker merchants that promoted commercial enterprise among brethren. The sessions also brought female Friends together. Especially at the local monthly meeting, women had a voice in decisions about admission, discipline, and charity. When one adjusts the focus from ministers, "pillars," and deacons to the lay rank and file, women emerge as the soul of eighteenth-century New England religion.

NATIVE PEOPLE: SURVIVAL AND ADAPTATION

Gender imbalance increasingly marked New England's dwindling eighteenth-century Native population. Colonists continued to recruit Native fighters, many of whom lost their lives in military campaigns. Wampanoag warriors, for example, participated in warfare against the Abenaki in the 1720s on the Maine frontier. Need drove Native men to sea, where they performed risky work as mariners and whalers. Often manipulated into debt by whites, Native men left their families to escape creditors. A new type of "wandering Indian" appeared in eighteenth-century New England: footloose poor men moving through ports and the countryside in search of work. Women outnumbered men in Native home enclaves. In Natick at midcentury, women made up 59 percent of the adult population.

The gender disruption of families and bands reduced the Native birthrate in the eighteenth century. At the same time, the continuing surge in white fertility drove Native people down to the low single digits as a percentage of New England's population. It is difficult to establish accurate numbers; census reports typically undercounted Native people. In 1725, Connecticut's governor estimated that there were 1,600 Indians in the colony, many on Mohegan and Pequot reservations. During this period, the Narragansett reserve, Rhode Island's largest, held about 500 Natives; an equal number lived as servants in white households nearby or in Newport. With less than 300 people, Mashpee on Cape Cod was the largest Native enclave in Massachusetts by the 1720s. Indigenous people adapted to their diminished presence on the regional landscape. Despite their modest numbers, Natives remained vital participants in colonial life, not only as military recruits but also as indentured servants, wage laborers, or possessors of coveted tribal land.

Migration and the consolidation of villages represented one Native response to demographic decline. In southern New England some families retreated to reserves, where they sought shelter from English colonists and pursued a mix of Native and Anglo ways. In Maine, after English counterattacks in the 1720s, Abenaki moved to more northern tribal lands or near Jesuit missions, French praying towns, in Canada. The contested borderland between New England and New France harbored a diverse Native populace of indigenous tribes and migrants from the south—refugees from wars that went back to King Philip. Depopulation fostered intermarriage and the blending of tribal people. New England Natives had a long history of assimilating new members, including war captives. They would soon confront African-American men who began to marry into heavily female tribes.

Depopulation, the consolidation of villages, movement away from land-hungry colonists—all of this fed eighteenth-century New England perceptions of the "vanishing Indians." The colonial imagination was also at work. The rhetoric of disappearing Indians and census undercounting paralleled colonists' new invasions of remaining tribal land. In the Native enclaves of southern New England, land provided a livelihood for decimated bands. It was also a commodity that could generate credit or cash for the acquisition of English goods. In addition, land offered Natives some security against poverty, illness, and old age. Across southern New England, need and greed conspired to dispossess eighteenth-century Natives of land in old praying towns and in the new reservations created in the decades after King Philip's War.

In Natick, for example, white encroachers capitalized on Native poverty to transform John Eliot's original praying town into a community where Anglo newcomers gained control of the land and government. Natick Indians first used the sale or lease of tribal land primarily to finance individual and community improvements. As they pursued more English ways of farming, individual Natives sold land to buy items such as livestock and plows and to build houses and barns. Tribal land sales also financed civic improvements, from the construction of a new meetinghouse to the erection of a sawmill. Indian land sales had to be approved by the Massachusetts General Court. In Natick and throughout New England, appointed white "guardians" of Indians advised colonial governments over the sale of tribal land. The region's guardian system proved to be a thin legal garment that afforded Indians little protection in the eighteenth century. It was rent by ethnocentrism and self-interest. Declining, wandering, and debt-ridden Indian people, many of whom drowned their despair in abundantly available rum, seemed doomed to extinction. Guardians embraced English development of badly needed reservation land, which frequently benefited themselves or their relatives and neighbors.

Despite the advance of Anglo ways, Natick persisted as an Indian town into the 1720s. A succession of Native preachers served the community until 1721; many people continued to live in wigwams, and the sale of land to whites remained limited. Over the next thirty years, settlers from populous eastern Massachusetts "reconquered" the mixed bands that constituted Natick's Indian society.

Native residents expanded the sale of their land to finance an ongoing transition from an Indian to a more English and material way of life. Natives lost control of their land primarily because they were increasingly forced to rely on it as a "source of social welfare," as one Native historian has put it.[7] Natick's problems were shared by other eighteenth-century enclaves. Some young men lost their lives in military service or seafaring. Returning soldiers often brought disease back to enclaves. Epidemics ravaged Natick at midcentury, including an outbreak in 1745 that took fifty-one Indian lives. Natives incurred debt not only to acquire English goods but also to pay medical and burial expenses. Court proceedings for debt or land disputes created additional legal costs. Not surprisingly, beginning in the 1730s, petitions to sell land surged as Natives scrambled to satisfy English creditors. By the end of the next decade, Natick's Indian population of 168 was mostly women (51) and children (73). John Eliot's pioneering experiment was on the verge of collapsing into the lap of white freeholders.

Native land in the Narragansett reserve in Charlestown, Rhode Island, also passed into the hands of colonists in the eighteenth century. Social and political turmoil ensued, undermining the stability of a tribe that still numbered well over a thousand members. The Ninigret family, "the King-sachems" of the Narragansett, gained legal control over thousands of acres of tribal land. They used it not on behalf of fellow reservation Natives but to finance a lavish Anglicized way of life that emulated the colonial gentry and aspired to European royalty.

From the earliest days of trade and settlement, Natives incorporated European goods into their villages. Sachems, who usually possessed large wigwams, were in the forefront of this material cultural exchange. By the eighteenth century, at least some sachems and other Natives inhabited wigwams with highly Anglicized interiors. Boston magistrate Samuel Sewall visited a sachem's wigwam on Martha's Vineyard in 1702 and described how it was filled with "Furniture . . . [and] Two great Spinning Wheels, one small for Linen, and a Loom to weave it."[8] Later New England accounts described wigwams that housed chests and even tea tables. Traditional dwellings equipped with English artifacts captured in material ways the hybrid culture that developed in Native enclaves. While most eighteenth-century Indians continued to live in wigwams, some took the next step toward Anglicization: as in Natick, they built timber-framed, English-style clapboard houses. The Ninigrets went even further; they aspired to live like English royalty. With the complicity of tribal guardians and colonial authorities, the Ninigrets appropriated and disposed of Narragansett land for their personal benefit.

The Ninigret family consolidated its authority by claiming to be "Indian Kings" of the Narragansett. This Anglicization of the traditional Native sachem clan served both the needs of Rhode Island officials and the self-interest of the Ninigrets. Sachems, even the so-called King Philip, never held royal-like authority over tribal land, though they sometimes cited European notions of monarchy to bolster their power. Colonial officials often welcomed this political fiction because it isolated a single authority who could negotiate land transactions. In 1709, Indian King Ninigret relinquished 135,000 acres of land to Rhode Island; an expanse of twenty-five square miles was reserved by the colony for his descendants.

Through the middle decades of the eighteenth century, Ninigret's heirs relied on Narragansett land to subsidize their quest for gentility. Like growing numbers of Natives, Ninigret's offspring adopted English first names. His sons, Charles and George, and his grandson, Thomas, rented land to English tenants and sold parcels to other colonists. Profits from land enabled Charles to abandon his wigwam in 1736 for a palatial stone house. Upon Charles's death that year, his brother inherited the Narragansett "throne." George indulged his taste for imported wine and fancy clothes. "His queen," one traveler reported, "goes in a high modish dress in her silks, hoops, stays, and dresses like an English woman."[9]

To appease their appetite for genteel living, the Ninigrets consumed thousands of acres of Narragansett land. Their subjects, who eventually rose up against the would-be Native royalists, lived marginal lives on the reservation. The bulk of the tribe, however, had wandered off their official homeland. Narragansett men, women, and children survived as wage or indentured laborers in white communities and households. Throughout eighteenth-century southern New England, white indentured servitude had evolved into a social welfare/apprenticeship practice. In contrast, Native bondage became part of a valuable labor system that rested on debt peonage.

As the plight of the Narragansett suggests, not all Natives had access to large land reserves that could be used to satisfy creditors, even if only temporarily. Native farmers of all sizes fell into debt as they adopted more Anglo ways of cultivating their land and purchased widely available English manufactured products. Alcohol was one of the most abundant of these goods. Alcoholism wracked Native families; it also made Indians more susceptible to sickness and death, which only deepened indebtedness. Fines and court costs for petty offenses or crimes such as stealing added to Natives' financial obligations. In other words, colonists exploited legal and extralegal ways of controlling Indians through debt and securing claims on their labor. Without valuable land or unwilling to lose whatever limited property they possessed, Natives were forced to "sell" their labor. They "worked off" their debts through creditor-servant arrangements that often prolonged Indian dependency on whites.

Debt-servitude fractured Native families. Some fathers made informal, easily manipulated labor agreements with creditors to discharge their debt. Others were taken to court and legally bound out. Creditors sometimes sold indentures to merchants in port cities or other colonies. Unable to support their families, unmarried, abandoned, and widowed Native mothers bound themselves, and frequently their children as well, to white families. Indian parents often relied on their children to pay off debts. From Natick to Cape Cod, Rhode Island, and Connecticut, hundreds of young Natives were raised in English households. "There is scarcely an Indian Boy among us not indebted to an English master," the missionary minister in Mashpee reported in 1730. "Their neighbors find means to involve the Indians so deeply in debt as they are obliged to make over their boys, if they have any, for security till payment."[10] Families usually forfeited their "security." A generation of Indian boys and girls, Anglicized in colonial households, lost their knowledge of Native language and culture.

In the eighteenth century, whaling developed into a lucrative maritime industry that heavily depended on Indian debt servitude. Native people in New England had long pursued seasonal shore whaling. When the colonists began organizing local shore whaling in the 1690s, Indian men supplied the brawn of this famous "Yankee" enterprise. By the middle decades of the eighteenth century, the quest for profitable whale oil and bone pushed the hunt up to fifty miles off the coast. Ships returned to shore every few weeks to process blubber. The erection of brick tryworks on whaleships after 1750 further transformed what had begun as a local fishery. Whalers now boiled blubber on deck and stored oil in casks; the first factory ships appeared in maritime New England. Captains were now free to roam the sea in voyages that lengthened into months. The production of whale oil surged; the output of Nantucket grew from 11,250 barrels in 1748 to 30,000 barrels by 1775. Whaling emerged as one of New England's most important and profitable maritime enterprises.

As the eighteenth-century whale industry expanded, ship owners and captains confronted a shortage of workers. After all, the hunt and the processing of blubber and bone were hazardous, dirty activities that required periods of intense labor far from home. Cape Cod, Martha's Vineyard, and Nantucket, where the bulk of the New England whale fleet anchored, held declining Native populations. The 800 Indians on Nantucket in 1700 slid to 358 by 1763. Yet Native whalers persisted as a vital element in the labor-hungry industry. Whaling may have appealed to Indians as a reenactment of the male-centered tribal hunt, it is sometimes suggested. But it was mostly debt that forced Natives to sea.

On Martha's Vineyard and Nantucket, the familiar pattern of indebtedness produced indentured Native whalemen. In their search for whale hands, merchants eagerly offered Natives credit for the purchase of English goods, especially clothing, or to pay for medical and legal expenses, which included fines. The consumption of alcohol spurred debt. Besotted Indians were easily tricked into credit transactions designed to gain a claim on their labor. Merchants either enforced these claims or sold them to another creditor. Either way, Native men found themselves at sea. In some cases, they were in effect "shanghaied," forced to serve on a ship. Creditors received the wages of bound Native whalemen, who toiled at sea for two- or three-year terms. Without the benefit of earnings to support themselves, whalemen once again needed credit, which continued the cycle of debt peonage.

Whaling contributed to the gender imbalance of Native enclaves on Cape Cod and the islands. A heavily female Native population throughout southern New England coexisted with a predominantly male African-American populace, whose numbers reached a colonial-era high point at midcentury. Native women began to find mates among free and enslaved blacks. Some free and bound blacks sought refuge from white society in Indian enclaves. Native women met African mates off reservation land and returned home with them. In at least several cases, Indian women purchased black slaves who then became their husbands. The children of women who married slaves were born free. White officials reported increasing numbers of "mulatoes" in Native enclaves. Evidence suggests that Crispus Attucks, the African American killed in the Boston Massacre of 1770, was a mulatto mariner of Natick Indian ancestry.

SLAVE MERCHANTS AND AFRICAN AMERICANS

Not just on Indian reservations but also in the port cities and on agricultural estates in Narragansett country, the lives of Native and African people intersected. In Boston, Newport, and other seaports, the two groups labored and lived side by side. Reacting to racism and skewed gender ratios, Natives and blacks socialized, mated or married, and bore children. At midcentury blacks represented 10 percent of the population in Rhode Island, 3 percent in Connecticut, and 2 percent in both Massachusetts (including Maine) and New Hampshire. On the whole blacks made up 3 percent of the region's residents, the lowest figure in British colonial America. From 8 percent of the population of the Middle Colonies, the number of black slaves soared as one moved south: Maryland (31 percent), Virginia (46 percent), and South Carolina (61 percent).

Nevertheless, a simple numerical comparison tends to downplay the dimensions of eighteenth-century New England's engagement with slavery. The region's merchants were in the forefront of the American phase of the Atlantic slave trade. In the first half of the eighteenth century, half of New England's slaves were native-born African-American "creoles." The other half were foreign-born Africans, bound imports who reflected the region's expanded involvement in the slave trade. Furthermore, New England's 11,000 black slaves in 1750 were not dispersed evenly across the landscape; they clustered in particular locations.

Highly visible and economically important concentrations of black slaves labored in port cities and towns as domestic servants and maritime hands.

New Englanders' traffic in black souls must be understood in the larger context of the multi-nation, 200-year-old Atlantic slave trade. In the eighteenth century more than five million Africans were forcibly transported to New World slave societies. Britain, Portugal, and France dominated the trade. The overwhelming majority of bound Africans—96 percent—arrived on sugar plantations in the Caribbean and Brazil. Brutal working conditions and disease devoured African lives; handsome profits enabled plantation owners to import "cheap" slaves to replenish the labor forces in the sugar colonies.

The remaining four percent of eighteenth-century African captives, approximately 200,000, came to Britain's North American colonies. The slave population of the mainland American colonies originated from modest, not mass, importation; it grew from natural increase in settings that were far less deadly than the sugar plantations. Merchants from Massachusetts, Connecticut, and especially Rhode Island established New England's ascendancy over an "American" phase of the eighteenth-century Atlantic slave trade. By midcentury, Newport had secured its claim as the region's slave trading capital.

Newport merchants and their counterparts in other New England ports constantly prowled the Atlantic world in search of commodities to add to their stapleless systems of exchange. In the West Indies they had early discovered a profitable market for fish, farm products, and lumber. Trade in slaves began as an incidental part of this exchange. During the eighteenth century, the slave trade remained only one aspect of the region's diverse, complex maritime commerce. But it was no longer an incidental by-product of the West Indies exchange. New England merchants outfitted ships for the purpose of transporting bound Africans to the New World. More than any other form of maritime commerce, the New England traffic in slaves conformed to the famous "triangle trade" pattern. Slavers shipped rum to the African coast for "captives," who were transported to the West Indies and exchanged for molasses, sugar, money, and bills of credit. Molasses made the return trip to New England, where scores of distilleries turned it into rum for home consumption and ongoing trade.

Slavers also brought back some of their human cargo. They privately sold Africans to New England merchants, ship captains, tradesmen, and farmers. Newspapers announced public auctions of small groups of slaves, usually fewer than ten. Africans were auctioned off on ships, in taverns and warehouses, and near open sites such as burial grounds. One measure of the slave trade's acceptance was revealed in Boston and Newport, where importers even sold new slaves out of their homes.

With the exception of some Quakers, the slave trade and black bondage grew largely unchallenged before the Revolutionary Era. New England's first antislavery tract was published in 1700. *The Selling of Joseph* came from the hand of a prominent Puritan rather than a Quaker. Judge Samuel Sewall refuted the conventional justifications for slavery, including the argument that strangers to Christianity who were captured in just wars might be lawfully enslaved. Sewall described the spiritual equality of Africans as "Sons of *Adam*," but he had no illusions about their racial difference, their ability to succeed in freedom, or their acceptance by white New Englanders. "They can never embody with us, and grow up into orderly Families, to the Peopling of the Land: but still remain in our Body Politick as a kind of extravasat [spreading] Blood."[11] The preservation of New England's social and civic order required a halt to the importation of slaves.

Sewall's notable early antislavery arguments had little impact either on his contemporaries or on the ensuing history of the New England slave trade. Well before midcentury, Rhode Island, led by Newport merchants, eclipsed Massachusetts and Connecticut in slave importations. By 1750 the ocean colony dominated the American involvement in the "Guinea trade." Between 1709 and 1775, Rhode Island slavers delivered nearly 60,000 Africans into New World bondage. Two-thirds of the human freight ended up in the West Indies; another third was sold to Britain's mainland colonies. Rhode Island slavers also marketed their imports at home, bestowing on the colony what was by far the highest proportion of African slaves in all of New England.

In the eighteenth-century quest to plow the seas for profit, necessity and ingenuity propelled Rhode Island to the vanguard of the American slave trade. Maritime historians have explained how prosperous entrepôts, places where goods are exchanged, shared common elements. They boasted access to the sea, protected harbors, and connections to a hinterland whose inhabitants supplied and consumed trade goods. Colonial New England was blessed with ports that were defined by such geographical characteristics: New London, Boston, Salem, Portsmouth, and Falmouth (Portland), to name some of the most important or emerging eighteenth-century entrepôts. Though it rose to commercial prominence, Newport had to overcome a major geographical obstacle. It possessed access to open ocean and a sheltered harbor, but Newport was situated on the tip of Aquidneck Island, with only a severely limited hinterland at its back. Across the bay in Narragansett country, wealthy families with ties to Newport created, on former Native land, one of colonial New England's distinctive socioeconomic landscapes: a society of plantation-like farms with labor gangs as large as 20 to 30 slaves.

Yet the Narragansett planter-grandees only partially solved the problem of Newport's lack of a hinterland. As they had in the past, Newport merchants displayed skill, opportunism, and creativity in patching together their diverse system of trade. Enterprising merchants in other New England colonies did the same. Still, with a limited hinterland, Newporters "out-Yankeed" their competitors, as dominance of the American slave trade suggests.

Merchants in Newport and other Rhode Island ports commissioned small, swift craft that typically carried between 75 and 150 slaves, one third of what British ships in the Atlantic trade transported. Newporters' brigs were quickly filled on the African coast, which diminished the crew's exposure to disease. Most important, the colony's slavers sped up the Atlantic crossing, reducing the loss of their perishable human commodity during the deadly "middle passage." A sea of rum buoyed the Rhode Island slave trade. In 1756, the colony's slavers unloaded more than 155,000 gallons of rum on the African coast. Newporters alone operated sixteen distilleries. They became skilled at producing large quantities of rum that was of higher proof than competing brands. White and black slave traders in Africa preferred this potent Rhode Island spirit.

Newport and the Narragansett country contained the highest

concentrations of bound Africans in New England, one consequence of the colony's command of the American slave trade.
At midcentury, almost 40 percent of the residents of Charlestown, in the Narragansett region, were black and nearly 30 percent of the population in neighboring South Kingstown. Newport held the highest proportion of African-Americans among
New England's port cities and towns, 20 percent; Boston was second with 10 percent.

With the major exception of Narragansett plantation agriculture, which extended into eastern Connecticut, New England's
relatively small black population was heavily concentrated along
the coast. From Fairfield and New London to Portsmouth, maritime communities contained a high proportion of the black
slaves in their respective colonies. One third of all Massachusetts
slaves lived in Boston, and the same share of New Hampshire's
smaller black population resided in Portsmouth. Black slaves
strode the wharves of New England ports and served as mariners on ships engaged in coastal trade. They worked alongside
white masters and laborers in shipyards, sail factories, and ropewalks. Masters often arranged such maritime employment and
collected their slaves' pay. Some slaves even found opportunities
to earn a little money of their own.

The intimacy between blacks and whites extended beyond the
maritime marketplace. The majority of slaves worked as domestic servants and lived with their white masters' families. Like Native indentured servants, domestic slaves faced pressure to Anglicize, as the case of Phillis Wheatley, colonial America's first
published black poet, illustrates. Wheatley was one of a group of
Africans advertised for sale in the *Boston Evening Post* in August
of 1761. Purchasers were informed to inquire at a certain slave
trader's house or at his store, which was attached to a distillery.
Susannah Wheatley, the wife of a successful tailor, acquired a
slave child and named her Phillis. The girl had shed her front
teeth, and it was determined that she was about seven years old.
Young Phillis displayed high intelligence and quickly learned English. The Wheatleys relieved her of domestic work, tutored her
in literature and languages, and paraded her in Boston's social cir-
cles. Phillis published her first poem when she was thirteen. *Poems on Various Subjects, Religious and Moral* (1773) was the first book
published by a black American writer. She composed classical,

Anglicized verse for a white audience, but not without race consciousness. In her poem "On Being Brought from Africa to America," Wheatley admonished her pious white readers: "Remember, *Christians, Negroes,* black as *Cain,* / May be refin'd, and join th' angelic train."[12]

With her impressive intelligence and her emergence as an African curiosity, the poet was essentially adopted into the Wheatley family while remaining a slave. Phillis's circumstances were exceptional. But because slavery in New England was heavily urban and domestic or tied to maritime trades, historians have usually characterized it as "mild" in comparison to black bondage in the plantation South and the West Indies graveyard. The greater part of New England blacks performed nonmarket labor similar to the work of southern house slaves. Domestic slaves, urban and rural, were typically cramped into attics and small back rooms. One Bostonian traveling to New York found the black-white intimacy in New Haven appalling. Masters allowed slaves "to sit at Table and eat with them, (as they say to save time,) and into the dish goes the black hoof as freely as the white hand."[13]

Some New England maritime slaves were able to earn small amounts of money for themselves. Through enterprise and frugality, some slaves bought their own freedom, along with, on occasion, that of a black spouse. New England slaves also had limited legal rights. They could take whites to court and testify against them. Only Massachusetts prohibited whites and blacks from marrying.

Slavery nonetheless remained slavery, and its comparative mildness in New England has sometimes been exaggerated, beginning with nineteenth-century regional abolitionists. Intimate master-slave relationships carried their own burdens—constant scrutiny, for example. Masters kept their slaves in line by threatening to sell them to the dreaded West Indies. New England slaves struggled to maintain Christian or common-law marriages across their masters' households; black husbands and wives had no protection against their sale. Whatever legal rights slaves might claim, Africans, like Native people, were highly unlikely to make progress in New England's court system without the strong support of influential whites. In addition, the risks of maritime work and the heavy labor demands on domestic slaves, which made them more vulnerable to disease, significantly increased the black death rate. In port cities, blacks died at almost double the rate of whites.

Close interaction between white colonists and African slaves in New England encouraged Anglicization. The clustering of slaves in maritime communities also fostered the development of African-American ways. Blacks blended customs derived from different African societies of origin with Anglo practices. Negro Election Day best exemplified the mixing of African and American cultures that defined the colonial New England slave's world.

Eighteenth-century blacks adapted the longstanding Anglo celebration of annual colony-wide elections, held in the spring. Puritan Massachusetts and Connecticut had initiated these occasions and solemnized them through election sermons. In the eighteenth century, the growing black population of the New England capitals was augmented at election time by masters from surrounding towns who often brought their slaves with them to the official event. By midcentury, African Americans had created their own election day ceremonies and festivities in Boston, Salem, Newport, Hartford, and some other large towns. The assembled blacks elected governors in charter colonies, kings in royal colonies, and judges. African natives with royal ancestry or slaves of wealthy masters who showed good character often saw electoral success. In white eyes, elected black officials held no power. Yet among African Americans, these kings, governors, and judges seem to have been accepted as leaders—even as arbiters of disputes.

African-American festivities paralleled the white commemorations on election day. From colorful parades to African music, dance, and sporting contests, blacks offered a boisterous alternative to more staid Anglo celebrations. The expressive activities of black election, especially its profane side, drew the attention of whites. One white witness to festivities in Newport remembered that "All the various languages of Africa, mixed with broken and ludicrous English, filled the air, accompanied with the music of the fiddle, tambourine, the banjo, drum, etc."[14] Bystanders in Newport joined the procession as it ambled to the house of the "governor's" master, where the celebration continued with races, African wrestling matches, and toasts to the newly elected.

Masters paid for the "inauguration" celebrations of their own slaves, even providing horses, guns, and swords to marchers on Negro Election Day. Some whites complained about the seeming disorder of election day and the presence of armed slaves. Masters who supported the festivities undoubtedly saw the carnival-like events as a ritual that briefly overturned the order of things in a way that strengthened the paternalistic exercise of power within the slave system. For African-American participants who appropriated election day, the celebration promoted a sense of community and the preservation of collective customs.

Though their numbers were comparatively small for colonial America in the middle of the eighteenth century, African slaves and Native servants supplied valuable market and nonmarket labor in New England. The size of the black population in the region's cities and large towns also enabled slaves to fashion African-American ways of coping with life in New England. The region's Native people continued to decline, but they did not disappear. They remained prize subjects for debt peonage, either as domestic servants or mariners.

The Natives' consumption of English goods and adoption of English customs in dress, housing, and farming reflected a much larger process of Anglicizing eighteenth-century New England life. More than 90 percent of the inhabitants of midcentury New England claimed white ancestry. However divided by class, religion, or profane ways, at least 80 percent of the region's people were English. Puritanism remained an integrating force in much of eighteenth-century New England, especially after migrants expanded its civic-religious institutions and practices in New Hampshire and Maine. More than Puritanism, midcentury New Englanders continued to share a common English descent. Colonial integration into an expanding British Empire and the related forces of Anglicization had perhaps their greatest impact on eighteenth-century America's whitest and most English region.

# SIX

# Provincial New England

## The Eighteenth-Century Empire of Liberty, Commerce, and Protestantism

NEW ENGLAND ORIGINATED as a cluster of separate, even distinctive, English colonies. In the decades between the Glorious Revolution and the expulsion of the French from North America in 1763, New England evolved into a province within the British Empire. Expanding political, commercial, and cultural ties to the homeland swelled Anglo New Englanders' pride in the British safeguards of civil and religious liberty. A new phase of transatlantic warfare with France, which began at midcentury, further strengthened links between England and New England. Eighteenth-century white New Englanders increasingly saw themselves as proud British citizens of a rising English empire defined by liberty, commerce, and Protestantism.

Historians have often used the term Anglicization to describe the political, economic, and cultural integration of eighteenth-century colonial America into the new imperial order. Anglicization affected all colonial regions—and none more than New England. Populous New England was geographically overexposed to attacks from the heartland of New France, as Queen Anne's War demonstrated. French political and religious absolutism posed their greatest threat to New England's Anglo-American civil and Protestant liberty. Furthermore, eighteenth-century New England remained the most English region in British America.

Indeed, "Anglicization" does not precisely describe the British patriotism and investment in English culture that infused eighteenth-century New England. These developments should be more properly called "re-Anglicization," a return to the region's English origins. The region had been founded as a "new" England, a place where Reformed English Protestant ways would be planted and reexported to the homeland. To be sure, second-generation Puritan "creoles" had Americanized regional identity through the jeremiad and other epic, idealized historical accounts of New England's founding. In the eighteenth century, however, Puritan narratives of regional identity retraced New England's English origins. Inspired by the events surrounding the Glorious Revolution, Puritan descendants re-Anglicized the story of their ancestors' "errand" into the New World wilderness. The founders had come to New England in search of the *English* civil and religious liberty that the Glorious Revolution finally established in the homeland.

The legacy of England's Glorious Revolution shaped the political culture of every New England colony, but it was only one source of eighteenth-century re-Anglicization. At the same time, English manufactured goods poured into colonial markets. An empire of commerce created pathways for traffic in English books, periodicals, ideas, values, and aesthetic tastes. Even the midcentury religious revivals known as the Great Awakening occurred in a transatlantic imperial context. They were, in part, a reaction to the growing consumption of English imported goods and the resulting alterations in colonial material life. The final war for empire with the French and their Indian allies redirected much of the moral fervor of New England revivalists. Imperial victory marked the triumph of "British Israel," an expanding Anglo-American Protestant realm of civil and religious liberty.

## BRITISH POLITICAL CULTURE:
## ENGLAND OLD AND NEW

The events surrounding and following the Glorious Revolution formed a constitutional turning point in England whose influence pervaded American colonial politics through independence and promoted the re-Anglicization of New England regional identity in the eighteenth century. The English constitution did not consist of a single written document. Rather, the "constitution" referred to an accumulation of documents, precedents, and arrangements that stretched from the Magna Carta

(1215) to the Glorious Revolution. The overthrow of James II in 1688, it will be recalled, reestablished Protestant succession to the English throne and produced sweeping political change. The revolutionary settlement created a limited monarchy that recognized parliamentary authority, instituted religious toleration, and approved an English bill of rights.

The Glorious Revolution, then, was legitimately enshrined as a constitutional landmark that secured the civil and religious liberty of British citizens on both sides of the Atlantic. For most of the seventeenth century, people in England and New England had struggled against the despotism of Stuart monarchs. With a constitutional monarchy and a bill of rights, England now stood politically separate from the other major European powers. No wonder the Glorious Revolution inspired British patriotism and tributes to a national character distinguished by its devotion to liberty.

In England and the colonies, leaders hailed the "mixed government" or "balanced constitution" that the revolutionary settlement institutionalized. New political arrangements incorporated distinct social elements into a government that balanced monarchy (the king), aristocracy (House of Lords), and democracy (House of Commons). This mixed government dispersed authority across countervailing sociopolitical branches. At least in theory, neither the king nor the nobles and commoners were in a position to acquire dominating political power that might lead to the tyranny of one branch of government. Thus the balanced constitution protected citizens against governmental encroachment on their liberty.

Despite its conceptual elegance, England's much-admired government encountered critics in the eighteenth century. They were not just Tories, who lamented the decline of royal authority. Radical dissenters or Commonwealthmen such as John Trenchard and Thomas Gordon warned against a complacent pride in the balanced constitution. In *Cato's Letters,* essays written in the early 1720s and named after the Roman statesman, soldier, and writer, Trenchard and Gordon insisted that factions within government always seek to hoard power. To prevent the corruption of the balanced constitution, England needed public-minded, virtuous citizens like Cato who were ever vigilant of government operations. *Cato's Letters* were quoted and reprinted in the colonies, where the dissenting Commonwealthmen found a larger audience than in the imperial homeland.

Colonists in America saw themselves as British citizens entitled to the rights secured by the Glorious Revolution. They also came to view colonial governments as scaled-down versions of England's balanced constitution. The Massachusetts House of Representatives claimed the same "powers & privileges as the house of commons in England."[1] In New England and other colonies, political leaders increasingly defended their mixed governments as "parliaments" in their own right. In other words, the Glorious Revolution and its legacy served as the prism through which colonials viewed their political institutions and practices. Yet, in spite of this re-Anglicization, New England politics did not neatly fit the English model, as a brief review of colonial government shows.

By the end of the seventeenth century, all the New England colonies had developed tripartite or mixed forms of government, though electoral practices and political structures varied from colony to colony. Eighteenth-century political leaders, especially in the royal colony of Massachusetts, repeatedly invoked comparisons to England's balanced constitution as an expression of pride and as a vehicle of political self-understanding and self-interest. In reality, the English idea and practice of balanced constitutionalism was unevenly applied in New England. Every New England colony had an elected lower house of representatives. Citizens in the charter colonies of Connecticut and Rhode Island also elected upper houses or councils and governors. In the royal colonies of Massachusetts and New Hampshire, the Crown appointed governors. On the recommendation of New Hampshire's governor, the Board of Trade in London approved appointees to the council. All royal colonies followed this practice of seating upper houses, except for Massachusetts. Its lower house chose the council with the approval of the royal governor.

What these details suggest is that, as much as New Englanders looked to postrevolutionary England for political ideas and models, their colonial governments were far from embodiments of the homeland's revered balanced constitution. Of course, a similar conclusion might be drawn for the other mainland colonies. After all, local elites who were not comparable to the nobles in the House of Lords filled the upper houses of colonial assemblies. Still, eighteenth-century New England endured as the most representative republican political region in British America. In addition to local self-rule through town meetings and selectmen, the region boasted the only two colonies that elected all branches of government. In fact, eighteenth-century English authorities, disturbed by this imbalance of power, repeatedly threatened to revoke the charters of Connecticut and Rhode Island.

English concepts of mixed or balanced government made more sense in the royal colonies, where the governor represented the authority of the Crown. But even here strong representative assemblies stymied royal authority. History and tradition had molded the Massachusetts lower house, whose deputies represented towns, into one of the most assertive in the colonies. The deputies' unique role in choosing the Bay Colony's council enhanced the power of the house at the expense of the royal governor.

Massachusetts was in the forefront of a larger eighteenth-century political development: the emergence of lower houses as a powerful branch of colonial governments. These representative bodies were certainly emboldened by the rise of Parliament after the Glorious Revolution. The source of their new authority, however, resided in the "power of the purse." Lower houses collected taxes and appropriated money for government operations including military campaigns. In the royal colonies, they paid the governor's salary. Many royal governors were poor representatives of the king's authority. Only the most skilled royal appointees succeeded in a political context where colonial assemblies exercised considerable leverage over them.

In royal colonies with strong representative assemblies, as in Massachusetts, political leaders adopted the ideas of England's dissenting Commonwealthmen. Drawing on works such as *Cato's Letters,* critics assailed royal governors who attempted to shore up or just exercise their executive power. They were perceived as corrupting the colonies' balanced constitutions and conspiring to undermine this safeguard of British liberty in America. Colonial critics did not blame the king. They professed their admiration of the Crown and of the balanced constitution, which limited monarchical authority. Instead, they attacked royal governors in defense of the rights of colonial "parliaments."

Beyond its town governments, two charter colonies, and the

distinctive representative elements of royal Massachusetts, the right to vote in New England strengthened the region's republican political culture. In England, property requirements and a system of "rotten boroughs," districts with small numbers of eligible voters that were allowed to send representatives to Parliament, sharply restricted suffrage. Twenty-five years after the Glorious Revolution, only 20 percent of adult males in England were qualified to vote. The so-called House of Commons failed to represent anywhere near a majority of England's adult males, let alone the larger body of English people. Though colonial America denied women, blacks, and Indians the right to vote, suffrage was widespread among white adult males, especially in New England. With extensive freeholding and abundant shopkeepers and tradesmen, large majorities in the region met property qualifications for suffrage. Estimates vary, but in the middle decades of the eighteenth century perhaps more than 80 percent of adult white males in New England were eligible to vote. This "democratical" element further distanced New England from both the theory and the practice of mixed, balanced government in England.

Nevertheless, eighteenth-century New England voters did not think and act like democrats at either the town or the colony level. In colonial elections less than half of eligible men typically voted. Midcentury gubernatorial contests in Connecticut and Rhode Island often drew only 20 to 38 percent of qualified voters. Elections installed men of social standing and at least modest wealth as political leaders. The eighteenth-century rise of the colonial assemblies coincided with the emergence of successful merchants and professionals, who saw themselves as British gentlemen, the colonial equivalent of parliamentary leaders in England.

Consider the case of James Otis Sr., a member of a prominent family in Barnstable on Cape Cod who was elected to the Massachusetts House in 1745. Otis launched his political career by first consolidating his social and economic claim as a member of the gentry. A merchant, Otis ran the family business in Barnstable and inherited his father's two-story gambrel-roof house. He pressed charges against Mashpee Indians accused of stealing from the family store. The Otis household included Native indentured servants and slaves, one named "London." Otis also practiced law, serving clients throughout Barnstable County. By his early forties, Otis had secured his standing as a prominent member of the Cape Cod gentry. He stood for election to the Massachusetts House; his victory confirmed his status and opened up prospects for political and economic advancement. He was chosen speaker of the house in 1760 and later served on the Massachusetts Council, the upper chamber of gentlemen. His political investment paid dividends. In Barnstable, Otis became a guardian of the Mashpee Indians, he sold whaleboats to the military to prosecute war against France, and he outfitted local soldiers from his store. Otis remained an opportunistic Yankee merchant. Yet like other members of the eighteenth-century gentry who filled colonial houses and councils, Otis saw himself as a participant in a little Parliament. He sought the recognition and esteem of others for his leadership, a leadership that took place in a political culture in which personal and public interests intersected.

In New England and other American colonies, elites similar to Otis wielded political power and jockeyed for status and advantage. They often behaved like members of a colonial aristocracy. But as shadows rather than mirrors of the nobles in the House of Lords and the gentry in the Commons, elite colonial officeholders did not embody the sociopolitical principles of English constitutional thought. In a variety of other ways, New England's mixed governments failed to approximate the balance extolled in English constitutionalism. The legacy of the Glorious Revolution still persisted as a means of political re-Anglicization.

## RE-ANGLICIZING REGIONAL IDENTITY

English constitutionalism also supplied a new lens through which eighteenth-century Puritan writers and speakers reexamined New England's heroic past. They re-Anglicized the historic errand into the wilderness as a quest for the kind of English religious and civil liberty that was achieved through the Glorious Revolution. Eighteenth-century Puritans modified, and in some cases abandoned, second-generation notions of New England as a place-bound New Israel—the home of God's "peculiar" people. Third- and fourth-generation Puritans shared a pride in the transatlantic British empire of Protestant civil and religious liberty. They embraced their British identity even as they labored to preserve elements of New England's distinctive historical self-image.

"New England" proclaimed the early colonists' quest for cultural continuity with the homeland. The Great Migration transplanted English people who sought to create a reformed society that they associated with the mother country of an earlier era. Their native-born sons and daughters inhabited a Puritan world more culturally and morally distant from the homeland. They lived through the collapse of the Puritan Revolution and the restoration of the Stuart monarchy in England. The jeremiad and inspirational historical accounts propagated narratives that stirred an Americanized interpretation of New England's meaning. Eighteenth-century re-Anglicization involved a return to New Englanders' conception of themselves as members of a transatlantic kingdom: a British Protestant empire of liberty.

In the Congregational strongholds of Massachusetts and Connecticut, civic preaching and the Puritan culture of print negotiated revisions of regional identity that accommodated a new imperial reality. Fast, thanksgiving, and election sermons as well as jeremiads recorded a renewed investment in English culture and history. This process of re-Anglicizing New England's collective identity began in the 1690s with defenses of the new charter that made Massachusetts a royal colony and established religious toleration. After the overthrow of King James in the Glorious Revolution, Increase Mather spent two years in England working unsuccessfully for the restoration of the old Massachusetts charter under which John Winthrop had governed. Mather then reconciled himself to the new charter of 1691 and defended its promise.

This late-seventeenth-century leader of the formidable three-generation clerical clan reminded critics of the new charter how their Puritan forebears had been persecuted in England. Mather insisted "that by this Charter great privileges are granted to the People of New England, and in some particulars, greater than any they formerly enjoyed: For all English liberties are restored to them."[2] New England Congregationalism would now exist not by royal forbearance but by constitutional protection. The charter represented a fulfillment of the original Puritan errand into the wilderness, for the founders had journeyed to New England in pursuit of English civil liberty as well as the freedom to worship in their own way.

Eighteenth-century speakers and writers extended this type of re-Anglicization of the Puritans' epic errand. Increase Mather's son Cotton produced the most impressive and exhaustive history of any region in the Colonial Era. His seven-volume history of seventeenth-century New England, titled *Magnalia Christi Americana* ("the Great Works of Christ in America"), was published in 1702. Mather asserted that the Massachusetts General Court possessed "as much Power in New-England as the King and parliament have in England."[3] The Bay Colony's new charter came to be viewed as New England's "Magna Carta" in the eighteenth century. This perspective compelled Mather to retell the story of New England's founding with the Glorious Revolution as a foundational event.

Mather stressed that the region's first settlers were nonseparating Congregationalists, evidence of their continuing loyalty to the English church and nation. They were persecuted and driven "into the horrid thickets of *America*" not by the Church of England but by a "party" within the religious establishment that was abetted by Stuart tyranny. In the afterglow of the Glorious Revolution, Mather declared that "the planters of New-England were *truer* sons to the Church of England than that part of the church which . . . banished them into this plantation." The errand into the wilderness and the Glorious Revolution were inspired by a common quest to secure English civil and religious liberty in the face of royal and ecclesiastical tyranny. Picking up on the *Magnalia*'s historical narrative, a group of Connecticut ministers pointed out in 1708 that had religious toleration prevailed in England during the 1630s, neither the Puritan errand nor other "Memorable Providences relating to our *English Nation* in the last *Century*" would have occurred.[4]

Eighteenth-century writers and speakers contrasted the England that emerged from the Glorious Revolution with the homeland that had hounded New England's founders into exile. Under the Stuart monarchy England had been a "Land of Egypt." Beginning with the "ever memorable King William," the mother country had become a domain of Protestant civil and religious liberty.[5] Common constitutional rights forged a transatlantic united kingdom, a British citizenry bonded by blood and a historic love of liberty. Not surprisingly, eighteenth-century New England leaders often cast restraint aside when they publicly professed their loyalty to the Crown.

Pride in a rising British Empire also infiltrated re-Anglicized interpretations of New England's history. The 1730s marked the arrival of the centennial of such seminal historical events as the Great Migration. Election speakers commemorated these anniversaries, and ministers produced new histories of New England. Commemorative dates inspired a renewed historical awareness, and they provided opportunities for the re-Anglicization of the collective memory. Some speakers and writers positioned New England's past within an imperial context. One goal of the region's colonists, a clerical historian noted in 1730, was "to enlarge the British Dominions." With an eighteenth-century sense of imperial purpose and pride, historians reimagined the Puritans as agents of empire. The early colonies, an election speaker claimed in 1734, represented "the first founding [of] the British Empire in this distant part of the world."[6]

Imperial rhetoric invaded eighteenth-century historical accounts. Yet anniversaries also became occasions for commemorating New England's distinctive past. That is, re-Anglicization of regional identity complicated but did not erase the second generation's mythologized narrative of New England as New Israel, a covenanted people in special relationship with God. To be sure, some ministers, especially in gentrified places like Boston, challenged any direct association between New England and ancient Israel. Such thinking smacked of backwater provincialism and sectarian self-righteousness rather than British cosmopolitanism and enlightenment. After ancient Israel, the minister of Boston's urbane Brattle Street Church pointed out in 1723, "God has *never* . . . assayed to go and take him a Nation from the midst of another nation, by temptations and signs and wonders, by a stretched out arm and great terrors."[7]

Eighteenth-century writers who enthusiastically adopted this view stressed that all nations lived under a providential covenant. Throughout history countries have been afflicted or blessed according to their behavior. Unlike human beings, nations are not judged in an afterlife; they have to be punished or rewarded in this world to preserve God's moral order. Universal divine law rather than a special covenant determined that countries would prosper or be afflicted based on their behavior. New England history recorded many divine blessings (and some afflictions) not because its people were among the chosen but because they were pious.

For most eighteenth-century Puritan ministers and historians, New England's glorious past was not so easily subordinated to universal divine law. Mythologized New England retained much of its inspirational capital—testimony to the cultural achievement of the second generation, whose works were reprinted and quoted in the eighteenth century. In times of moral exhortation and historical commemoration, invocations of the New English Israel proved more effective than appeals to universal divine law. Fast, thanksgiving, and election day speakers summoned the traditional language of New England's communal covenant. "And here I cannot forbear observing," an election preacher intoned in 1730, "that never was any People on Earth so parallel in their general History to that of the ancient *Israelites* as this of *New England*."[8] The region's provincial spokesmen strove, in not always consistent ways, to reconcile eighteenth-century re-Anglicization with a historical awareness of New England's distinctive past— their ancestors' heroic errand into the wilderness. The final imperial conflict with France in North America would help resolve that interpretive dilemma. Colonies and homeland came to be imagined as one British Israel, a transatlantic empire inhabited by a "peculiar," liberty-loving Protestant people.

Eighteenth-century Puritan efforts to revise regional identity shed light on several aspects of New England's colonial history. Re-Anglicization qualifies the frequent assumptions people make about the region being a "city upon a hill." Winthrop's original utterance and the pronouncements of subsequent generational leaders document no steady growth in the Americanization of regional identity. Colonial New England was not consistently imagined as a moral beacon to the world. Furthermore, the region's encounter with the forces of re-Anglicization in the eighteenth century compelled revisions of familiar historical narratives. A new phase in the cultural reinterpretation of its past buttressed New England's standing as colonial America's most historically conscious region. With a population heavily composed of the founders' descendants, history mattered in New England. Standing on the shoulders of the historically minded second generation and living through centennial anniversaries, eighteenth-century Puritan leaders widened the river of ink devoted to New England's meaning. However Puritan-centered it remained, the region's collective identity endured as the most fully wrought in colonial British America.

## COMMERCE AND CULTURE

The winds of trade advanced the re-Anglicization of eighteenth-century colonial life. New Englanders were drawn into what historians have described as an "empire of goods" sustained by a "consumer revolution."[9] Despite growing urban poverty, provincial colonists' demand for manufactured goods reflected a rising standard of living and an admiration of all things British. The appetite for imported goods re-Anglicized colonial material life. It also increased the American colonies' commercial importance to the homeland. They were no longer valued primarily for the staples—tobacco, sugar, rice—that they supplied to the mother country. With burgeoning populations, the American colonies evolved into major markets whose consumers were critical to British prosperity. This commercial change dramatically altered New England's position within the empire.

Seventeenth-century royal officials did not highly value the New England colonies. The region's merchants found markets for fish, foodstuffs, and lumber; they also supplied masts to the English navy. But New England yielded no staple products comparable to those of the colonial South or the West Indies. For all the Puritans' self-importance, English officials disparaged seventeenth-century New England as commercially marginal. One prominent writer in the homeland belittled New England in 1684 as "that unprofitable Plantation, which now brings nothing to this Nation, but to the contrary buries Numbers of Industrious People in a Wilderness, that produceth nothing but Provisions to feed them."[10] As late as 1691, a major writer on the empire and trade in England proposed the removal of colonists from "unprofitable" New England and their resettlement in the Caribbean or Ireland.

During the second half of the seventeenth century, Parliament approved Navigation Acts for the tighter regulation of trade within the empire. Legislation passed in 1696 expanded to the colonies both the British customs service and the admiralty court system to try violators of navigation law. Trade regulations did not significantly hinder New England commerce, mainly because they were not consistently enforced. Navigation laws also conferred benefits on the colonies. Both New England shipbuilding and commerce thrived, for example, in an empire that banned non-British ships from its ports. Maritime expansion generated the profits and the transatlantic structure of credit that underpinned the empire of goods in New England. Eighteenth-century consumption of English products in populous New England elevated the region's profile and boosted its importance within the empire.

Colonial consumers interacted with the homeland through the purchase of imported goods. Colonial officials and merchants also cultivated direct ties to the empire's metropolitan center. By the early eighteenth century, all the New England colonies appointed permanent agents in London, where political and economic decisions affecting lives and fortunes three thousand miles away were handed down. Paid agents, what we would call lobbyists, advocated for the interests of the colonies they represented. They were often joined in London by New England merchants and politicians on personal missions of self-interest. Colonial visitors frequently met on London's "New England Walk" or at establishments like the "Sun of New England Coffee House." The growing number of New England travelers to London transported back to the colonies manners and tastes of the imperial metropolis.

One colonial agent who represented, at different times, Massachusetts, Connecticut, and Rhode Island in London summarized the progress of the empire of goods in 1721. He was defending Connecticut and Rhode Island against renewed English efforts to abolish their independent charters. Why punish "loyal consumers" who contributed to British prosperity? "There is no sort of manufacture, but what the subjects there demand in greater or lesser proportion, as they have the ability to pay for it; everything for the use, convenience, ornament, and (I say it with great regret) the luxury and pride of life."[11] Importation accelerated in the following decades, transforming the balance of trade and creating a trail of debt that stretched from London, Liverpool, Bristol, and Glasgow into the colonial countryside.

Between 1740 and 1770, it has been estimated that British imports surged by 360 percent.

This eighteenth-century consumer revolution and its attendant re-Anglicization of material life registered their greatest impact in ports such as Boston, Newport, Salem, New London, and Portsmouth. The political, economic, and imaginative integration of the colonies into the British Empire encouraged New England merchants to emulate the English gentry. The material markers of gentility proliferated, led by Georgian "mansions" (so named for the three successive Hanoverian kings named George, who reigned in England from 1714 to the American Revolution). These large, symmetrical, two- and three-story homes with prominent central halls were based on designs from English architectural books. Genteel inhabitants displayed or stored imported British goods in the spacious rooms of Georgian houses. In the eighteenth century tea-drinking emerged as an important Anglo-American social ritual that required material acquisitions, from tea tables to Staffordshire China. Plates, which replaced the traditional bowl, led to the purchase of knives, forks, and wine glasses. The inhabitants of Georgian houses and other eighteenth-century New Englanders dressed in clothing made from imported cloth. The men donned wigs, emblem of English gentility. Through large dwellings and "big wigs," merchants burnished their self-image as members of a colonial gentry. The vogue of portraits did more than frame that identity. They served as yet another material component of the elite self-image. Indeed, portraits often captured many of the material artifacts that constituted gentility: wigs, imported furniture, and clothing made from British textiles. House slaves broadened the gentry's investment in domestic comfort and social privilege.

Newspaper advertisements document the progress of the empire of goods in eighteenth-century colonial America. The first significant paper, the *Boston Weekly News-Letter*, began publishing in 1704. In the decades before the Revolution, commercial, literate New England remained in the forefront of newspaper publishing. Twelve weekly newspapers were published in the American colonies in 1739, five of them in Boston. These weeklies carried news from London. They helped colonists think about themselves as members of a transatlantic empire. Newspapers also ran advertisements from merchants describing the latest imported British goods. One examination of colonial weeklies concluded that between 1736 and 1773 the number of British goods advertised in the *Boston Evening Post* increased from approximately ten to more than five hundred items.

Handbills, printed flyers distributed in the street, also announced the latest goods "imported in the Last Ship from LONDON." Handbills and advertisements reveal the significant involvement of women in the commercial life of port cities. Widows dominated the ranks of female shopkeepers; single women also ran businesses. Referred to as "She Merchants," these "Betty Diligents," as Benjamin Franklin labeled them, operated successful millinery shops that catered to women customers.[12] In the middle decades of the eighteenth century close to one hundred woman owned shops in Boston. At midcentury, Abigail Whitney ran a shop in the city with her nineteen-year-old daughter. The Whitneys sold a range of goods from cloth to shoes. When Abigail died in 1768, her daughter took over the business.

The availability of imported goods stretched well beyond New England's port cities and towns. The empire of goods penetrated the backcountry, the region's abundant waterways assisting the growth of a commercial network that linked inland communities, port cities, and the British metropolitan world. Lines of credit, the lifeblood of this transatlantic commercial network, extended from London to country towns all over New England. British wholesalers offered credit to large colonial merchants, who in turn extended it to customers. Many of these customers were inland shopkeepers who set up their own stores, sometimes in their homes. One rural Connecticut store's inventory in the 1730s and 1740s listed items ranging from "lace," "gloves," "mohair," "tiles," "earthenware," "pots," and "pans," to "tea," "buckles," "silk," "spectacles," and "looking glasses." Complaints like this one that appeared in the *Connecticut Courant* in 1765 were commonly voiced in newspapers and from pulpits at midcentury: "Throughout the Whole, there are zealous Efforts in every single Person to imitate the person next above him, and in every Town to equal [the] next [highest] in Wealth, Popularity, and Politeness," chided the writer, who used Cato's name. "Thus by a [spread] of the most ridiculous Mimickry, the Fashions of London are communicated to the poorest, meanest Town in Connecticut."[13]

Peddlers added to the availability of goods. Traveling by foot or on horseback, they lugged merchandise to country consumers across New England, often earning the enmity of local shopkeepers. To protect their markets and perhaps hide their own shrewd dealings, local merchants maligned the character of their traveling competitors. The reputation of the calculating Yankee peddler was born, and laws were enacted to control the trade. In 1721, the officials of Berwick, Maine, arrested a hapless peddler, seized his sack of goods, and brought him to court for selling without a license.

Given the sweeping commercial, political, and imaginative incorporation of New England into the empire, it should not be surprising that re-Anglicization also encouraged new religious fashions within the Congregational Church. In the first half of the eighteenth century, commercial towns launched a development that would take a century to complete: the evolution of plain, steepleless meetinghouses into the churchly structures that would become New England's most esteemed regional icon. In 1699, Boston's Brattle Street Church built the first Congregational meetinghouse with a bell tower and spire. The construction of Anglican churches in eighteenth-century New England encouraged some Congregationalists to continue the modifications of the traditional Puritan meetinghouse that Brattle Street had initiated. Boston's Christ Church, a Georgian structure with a spire that soared nearly two hundred feet, was built in 1723; it became an impressive architectural model as well as a symbol of the power of the Church of England and its culture. Two years later, Newport Anglicans began construction of a new Trinity Church, a steepled wooden building that resembled Boston's Christ Church. Eighteenth-century Anglican churches influenced the architecture of Congregational meetinghouses built in ports and large inland towns. Boston's Old South Church, completed in 1730, featured a stately spire.

The new commercial wealth and the re-Anglicization of the Puritan tradition also introduced changes to meetinghouse interiors. Box pews with cushions, expanded pulpits, and arched windows reflected an eighteenth-century desire for more comfort and style in meetinghouses that now appeared too primitive and austere—an unwelcome reminder for some New Englanders of Puritanism's sectarian past. In particular, the construction of new box pews to be sold to families announced the creation of new wealth. In their quest for English-like gentility, successful entrepreneurs sought churchly recognition of their recently attained status. Despite the material changes to meetinghouse interiors and exteriors, Puritan traditions did persist in the eighteenth century. Worshippers did without instrumental music and heat in their remodeled meetinghouses.

Moreover, physical alterations to houses of worship occurred primarily in cities and large towns, where commercial wealth, re-Anglicization, and the consumption of imported goods were most pronounced. In these locations, some churches began to re-Anglicize Congregational worship itself. A group of rationalist, even post-Calvinist, clergy who were heavily concentrated in eastern Massachusetts emerged by midcentury. They often preached to congregations filled with merchants engaged in the empire of goods and the quest for gentility. These "catholick" Congregational clergy were influenced by Anglican writings and shaped by the Enlightenment: the explosion of rationalist thought that offered reasoned explanations of how God, nature, and the human world operated. Rationalist Congregational clergy distanced themselves from Puritanism's sectarian past. Most spurned any easy identification between New England and ancient Israel, and they cultivated a tolerant attitude toward non-Congregational Protestants while clinging to the region's longstanding animosity toward Catholics.

The rationalist clergy stood in the vanguard of religious re-Anglicization. The Brattle Street Church, for instance, instituted public recitation of formal prayers such as the Lord's Prayer. This practice contradicted the traditional Puritan hostility toward Romanist "set forms" in either prayers or hymns. Brattle Street and other congregations under rationalist ministers also abandoned public accounts of conversion. They either heard testimony of spiritual rebirth in private or eliminated it as a requirement for church membership. Public conversion accounts, like the stark New England meetinghouse, seemed to strike many rationalist, re-Anglicized Congregational clergy as another expression of sectarian Puritanism, which they hoped an age of reason would relegate to an historical relic.

Practical considerations as well as rationalist thought impelled the changes that the more religiously liberal Congregational clergymen oversaw. Both alterations of worship and the material setting in which it occurred addressed a growing midcentury concern: the defection of Congregationalists to the Church of England. By re-Anglicizing worship and meetinghouses in commercial towns, antisectarian Congregational leaders tried to preempt the new appeal of the Church of England to some New Englanders. The most stunning defections occurred at Yale College in 1722. Yale itself, the third colonial college, had been founded in 1701 partly in reaction to the growing rationalism at Harvard. Yale and much of the Congregational establishment reacted with shock in 1722 when seven ministers and tutors announced at commencement that they were converting to Anglicanism and would pursue ordination by a bishop in London.

Despite this defection and the continuing growth of the Anglican Church in New England, the region would remain overwhelmingly Congregational. With 420 churches in 1740, Congregationalism was by far the largest denomination in colonial America, well ahead of the Church of England, the second largest, with 300 churches, most of those in the South. Furthermore, shortly after the distressing Anglican betrayal in New Haven, Yale graduates provided the leadership for an unprecedented series of religious revivals that have come to be known as the "Great Awakening." Like the disquiet of the Salem witchcraft era, this religious outburst thrived on unease, which some ministers channeled into local revivals. New concerns accompanied the process of eighteenth-century re-Anglicization. Revivalists reacted to the advance of religious rationalism fostered by Anglican books and ideas and to the explosion of English imports that challenged familiar notions of competency and the stewardship of wealth. With a new emphasis on the need for spiritual rebirth, revivalists rearranged New England's religious landscape.

THE EMPIRE OF PROTESTANT PIETY

The term "Great Awakening" has been often employed in misleading ways. The religious revivals that flared between 1739 and 1743 made up a single historical intercolonial event. Revivals occurred in many locations, but they did not sweep through all, or even most, of the colonies. The midcentury religious awakening spurred by widespread local revivals was limited to Pennsylvania, New Jersey, and New England. In the two Middle Colonies, Scottish Presbyterians dominated the revivals. Neither New York nor the Anglican and "unchurched" colonies of the South experienced major religious stirrings in the 1730s and 1740s. Baptist-led revivals in Anglican Virginia only erupted in the two decades before American independence. The Great Awakening shook New England most of all. With colonial America's largest denomination, the region emerged as the spiritual and intellectual seat of the religious movement. Still, revivalism did not scorch the entire region. "Seasons of grace" roared through scores of churches in Massachusetts and Connecticut. They were less extensive in Rhode Island and rather brief in northern New England. Whether among Congregationalists and Baptists in New England or Presbyterians and the Dutch-Reformed in the Middle Colonies, the awakening sprang from common theological soil: the Calvinist belief in original sin and the need for a transforming spiritual rebirth.

Just as the Salem outburst of 1692 outstripped previous witchcraft episodes, the Great Awakening far surpassed New England's earlier history of revivalism. With so many of the region's Puritan founders already reborn, revivalism did not shape the first generation's piety. Local revivals became more common in the second generation. Church records reveal how admissions spiked especially during times of crisis, when skilled pastors responded to lay concerns. The turmoil of the 1680s and early 1690s ignited local revivals, and so did the late-night earthquake that rocked New England in October of 1727. Diarists recorded how the earth trembled on a Sunday night, and ministers reported that New Englanders flocked to meetinghouses the next morning. They interpreted the quake as a divine affliction for violations of the communal covenant.

Reverend Solomon Stoddard of Northampton, Massachusetts, compiled New England's most impressive record of revivalism prior to the Awakening. Stoddard served his church for sixty years, from 1669 to 1729. A talented preacher, Stoddard placed so much pastoral emphasis on spiritual rebirth that he opened communion to halfway members. He provoked clerical controversy with his claim that the sacrament was a "converting ordinance" rather than a privilege for those already reborn. His evangelical ministry bore spiritual fruit. Five local revivals, which stretched from 1679 to 1718, continually renewed church membership. Under his ministry the Northampton church grew into the largest in the Connecticut Valley. Stoddard added to his reputation with publications that offered advice to ministers and students on effective preaching. In spite of controversial ecclesiastical innovations, through his preaching and writings Stoddard represented the most prominent tradition of revivalism in New England before the Awakening. Upon Stoddard's death in 1729, Jonathan Edwards, his grandson, succeeded to the prestigious Northampton pastorate. The church and the town would soon achieve international recognition under the grandson's revivalism.

Edwards (1703–58) and the traveling English evangelist George Whitefield (1714–70) were the two most important leaders of the religious awakening that, like so much else in eighteenth-century colonial life, had important transatlantic connections. It is no exaggeration to observe that Edwards achieved an unprecedented international reputation for a colonial American religious leader —a transatlantic acclaim that eclipsed the earlier recognition of Cotton Mather, who was elected a fellow of the Royal Society in London and awarded a doctor of divinity from the University of Glasgow. At midcentury, perhaps only one other colonial American acquired an international reputation that exceeded Edwards's notoriety. Benjamin Franklin's scientific accomplishments were widely acknowledged on both sides of the Atlantic, and he received honorary doctorates from Oxford and St. Andrews universities. Though his fortunes in Northampton rose and fell with the course of revivalism, Edwards's writings and ideas remained popular with evangelical audiences in England, Scotland, and continental Europe. In other words, the provincial pastor became an imperial figure—a towering religious intellect in a transatlantic community of Protestant pietism.

Edwards's brilliance illuminated his path into one of the most prominent pulpits in New England. Born in East Windsor, Connecticut, in 1703, Edwards displayed his discerning intelligence at Yale, where between 1716 and 1722 he earned his bachelor's degree and completed postgraduate studies in divinity. In 1726, after an eight-month ministry in New York and an appointment as a tutor at Yale, Edwards moved to Northampton and served as an assistant to his grandfather. A year later, he married seventeen-year-old Sarah Pierpont of New Haven, with whom he had fallen in love when she was only thirteen. Edwards would describe her conversion and the exemplary piety of other females in his writings on revivalism in the 1730s and 1740s.

The grandson quickly disengaged his ministry from Stoddard's shadow. Edwards would become colonial America's greatest and most prolific theologian. With intellectual skill unmatched in the eighteenth century, he used rationalist thought to shore up rather than undermine evangelical Calvinism. His theological labors stressed the importance of "experimental religion." Salvation and true religious virtue, as opposed to mere morality, required a spiritual transformation. Believers had to experience divine grace in personal, interiorized ways. Edwards spoke for other revivalists when he declared that "our people do not so much need to have their heads stored, as to have their hearts touched, and they stand in need of that sort of preaching that has the greatest tendency to do this."[14] Edwards first achieved colonial and transatlantic notoriety as a revivalist, not as a theologian.

Five years after he replaced his grandfather, Edwards helped spark the most significant revivals in New England up to that time, a harbinger of what would occur in the Awakening several years later. In Northampton a local revival among young people broke out under his preaching in 1734. News of the Northampton revival spread to nearby valley towns in Massachusetts and Connecticut. By the time revivalism subsided in mid-1735, thirty-two towns had been awakened, and several hundred reborn people joined churches in full membership. Edwards claimed that Northampton alone witnessed three hundred conversions. Tragedy marked the revival's decline, however. Joseph Hawley, a lawyer, wealthy Northampton merchant, and uncle of Edwards, slashed his throat in despondency over the state of his soul.

Edwards wrote a detailed account of the Connecticut Valley revivals. *A Faithful Narrative of the Surprising Work of God* was published in London and Glasgow in 1737; American editions appeared the next year. Edwards's volume marked the birth of a new religious form: the revival narrative, an informative, inspirational recounting of a local spiritual awakening. Such narratives would soon emerge as an important means of linking local revivals that took place in different colonies and across the Atlantic into the perception of a "general" awakening. Evangelicals in England and Presbyterians in Scotland fully recognized the novelty of Edwards's *Faithful Narrative;* they published seven editions by 1750. Anglican books, rationalist tracts, revival narratives, Edwards's doctrinal tomes—all became intellectual commodities in the eighteenth-century transatlantic exchange of religious ideas. English revivalist George Whitefield read the *Faithful Narrative* before he launched his famous colonial preaching tour in 1739. In the northern colonies, the "Grand Itinerant" attracted thousands of listeners and inspired local revivalists. The events that made up the Great Awakening unfolded between 1739 and Whitefield's return visit to the colonies in 1744.

Although he was only twenty-four years old when he began his preaching tour in the colonies, Whitefield had already experienced remarkable success in England. He pioneered the role of itinerant revival preacher. A Calvinist who was ordained as a preaching deacon in the Church of England, Whitefield traveled from town to town speaking in open fields to crowds as large as twenty thousand. His itinerancy proclaimed that local ministers were no longer solely responsible for stirring up revivals. With a thundering voice and a theatrical flair, the youthful preacher connected with his audiences by speaking extemporaneously, without notes, as if guided by divine inspiration. Colonial newspapers published reports of Whitefield's triumphs in England. His well-publicized travels through the colonies drew throngs, from the pious to the curious. Whitefield's preaching tour also spawned imitators, who carried itinerancy and spontaneous inspiration in troubling directions.

Whitefield spent most of his first year preaching in the Middle Colonies, especially Pennsylvania. In the fall of 1740 he disembarked at Newport to commence his grand tour of New England. Whitefield focused his preaching on the region's cities and large towns, as he had in the Middle Colonies. From Newport, the "divine dramatist," as he has been called, journeyed to Boston. In the city and surrounding towns large audiences turned out to see the young celebrity. He traveled north into coastal New Hampshire and Maine and returned to Boston. Whitefield's farewell sermon in the city drew twenty thousand people to the common. He then headed west to Worcester and towns along the Connecticut River. At Northampton he stayed long enough with Jonathan Edwards to conclude, "I think, I may say I have not seen his fellow [equal] in all New-England."[15] Whitefield preached at Yale on his way to New York. He delivered nearly ninety sermons during a sweep of New England that lasted approximately six weeks.

Quoting a Massachusetts critic of revivalism, one historian has suggestively described Whitefield as a "pedlar in divinity." The itinerant preacher borrowed advertising techniques from promoters of the eighteenth-century consumer revolution. Colonial newspapers publicized his triumphs, and handbills announced his appearances well in advance. Whitefield followed trade routes mapped out by merchants and peddlers to reach his religious market in the most populous places. The touring revivalist delivered what one sympathetic Boston minister described as "Holy Merchandize."[16]

Whitefield's activities, then, drew on the same imperial networks of trade and print that served as a conduit of colonial re-Anglicization. Yet he instigated revivals that attacked the consequences of re-Anglicization: a growing rationalism, formalism, and gentility in colonial religion and a corrupting consumption of imported luxuries. The progress of Enlightenment rationalism at Harvard unhinged Whitefield. "Bad books are become fashionable among the tutors and students," he bemoaned. Whitefield assailed "the Polite, the Rich, the Busy Self-righteous Pharisees of this Generation" who preferred to acquire "Merchandize" rather than saving grace.[17] However much he appropriated promotional techniques of the eighteenth-century marketplace, Whitefield dealt in spiritual goods: the necessity of rebirth in an era that had become too defined by rationalism and materialism. During the three years after his departure from New England, pro-revival ministers and lay preachers sounded Whitefield's refrains, revitalized the jeremiad, and won converts' souls across the region. The quickened pace of the Awakening also sowed discord that would divide families, churches, towns, and the Congregational establishment.

The "general" awakening of the early 1740s affected all the New England colonies, but revival zones defined its scope. Some successful local Congregational revivalists from those areas adapted aspects of Whitefield's itinerancy. Edwards received numerous invitations to preach, and the Connecticut Valley remained a hothouse of evangelical piety. Eastern Connecticut and adjacent towns in Rhode Island demarcated another revival zone. Eleazar Wheelock, a Yale graduate and pastor in the eastern Connecticut town of Lebanon who later founded Dartmouth College, was perhaps the most energetic Congregational itinerant. He preached all over southern New England, including in Boston and its neighboring towns, a third hub of revivalism. The Awakening made more modest inroads in less populated northern New England. Whitefield's tour of New Hampshire and Maine lasted only three days. On his first visit to Portsmouth he encountered much indifference. He moved on to Maine and never traveled beyond York. When he returned to Portsmouth on his way back to Boston, he did receive a warmer welcome. But the Awakening did not engage churches in the north until a year later. In the fall of 1741, a major revival consumed emotions in York and spread to other towns in Maine and New Hampshire. A year later conversions plummeted. Though pockets of radical piety persisted, on the whole the Awakening in the north proved to be short-lived.

In the revival zones and throughout New England, evangelical Jeremiahs castigated the "worldliness," "extravagance in fashions," and "covetousness" of the midcentury consumer revolution. "The land is becoming exceedingly extravagant," Edwards rebuked churchgoers from his Northampton pulpit. "Common people show an affection to be like those of high rank; country towns . . . affect to be like the metropolis." Revivalists, like earlier Jeremiahs, often traded in overheated rhetoric to awaken people from their spiritual complacency. Nonetheless, Edwards, Whitefield, and other "great awakeners" offered social criticism that did not simply spring from fevered imaginations. Revivalists reacted, albeit sometimes hyperbolically, to grounded social change in places like the Connecticut Valley. The majestic Connecticut River linked inland New England to the metropolitan world via a trail of English goods, tastes, and ideas. A group of so-called River Gods—a handful of families with interlocking control of land, trade, and political power—formed the local gentry. The commercialization of the Connecticut Valley and of Northampton provoked Edwards's pulpit admonitions. He chided his parishioners for ignoring religion; they were "full of talk about worldly business, about this and the other worldly design, about buying and selling."[18]

Of course, revivalistic meetings, held night and day, temporarily disrupted commerce and work. Across New England conversions peaked in 1742. Revivals speeded up the conversion process, which in other times might take months or even years as a believer moved through the stages of rebirth: from complacency to awakening, despair, hope, and salvation. Church records indicate that, among Congregationalists, preachers of the new birth harvested converts from the large pool of halfway members. Revivals brought into full communion many worshipers who might have remained in their halfway status. Men and young people disproportionately filled the halfway ranks, and they joined the church in new numbers. Women continued to dominate church membership, however. The Awakening solidified the faith of those already converted, a majority of whom were women. Revivals strengthened women's roles as leaders of prayer groups and as spiritual exemplars for family members. The Awakening even empowered some Congregational and many Baptist women to take up lay exhorting.

When revivalism reached its crest in New England in 1742, it fueled a millennial expectation among the awakened. Reports of transatlantic revivals in the colonies, England, and Scotland raised hopes that Christ's return was imminent. His thousand-year reign on earth, foretold in the Bible, would spread from Great Britain to the world. To critics of the Awakening, such thinking unveiled what was called "enthusiasm," overwrought religious emotions rooted in base affections, reminders of humans' carnal nature.

By 1742, enthusiasm, itinerancy, lay preaching, church disputes, and attacks on ministers hardened clergy and laity into anti-revival Old Light and pro-revival New Light parties. Old Lights, some of whom initially supported the revivals, concluded that it had descended into disorder, driven by religious enthusiasm and delusion. New Lights defended the Awakening as a work of God. The dominant group of moderates, for whom Edwards served as a major spokesman, acknowledged and repudiated revivalism's excesses while they maintained that God was shedding new spiritual light on the world. Radical New Lights, both Congregationalist and Baptist, exhibited more populous, even antinomian beliefs and behaviors. They publicly attacked ministers who were allegedly unconverted, for example. Divisiveness among revivalists gave birth to a new radical Separate Congregational movement.

The Awakening, then, diversified New England's religious market. A people who had already acquired the habits of consumers, learning to choose among imported goods, now faced an array of religious choices: Old Light, New Light (moderate and radical), Congregationalist, Separatist, Baptist, Anglican, and Quaker faiths. These new religious choices may have paralleled, and even intersected with, the consumer revolution, but they were not inspired by it. Rather, the Awakening's emphasis on the new birth empowered the laity. Revivalism located religious authority not in ministers, churches, and sacraments, but in the individual's interiorized experience of God's grace. Thus the Awakening revitalized the Protestant belief in the priesthood of all believers. Individuals were now freer to choose their path toward the celestial city.

Whitefield had sought to unify rather than divide Protestants. From England to Scotland and America, he preached an inclusive message of spiritual rebirth across denominational lines. Whitefield and transatlantic local revivalists were the architects of a new empire of Protestant piety. But the Awakening's experimental piety rejuvenated both religious individualism and brought out the "protest" inherent in Protestantism. Whitefield himself publicly identified ministers who had a sluggish spiritual pulse.

Both ordained and lay revivalists who followed in Whitefield's train escalated criticism of ministers who opposed or offered only tepid support for the Awakening. Gilbert Tennent, a Scots-Irish Presbyterian leader of revivalism in the Middle Colonies, numbered among the most controversial ordained itinerants. He toured New England with Whitefield's encouragement. In 1741 he published a controversial sermon called *On the Danger of an Unconverted Ministry*. He attacked ministers who possessed the external qualifications for the ministry—education and ordination—but lacked the internal requirement of rebirth. The New Light emphasis on the internal call to the ministry inspired countless other antiauthoritarian outbursts; a famous incident occurred at Yale in 1742, when a promising New Light student was dismissed for claiming that one of his clerical tutors had no more spiritual grace than a chair.

James Davenport, the most notorious itinerant minister, provoked a backlash from both pro- and anti-revival authorities. A Presbyterian from Long Island, New York, Davenport appeared at the Yale commencement in 1741 and tried to foment a student rebellion against the head of the college (his alma mater) and the pastor of New Haven's First Church. During a later visit to Connecticut, Davenport organized a protest against luxury and worldliness. At a revival in New London, Davenport urged his listeners to take off their fashionable accessories—stylish clothing, lace, and wigs, for instance—so that they could be destroyed in a bonfire. People complied, but their worldly vanities never actually went up in smoke. Between Davenport's visits to Connecticut, the General Assembly passed legislation that treated itinerants who had not been invited by a local pastor as "strangers." They were warned out, just as other "vagrants" were.

Moderate New Lights sought to contain the antiauthoritarian temper of revivalism within communal bounds, to harness spiritual rebirth to social renewal. Yet the new emphasis on an internal call to the ministry, part of the Awakening's larger interiorization of religious authority, generated ecclesiastical disorder in many towns. A perfectionist Separate Congregational movement, numbering more than one hundred churches, erupted in New England. These radical New Lights established spiritually "pure" churches with strict membership requirements. They purged the halfway covenant and infant baptism from Congregational practices and founded churches that restricted communion to adults who could testify to rebirth. The Separates preferred converted ministers whether they were educated or not. Separates adopted practices and beliefs that overlapped with New Light Baptist churches. Many Separate congregations eventually joined the Baptist faith.

Both Separate Congregationalists and New Light Baptists encouraged itinerant preaching and lay exhorting. Women as well as uneducated laymen took up the call. The spiritual testimony of women often began during the Awakening when they related their conversion experience in public rather than in private, as custom had previously dictated. Exhorting beyond the local church then followed. Sometimes what moderate New Light Congregationalists considered the contagion of female exhorting burst out in their own churches. Twice during the Awakening, Congregational authorities in the Connecticut Valley town of Westfield, Massachusetts, summoned Bathesheba Kingsley to account for the lay exhorting that ensued after her conversion. In 1741 she was charged with stealing a horse so that she could ride about the countryside bearing witness to the power of her new birth. Repentance before the congregation did not halt Kingsley's zealous activities. She apparently spent the next two years visiting homes in Westfield and other towns, where she accused individuals of wickedness and dispensed judgments against ministers. The Awakening empowered other Bathesheba Kingsleys, especially among Separates and Baptists. Boston's Charles Chauncy, the most powerful Old Light critic of the Awakening, reprimanded the revivalists: "The encouraging [of] WOMEN, yea GIRLS to speak in the assemblies for religious worship is a plain breach of that *commandment of the LORD,* where it is said, *Let your WOMEN keep in silence in the churches.*"[19]

Revivalists transgressed other social boundaries that had long defined New England worship. The social hierarchy codified in meetinghouse seating plans collapsed in outdoor meetings, where men and women, rich and poor, white and nonwhite mingled "promiscuously." Africans and Indians were released, at least temporarily, from the segregated worship that often confined them to meetinghouse galleries. Neither moderate nor radical revivalists in New England, however, translated the Awakening's spiritual egalitarianism into anything like true social equality. New Lights left slavery and the slave trade undisturbed. Prominent revivalists such as Jonathan Edwards continued to own black servants.

African-American engagement in the Awakening was uneven. Though it is often suggested that the emotional, expressive character of revivalistic religion widely appealed to African-Americans since it was more compatible with their spiritual traditions, the actual record is mixed. Revivals did attract the attention of blacks, some of whom defied Old Light masters. But African slaves often followed the religious preferences of their owners, as the life of Phillis Wheatley suggests. They even belonged to Anglican churches, which grew during the Awakening, as Old Lights feared, because of the way revivalism convulsed Congregationalism. African-Americans, then, worshiped in churches on both sides of the Awakening.

Native people in New England more fully participated in New Light religion, sometimes on their own terms. Local revivals broke out in Native enclaves and advanced the continuing Anglicization of Indian life. When the Mohegan reservation in eastern Connecticut was awakened in 1741, "the Indians brot in & gave up to the English a number of stone & wooden Idols & . . . worshipped none since," an observer reported.[20] James Davenport visited the area two years later, sparking a revival among the Pequot and Narragansett that spread from Stonington, Connecticut, to Westerly and Charlestown, Rhode Island.

On the Narragansett reservation, Natives who lived under the thumb of exploitative Indian and white leaders gained control over their own church. Conversion had begun under a Congregational minister in an Anglo-controlled church. After whites castigated exhorter Samuel Niles, a converted powwow who was unable to read, he and about one hundred Natives formed a Separate Baptist church. Under Niles's leadership, the Narragansett church seems to have found ground between the dreams, trances, and visions that some radical New Lights welcomed and the similar spirituality of the traditional powwow.

Samson Occom, the most famous New Light Indian convert, exemplifies a more common dimension of the "Indians' Awakening": the embrace of evangelical Christianity in the place of Native religious practices that had failed to protect indigenous people against disease, depredation, and decline. Occom became an international celebrity, the Native evangelical equivalent of Phillis Wheatley. His notoriety as an "Indian" preacher actually preceded the "African" poet's transatlantic acclaim. Born on the Mohegan reservation near New London, Occom converted during a local revival around 1740, when he was sixteen years old. The Awakening rekindled Congregational interest in Indian missions. Occom was tutored by Eleazar Wheelock in nearby Lebanon, Connecticut. Occom's success as a student and preacher encouraged Wheelock to train Native missionaries, and in 1754 he opened Moor's Indian Charity School. Occom preached to Native people on Long Island and throughout New York and New England. He was ordained by the Presbyterian Church.

Despite his success, Occom became embittered by the racism he encountered, even among his fellow evangelicals. The gospel society that sponsored his work with Natives paid him far below the rate that white missionaries earned. Occom's mentor ultimately betrayed him. In 1765, at Wheelock's behest, Occom toured Britain to raise money for Moor's Indian School. The first Native American to preach to a European audience, Occom drew large crowds attracted by his pulpit skills and a fascination with his New World exoticism. He returned to Connecticut with contributions of 11,000 pounds. Wheelock eventually used the money to found Dartmouth College. After Wheelock's early commitment to Native education, the new college became an institution primarily for whites. Nevertheless, with his transatlantic tour and fame, Occom had retraced the steps of Whitefield, who had also traveled to save souls and solicit money for his charitable causes.

Whitefield's American tour induced a religious awakening that faltered by 1743. When the Grand Itinerant returned to New England in the fall of 1744, the Great Awakening had collapsed. In his preaching from Maine to Boston, he heard "a general complaint of a withdrawing of the remarkable outpouring of the Spirit of God."[21] As religious ardor waned in Northampton, Edwards invoked the "city upon a hill" imagery, but not to uphold the town and New England as moral exemplars. Rather, the backsliding from the high spiritual promise of revivalism and the esteem conferred on the town and region meant that, as a city upon a hill, "we disgrace ourselves & expose ourselves to contempt."[22] Edwards knew that news traveled fast in those years, moving from colony to colony and from America to Britain along imperial routes of trade, communication, and cultural interaction. Edwards's church dismissed him in 1750, after he attempted to overturn his grandfather's open communion practices. He concluded that too many false saints had been admitted to the church during the Awakening. Edwards spent most of the next decade preaching to Indians in the western Massachusetts town of Stockbridge and composing many of the theological works that secured his international reputation as a religious thinker.

The "greatness" of the Great Awakening has sometimes been exaggerated. Its temporal and geographical limits are clear. Yet the Awakening did have enduring consequences for New England and colonial America. In spite of pietistic Calvinists' criticism of religious rationalism and their denunciation of the empire of goods, on the whole the Awakening moved colonial America forward, not backward. The new birth bolstered individualism and personal agency in an enlarged pluralistic religious marketplace. Even moderate evangelicals who labored to balance a re-Puritanized individualism with New England communalism had to recalibrate the relationship between the two religious-cultural impulses. Perhaps Jonathan Edwards failed to negotiate this adjustment within his own congregation.

The Awakening also had progressive educational and intellectual consequences. Moderate New Lights embraced piety and rationalism. Learning and spiritual rebirth were needed to combat the errors of radical pietists and rationalists. Presbyterian Princeton (1746), Baptist Brown (1764), and Congregational Dartmouth (1769) all grew from the Awakening's New Light religion. Furthermore, Enlightenment rationalism and the controversies surrounding the Awakening inaugurated the most prolific and creative outpouring of religious thought during the Colonial Era. Jonathan Edwards's theological works, especially his *Freedom of the Will*, and the writings of his closest clerical disciples explored, with considerable ingenuity, ways of reconciling Calvinist determinism with individual moral agency. The Awakening gave birth to what is called "the New England theology," the only homegrown school of Calvinist thought in America.

The New England theology extended the life of evangelical Calvinism, which suggests another consequence of the Awakening. As much as they took place in an imperial context and responded to transatlantic developments, the midcentury revivals marked the beginnings of evangelical America: the synthesis of conversionism, revivalism, and Biblicism that swept through the new nation in the decades after the Revolution. The leaders of the "Second Great Awakening" looked to these eighteenth-century revivals for precedent and inspiration; they reprinted and widely distributed devotional and doctrinal works, including many of Edwards's publications, in the process of evangelizing the new republic.

A final consequence of the colonial Awakening was more immediate. The midcentury revivals created a new "community" of British Protestants. Revivals seemed to dissolve colonial borders. The Awakening linked British America to England, Scotland, and Ireland. Whitefield, Tennent (who moderated his positions), Occom, and other itinerants crisscrossed denominational and geographic boundaries. They reinforced intercolonial and transatlantic Protestant bonds. Edwards, for instance, was called from the Stockbridge mission to the presidency of the Presbyterian College of New Jersey (later Princeton). The spread of news about local revivals and the publication of works like Edwards's *Faithful Narrative* and Whitefield's *Journals* enabled New Lights to envision themselves as part of an imperial community of pious Protestants. New warfare with France tapped into the moral fervor of evangelical religion. Resolutely British and Protestant, New Englanders and other colonials defended their empire of liberty and piety.

## BRITANNIA RULES

England had already declared war when Whitefield returned to New England in 1744. From the mid-1740s through the Seven Years' War, which began a decade later, conflict with France offered a crusade in which revivalistic zeal could be redeployed. New Lights resisted Anglican religious rationalism and criticized the expanding market for imported goods, but they shared the eighteenth-century pride in British constitutionalism and the understanding of New England's founding as a quest for English civil and religious liberty. As Edwards put it, English people did not have to fear "a papist king" or the kind of "despotick power" that ruled "the Turkish domains, Muscovy and France."[23] Imperial warfare encouraged Old Light and New Light Congregationalists to heal some of the wounds inflicted by the Awakening. Both factions rallied to defend their British heritage of Protestantism and constitutionalism against the prospect of French Catholic political and religious despotism.

Renewed war with France aided the ongoing process of re-Anglicization in other ways. New England's proximity to New

France and the French population center in the New World underscored the region's dependence on the homeland for protection. Military spending pumped money into the regional economy, which stimulated trade and consumption and eroded reforms brought about by the Awakening. Above all, final victory over France generated a groundswell of British patriotism.

Concentrated on the banks of the St. Lawrence River, from the capital of Quebec to Montreal, New France had developed in strikingly different ways from mainland British colonial America. In 1754, French settlements contained only 75,000 people; New England alone held more than five times as many colonists. A tradition of land tenancy among the French, in which farmers paid rent to wealthy "seigneurs," contrasted sharply with the free-holding that was widespread in New England and other parts of British America. A political as well as a social hierarchy prevailed in New France. The king appointed a governor-general and a handful of additional officials, including a bishop, to oversee the settlements. Representative government failed to take root in New France, either on the colonial or local level. French claims to the vast tracts of land that stretched beyond the St. Lawrence through the Great Lakes and down the Mississippi River Valley to Louisiana were secured by forts and trading posts. French traders carried on important exchange with the large numbers of Natives that inhabited the continental interior. But the French empire of goods was no match for the dynamic commercialism of British America. The St. Lawrence River, the artery into New France, froze over several months a year. The French crown valued its sugar islands in the Caribbean far more than sparsely populated, frigid New France.

A small colonial population did offer benefits that enabled the French to maintain a loose hold on their far-flung territory and to prosecute war against their English rivals. Far more than the English, the French depended on Native people, as the record of intermarriage suggests. The French were also less threatening to Natives than land-hungry British colonists, whose surging population, in contrast to that of New France, benefited from religious dissenters and thousands of immigrants. Whether in trade, warfare, or religion, the French learned from necessity to compromise with their powerful Indian allies. Jesuits resisted screening out all Native spiritual beliefs and practices from missionary

Catholicism. Military commanders accepted Indian-style warfare and ritualistic torture. Natives greatly augmented New France's military strength.

The prelude to the final campaign for imperial control of North America began in 1744, after England declared war on France for another attempt to install a Bourbon on an empty throne. A touring George Whitefield helped recruit colonial soldiers for the War of Austrian Succession or, as it was known in America, King George's War. Whitefield supplied a revivalistic war slogan for the crusade against France: "Christ leads, never despair."[24] Four thousand New England fighters supported by the British navy achieved a stunning victory in 1745. They seized Louisbourg, the so-called Gibraltar of the West, a massive fortress on Nova Scotia's Cape Breton Island that protected the Gulf of St. Lawrence. The celebrated capture of Louisbourg excited New Englanders' pride in the British Empire. When peace was finally negotiated in 1748, dismay and bitterness replaced celebration. Louisbourg was returned to France as England won what it considered more important concessions from its rival.

Peace was short-lived. The French feared for the future of the Ohio Valley. With a surging population and abundant imported goods to trade with Native people, an expansive British America seemed poised to gobble up trans-Appalachian territory. In the early 1750s, the French erected forts in the Ohio Valley to block the English colonial advance. The Virginia militia under George Washington responded in 1754, but their fort was overrun by French and Indian forces. That same year an election speaker in Massachusetts, Boston minister Jonathan Mayhew, described a potential Gallic horror involving "motley armies of French and painted savages taking our fortresses, and erecting their own, even in our capital towns and cities." He implored New Englanders to defend their British heritage against popery and tyranny, reminding his listening audience and readers that we "have always distinguished ourselves by a jealousy of our rights, by our loyalty, and our zeal for the common interest of his Majesty's dominions on the continent."[25]

New Englanders found further cause for alarm after more military setbacks preceded and followed the declaration of war. Twenty-five hundred British soldiers and colonists under the command of Major General Edward Braddock were routed in 1755 near the crucial French Fort Duquesne (Pittsburgh). The next year England officially declared war on France. Still, the Seven Years' War (1756–63), or what the colonists called the French and Indian War, continued to go badly for the English. Under the command of the Marquis de Montcalm, the French won major victories, especially in northern New York, where they captured one English garrison with 2,500 soldiers in 1757. Raids unsettled the colonial frontier from Maine to the Carolinas. New England contributed soldiers and words to the war effort. It has been estimated that during the course of the war, one out of every three men in the region who were physically able to fight joined the cause. New England ministers also drew on their rhetorical stockpile, from revivalistic jeremiads to fast, thanksgiving, and election sermons to inspire the region's defense of its British political and religious liberty.

The tide of war turned only after a major English military investment in North America, the kind of commitment of resources outside of Europe that France was unwilling to undertake. Under William Pitt, who became prime minister under George II in 1756, British imperial strategy focused on achieving a decisive military victory over the French in the New World. By 1758 the Anglo-American forces arrayed against New France numbered approximately 45,000 (24,000 British soldiers and the rest colonial militia), who were supported by the British navy. Under an assault by the army and navy, Louisbourg fell in 1758. With British warships patrolling the Gulf of St. Lawrence, New France was cut off from its homeland and left to fend for itself. Between 1758 and 1759, the French lost or abandoned forts from the Ohio Valley to the Great Lakes and northern New York. The French-Indian alliance was by then badly frayed. Montcalm's contempt for Natives damaged French-Indian relations. As one historian has aptly put it, Natives saw themselves "as free agents: allies, not servants, of the French."[26] Montcalm's treatment of them and then French losses led many Indians to withdraw their active support of the French cause after 1757 and negotiate peace with the English.

In September of 1759 both Montcalm and victorious English General James Wolfe perished in the famous Battle of Quebec. A year later the French army surrendered in Montreal. With the fall of New France, thanksgiving sermons and celebrations replaced fast days in New England. The Anglo-American triumph over popery and tyranny, a Connecticut minister enthused, was "of more Importance than has ever been made by the *English,* since *England* was a nation."[27] The peace treaty signed in 1763 lifted the French threat that had hovered over New England for three generations. France retained only its Caribbean sugar islands. Canada and all French territory east of the Mississippi River came under British control. Spain, France's ally, gained possession of Louisiana, the territory west of the Mississippi. France was driven out of mainland North America.

In New England, the successful culmination of the French and Indian War added a new epoch to the triumphant narrative of eighteenth-century Anglo-American identity. Thanksgiving sermons celebrated the chosen status of a transatlantic British nation. "Remarkable Providences" had been bestowed on "British Israel," divine blessings that extended from the Magna Carta to the Protestant Reformation, the Glorious Revolution, the "Growth and Flourishing of the New England colonies," and the conquest of New France.[28] Among descendants of the Puritans in particular, the imperial victory awakened millennialism—the intoxicating hope that Protestantism and political liberty would begin a steady progress around the world.

The French and Indian War strengthened New Englanders' sense of partnership in a British empire of liberty, commerce, and Protestantism. "Born and educated in this country," New Hampshire minister Jeremy Belknap confided to his diary in 1762, "I glory in the Name of Briton." As "British Brothers," the colonists could now live happily under the "glorious Throne of *Britannia,*" a New Hampshire editor proclaimed two years later.[29] Military victory invigorated such British patriotism, which had developed over the decades of re-Anglicization. New England even experienced a new burst in the growth of Anglican churches in the decade after the war. In Connecticut, for example, sixteen new churches were constructed between 1761 and 1774, and another twenty congregations became organized without church buildings.

Of course, as the Revolutionary Era dawned New England remained staunchly Congregational. The region also retained a collective memory of seventeenth-century English persecution. In addition, New England's politics and social structure diverged from the homeland. Nonetheless, the region's culture and identity had become more English than they had been since the founding generation.

# From the City upon a Hill
# to Plymouth Rock

On the eve of the Revolutionary Era, the English colonies had undergone decades of integration into a transatlantic imperial realm. Victory over France spurred unprecedented British patriotism. New Englanders did not embrace a morally exclusive *American* collective identity as a "city upon a hill." They saw themselves as part of a free Protestant British Israel.

Within a little more than a decade, resistance to new British policies undermined the effusive imperial patriotism that accompanied defeat of the French. Indictments of a corrupt mother country eroded British pride and eventually led to the proclamation of American independence. This epochal turn of events, of course, is the subject of countless books and interpretations. Moreover, the American Revolution has often shaped how we view the Colonial Era. After independence, the revolutionaries themselves, with historically minded New Englanders in the vanguard, retold the story of the Colonial Era from a patriotic American perspective. The need to explain the Revolution has tended to produce nationalist interpretations: accounts that examine the Colonial Era to uncover the roots of American independence. Consider again the image of New England as a city upon a hill. Winthrop's famous words, as we have seen, held shifting meaning in the Colonial Era. But they have been frequently cited in lineal narratives that trace American national identity back to New England's Puritan origins, ignoring or downplaying the first generation's affirmation of an English identity as well as the eighteenth-century process of re-Anglicization.

New England and the other English colonies developed in distinctly American ways from the seventeenth century through the eighteenth. Yet until shortly before independence, colonists justified political resistance to and economic boycotts of the mother country's policies as a defense of their "British" rights. One historian has recently pointed out that on his famous ride in 1775, Paul Revere proclaimed not, as American mythology holds, "The British are coming," but rather "The Regulars are coming." Revere and most of his contemporaries continued to see themselves as British.[1] It took repeated conflicts in the 1760s and early 1770s to dissolve the colonists' illusion that they were "British Brothers" with their transatlantic English compatriots. After a decade of defending their hard-won British rights, many colonists accepted the facts that defined their imperial position: the mother country viewed them, with undisguised metropolitan contempt, as subordinate subjects—coarsened inhabitants of a peripheral colonial world existing solely to serve the homeland's interest.

Colonial reservations about the imperial relationship actually flared during the French and Indian War, only to be smothered under triumphal British rhetoric. In New England, military officers and thousands of the rank-and-file redcoats displayed disregard, even contempt, for the colonists and such traditions as the Puritan Sabbath and the commemoration of election day. The colonial militia, mobilized more by voluntary contract than by state coercion, came in for special ridicule by a professional British army skilled at open field European warfare. A lack of discipline and cowardice in battle, the British continually sneered, were the trademarks of the colonial militia. Indeed, the French and Indian War marked the military birth of "Yankee Doodle," not as a colonial marching song but as a British satire of the New England militia. The opening stanza of the British "Yankee Doodle" summoned a mythical New Englander whose Old Testament name tied him to ancient Israel:

Brother Ephraim sold his cow and bought him a
  commission,
And then he went to Canada to Fight for the Nation,

But when Ephraim he came home he proved an arrant
    Coward,
He wou'd'nt fight the Frenchmen there for fear of being
    devoured.[2]

The lyrics went on to mock New Englanders in more general terms, portraying them as uncouth, rustic bumpkins. The Anglo-American Protestant crusade against French despotism exposed conflicts between the metropolitan and colonial worlds that intensified in the decade after imperial triumph.

At the same time, the decline of military spending sent an inflated commercial economy into a tailspin. Boston was especially hard hit; the cost of poor relief in the city soared. The postwar recession pinched maritime workers like those involved in what was labeled the "Boston Massacre" of 1770. New English taxes and duties threatened to impose additional burdens on an already slack economy. Political leaders and town meetings responded with non-importation agreements to secure their English rights. Resistance and recession disrupted the empire of goods.

Whatever the ineptitude of their implementation, British officials understandably saw postwar imperial policies as neither ill-timed nor unjust. The homeland had deployed thousands of British regulars and expended more than two million pounds to conquer New France. The army now had to garrison the expansive former French empire. Even after the peace treaty of 1763, British regulars contended with rebellious Native people in the American interior who feared an invasion of English settlers on the tribal land surrounding the Great Lakes. American colonists, imperial authorities reasoned, needed to pay for the continuing defense and orderly control of an extensive frontier. Changed circumstances compelled a readjustment of the imperial relationship. English efforts to find new sources of revenue, however, raised constitutional issues for colonial assemblies that claimed to be little Parliaments.

For many colonists, though far from all, the new imperial policies gnawed at the postwar faith in Britain as an empire of liberty and virtue. The eighteenth-century English radicals' Commonwealth critique of the homeland's balanced constitution acquired a new persuasiveness in the colonies after the war. *Cato's Letters* had warned British citizens that power-hungry ministers attached to private interests schemed to corrupt England's balanced constitution and the pursuit of the public good. Beginning in the 1760s, the real and perceived imperial threats to the colonies' little Parliaments—and thus to American liberty—far surpassed the regular plotting of individual royal governors that had been part of colonial politics. The king's "corrupt" ministers appeared to be engaged in a conspiracy against the colonists' English rights, including the right of no taxation without representation.

Colonists had long been instructed by English dissenters like the authors of *Cato's Letters* on the need for a vigilant, virtuous citizenry to preserve liberty. An attachment to luxury and the public complacency that resulted from a preoccupation with the pursuit of private interests invited government encroachment on liberty. In New England and other parts of colonial America, the postwar recession and non-importation agreements provoked new, politicized questions about the empire of goods, the corrupting effects of luxury, and the need to produce and not just consume manufactured items. Homespun clothing, which would soon adorn patriotic images of Yankee Doodle, became a sign of colonial virtue, industry, and public-mindedness.

In historically conscious New England, the imperial crisis encouraged a reinterpretation of the region's origins. Once again New England's founding provided edification and inspiration. With the invention of Forefathers' Day, Plymouth Rock finally entered the annals of New England colonial history. American revolutionaries fashioned a new Pilgrim-Puritan narrative of the colonial past. Plymouth Rock and the city upon a hill would develop into a powerful American narrative that continues to shape popular understanding of colonial New England.

Throughout the Colonial Era, the settlement of Plymouth had been overshadowed by heroic accounts of the Great Migration. Few recognized the Old Colony, as Plymouth came to be known after Massachusetts absorbed it in 1691, as the home of an historic lodestone. The story of Plymouth Rock had always been a vague local legend; the colonial descendants of the saints, strangers, and Native people who made up Plymouth's original population neither enshrined the boulder nor commemorated it in the Colonial Era. Indeed, in 1741 commercial progress in Plymouth nearly dislodged the rock. The town needed a new wharf to accommodate growing maritime trade and the boulder endured as a potential obstacle to economic development. Unable to budge the rock, town leaders built the wharf with the future "doorstep" to America protruding through its surface.

In 1769, protest, resistance, and non-importation stirred the historical imagination of a group of well-to-do Plymouth men who claimed descent from the colony's original settlers. They formed the Old Colony Club and created Forefathers' Day, December 22, to commemorate the arrival of the Mayflower in Plymouth Harbor and the establishment of New England's first permanent settlement. The celebration of 1769 included a public ceremony and a banquet that linked New England's founding to the imperial crisis. The banquet fare consisted of codfish, oysters, clams, and other seafood—reminders of the deprivation and struggle for survival of Plymouth's founders, who had been obliged to consume items more common to Native foodways. The banquet menu, like homespun clothing, made a political statement. The Old Colony Club vowed to avoid "all appearance of luxury and extravagance" in its celebration. The resistance movement enlivened discussion of a complex of beliefs about governmental power, vigilance, virtue, citizenship, and the public good that historians have labeled republicanism. Forefathers' Day acquired elements of an American republican commemoration of New England's origins: "May every person be possessed of the same noble sentiments against arbitrary power," one banquet toast proposed, "that our worthy ancestors were endowed with." Another toast linked colonial resistance to British policies with the persecution by the Church of England, headed by the first generation's most hated scourge, that gave birth to New England: "May every enemy to civil and religious liberty meet the same or a worse fate than Archbishop Laud."[3] The fate that Archbishop Laud ultimately met was execution.

The mythology of Plymouth and its historic rock emerged for the first time in revised narratives of the region's origins. These accounts depicted New Englanders as liberty-loving republicans who had successfully resisted the "iron jaws of English civil and prelatical tyranny" since 1620. The "Pilgrim Forefathers" were transformed from a mix of sometimes contentious saints and strangers into essential colonial New Englanders: simple, pious, virtuous, communal American republican prototypes. In 1774, firm in its resistance to England's new Coercive Acts (punishment for the patriot destruction of imported tea) but still seeking reconciliation, a Boston newspaper drew inspiration from the celebration of Forefathers' Day: "it may be safely affirmed, that all the potent thunders of Britain, cannot reduce us to more tremendous sufferings, than those distinguished patrons of religion and freedom, animated by sacred ardour, patiently endured."[4] Similar rhetoric surrounded the first major efforts to consecrate what came to be called Plymouth Rock—New England's republican cornerstone. In 1774 the resistance leaders guided a team of oxen to Plymouth Harbor, intending to transport the boulder to the center of town, where it would be stationed next to the liberty pole as a sacred artifact of New England's historic quest for freedom. As it was being lifted from its resting place, the rock split in two. One part remained at Plymouth Harbor, and the other was moved to Liberty Pole Square and deposited in front of the meetinghouse, where it would remain for two generations.

Forefathers' Day, Plymouth Rock, homespun, and the patriotic appropriation of "Yankee Doodle" at the Battle of Lexington and Concord in 1775 all suggest how New Englanders began to negotiate the transition from a British identity to an American one. The Revolutionary Era inaugurated an exclusive, nationalistic Pilgrim-Puritan narrative of the Colonial Era. Once independence was achieved, leaders such as John Adams saw New England's colonial past as a *republican* city upon a hill, a model for the new nation.

Pilgrim-Puritan narratives of American origins have often obscured the complexity of colonial New England. Saints clearly put their stamp on regional life and culture. Yet Natives, non-Puritans, the profane, white and nonwhite bound laborers, and other strangers also participated in the making of colonial New England. Separated from the homeland by three thousand miles of ocean, New England did not develop as an isolated American backwater. It became part of an Atlantic world, a dynamic mercantile region with far-flung commercial and racial crossings. Imperial membership bolstered the British patriotism of New Englanders and other colonials, necessitating a prolonged post-independence search for an American identity.

# Notes

PROLOGUE   City upon a Hill

1. Winthrop, "A Model of Christian Charity," in Alan Heimert and Andrew Delbanco, eds., *The Puritans in America: A Narrative Anthology* (Cambridge, Mass., 1989), pp. 82, 91.

ONE   Native New England

1. Samuel de Champlain, *Voyages,* translated by Charles P. Otis (Boston, 1878), pp. 66–70.

2. Ibid., p. 66; John Smith, *A Description of New England* (1616), in *The Complete Works of Captain John Smith (1580–1631),* edited by Philip L. Barbour, 3 vols. (Chapel Hill, N.C., 1986), 1:340.

3. Edward Winslow, *Good Newes from New England* (1624), in Alexander Young, ed., *Chronicles of the Pilgrim Fathers of the Colony of Plymouth, 1602–1625* (1841; rpt. New York, 1971), p. 363.

4. William Wood, *New England's Prospect* (1634), edited with an introduction by Alden T. Vaughan (Amherst, Mass., 1977), p. 89.

5. J. A. Leo Lemay, ed., "New England's Annoyances" (1643) in *"New England's Annoyances": America's First Folk Song* (Newark, Del., 1985), pp. 1–3.

6. Quoted in James Axtell, *The European and the Indian: Essays in the Ethnohistory of Colonial North America* (New York, 1981), p. 280.

7. Wood, *New England's Prospect,* p. 113.

8. Ibid.; Edward Johnson, *Wonder-Working Providence of Sion's Savior in New England, 1628–1651* (1654), edited by J. Franklin Jameson (New York, 1910), p. 211.

9. Daniel K. Richter, *Facing East from Indian Country: A Native History of Early America* (Cambridge, Mass., 2001), p. 49.

10. Wood, *New England's Prospect*, p. 85.

11. Winslow, *Good Newes from New England*, p. 338.

12. William Bradford, *Of Plymouth Plantation,* edited with an introduction by Harvey Wish (New York, 1962), p. 284. Native reaction quoted in Alfred A. Cave, *The Pequot War* (Amherst, Mass., 1996), p. 152. Captain John Underhill, quoted in Patrick M. Malone, *The Skulking Way of War: Technology and Tactics among the New England Indians* (Baltimore, 1993), p. 30.

13. Roger Williams, *A Key into the Language of America* (1643), edited by John J. Teunissen and Evelyn J. Hinz (Detroit, 1973), p. 237.

14. Ibid., p. 191.

15. John Bereton, "A Brief and True Relationship of the Discovery of the North Part of Virginia, 1602," in Henry S. Burrage, ed., *Early English and French Voyages* (New York, 1906), p. 337.

16. Bradford, *Of Plymouth Plantation,* p. 78.

17. Ibid., p. 176; Michael Wigglesworth, "God's Controversy with New England," in Heimert and Delbanco, eds., *The Puritans in America*, p. 232; and Robert E. Moody, ed., *The Letters of Thomas Gorges, Deputy Governor of the Province of Maine, 1640–43* (Portland, 1978), p. 110.

18. Winslow, *Good Newes from New England*, p. 352.

19. Smith, *Advertisements for the Unexperienced Planters of New England, or Any Where* (1631) in *Works,* 3:270.

TWO   Puritan New England, 1620–1660

1. Stephen Innes, *Creating the Commonwealth: The Economic Culture of Puritan New England* (New York, 1995), ch. 1.

2. William Hunt, *The Puritan Moment: The Coming of a Revolution in an English Country* (Cambridge, Mass., 1983), p. 146.

3. Quoted in Alan Heimert and Andrew Delbanco, eds., *The Puritans in America: A Narrative Anthology* (Cambridge, Mass., 1985), p. 1.

4. Winthrop, quoted in Everett Emerson, ed., *Letters from New England: The Massachusetts Bay Colony, 1629–1638* (Amherst, Mass., 1976), p. 30.

5. [Robert Cushman], "Reasons and Considerations touching the lawfulness of removing out of England into parts of America" (1632) in Dwight Heath, ed., *Mourt's Relation: A Journal of the Pilgrims in Plymouth* (New York, 1963), pp. 89–90.

6. Winthrop, "Reasons to Be Considered for . . . the Intended Plantation in New England" (1629), in Heimert and Delbanco, eds., *The Puritans in America,* p. 73.

7. Cotton, "God's Promises to His Plantations" (1630), in Heimert and Delbanco, eds., *The Puritans in America,* pp. 79–80.

8. Winthrop to [unknown] (1629), *Winthrop Papers,* 6 vols. (Boston, 1929–), 2:122.

9. William Hubbard, *A General History of New England from the Discovery*

*to 1680* (1682), in Massachusetts Historical Society, *Collections* 2 (1815), p. 545.

10. Nathaniel B. Shurtleff, ed., *Records of the Governor and Company of the Massachusetts Bay in New England,* 5 vols. (Boston, 1853–55), 1:159.

11. For the quotations from Hooker and Winthrop, see Gloria L. Main, *Peoples of a Spacious Land: Families and Cultures in Colonial New England* (Cambridge, Mass., 2001), p. 48; and Bruce C. Daniels, *The Connecticut Town: Growth and Development, 1635–1690* (Middletown, Conn., 1979), pp. 9–10.

12. Shurtleff, ed., *Records of Massachusetts Bay,* 2:6–7.

13. Originally coined by the Reverend Samuel Stone, one of Connecticut's founders, this phrase was repeated by other Puritans. Andrew Delbanco, *The Puritan Ordeal* (Cambridge, Mass., 1989), p. 11.

14. Marilyn J. Westerkamp, *Women and Religion in Early America, 1600–1850* (New York, 1999), p. 36.

15. Quoted in Edmund S. Morgan, *The Puritan Family: Religion and Domestic Relations in Seventeenth-Century New England* (1944; rpt. New York, 1966), p. 45.

16. *The Works of Anne Bradstreet,* edited by Jeannine Hensley (Cambridge, Mass., 1967), p. 241.

17. Bradstreet, "A Letter to Her Husband, Absent upon Public Employment," ibid., p. 226.

18. Ibid., p. 224.

19. Ibid., p. 241.

20. Nathaniel Mather (1651), quoted in Marian Card Donnelly, *The New England Meeting Houses of the Seventeenth Century* (Middletown, Conn., 1968), p. 61.

21. William Hooke, *New England's Tears for Old England's Fears* (1641) in Heimert and Delbanco, eds., *The Puritans in America,* p. 105.

22. [Anonymous], *New England's First Fruits* (1643), reprinted in Samuel Eliot Morison, *The Founding of Harvard College* (Harvard, Mass., 1935), p. 441.

23. Bradstreet, *Works,* p. 185.

THREE    Beyond Puritan New England

1. Bradford, *Of Plymouth Plantation,* edited with an introduction by Harvey Wish (New York, 1962), 141.

2. Hawthorne, "The Maypole of Merry Mount," in *Selected Tales and Sketches,* edited by Hyatt H. Waggoner (New York, 1964), pp. 145–46.

3. Quoted in Gloria L. Main, *Peoples of a Spacious Land: Families and Cultures in Colonial New England* (Cambridge, Mass., 2001), p. 50.

4. Everett Emerson, ed., *Letters from New England: The Massachusetts Bay Colony, 1629–1638* (Amherst, Mass., 1976), p. 176.

5. Quoted in Richard P. Gildrie, *The Profane, the Civil, and the Godly: The*

*Reformation of Manners in Orthodox New England, 1679–1749* (University Park, Penn., 1994), p. 53.

6. See David Cressy, *Coming Over: Migration and Communication between England and New England in the Seventeenth Century* (New York, 1987), pp. 176–77, for quotations. For sea deliverance tales, see Cotton Mather, *Magnalia Christi Americana, or the Ecclesiastical History of New England,* 2 vols. (1702; rpt. New York, 1852), 2:343–54.

7. See James T. Carlton, "Blue Immigrants: The Marine Biology of Maritime History," *The Log of Mystic Seaport* (Summer 1992), pp. 31–36, for all quotations.

8. Christine Leigh Heyrman, *Commerce and Culture: The Maritime Communities of Colonial Massachusetts, 1690–1750* (New York, 1984), p. 223. Daniel Vickers, *Farmers and Fishermen: Two Centuries of Work in Essex County, Massachusetts, 1630–1850* (Chapel Hill, N.C., 1994), informs my discussion of cod fishing and its workers.

9. William Wood, *New England's Prospect* (1634), edited with an introduction by Alden T. Vaughan (Amherst, Mass., 1977), p. 53.

10. Quoted in Margaret Ellen Newell, *From Dependency to Independence: Economic Revolution in Colonial New England* (Ithaca, N.Y., 1998), pp. 102–3.

11. Karen Ordahl Kupperman, *Providence Island, 1630–1641: The Other Puritan Colony* (New York, 1993), p. 178.

12. Quoted in Winthrop D. Jordan, *White over Black: American Attitudes toward the Negro, 1550–1812* (Chapel Hill, N.C., 1968), p. 67.

13. Quoted in Lorenzo J. Greene, *The Negro in Colonial New England, 1620–1776* (1942; rpt. New York, 1966), p. 60.

14. Kupperman, *Providence Island,* p. 213.

15. Quoted in Charles E. Clark, *The Settlement of Northern New England, 1610–1763* (1970; rpt. Hanover, N.H., 1983), p. 35.

16. Mather, *The Fisher-mans Calling* (Boston, 1712), pp. 42–43.

17. Mather, *Magnalia Christi Americana,* 1:66.

18. Joseph Conforti, *Imagining New England: Explorations of Regional Identity from the Pilgrims to the Mid-Twentieth Century* (Chapel Hill, N.C., 2001), p. 31.

19. Quoted in Bruce C. Daniels, *Dissent and Conformity on Narragansett Bay: The Colonial Rhode Island Town* (Middletown, Conn., 1983), p. 9.

20. John J. McCusker and Russell R. Menard, *The Economy of British America, 1607–1789* (Chapel Hill, N.C., 1985), p. 92.

FOUR   New England Besieged, 1660–1700

1. Calvin quoted in Karen Ordahl Kupperman, "Climate and Mastery of the Wilderness," in David Hall and David Grayson Allen, eds., *Seventeenth-Century New England* (Boston, 1984), pp. 26–27.

2. Theodore Dwight Bozeman, *To Live Ancient Lives: The Primitivist Dimension in Puritanism* (Chapel Hill, N.C., 1988), pp. 298–310.

3. Increase Mather, *An Earnest Exhortation* (Boston, 1696), pp. 9–10.

4. Mark A. Peterson, *The Price of Redemption: The Spiritual Economy of Puritan New England* (Stanford, Calif., 1997), p. 19, quoting John Cotton. Peterson's excellent book has influenced my discussion of declension.

5. Higginson, *The Cause of God and His People in New England* (Cambridge, Mass., 1664), pp. 9–10.

6. Samuel Danforth, *A Brief Recognition of New England's Errand into the Wilderness* (Cambridge, Mass., 1671).

7. Cotton Mather, *Things for a Distressed People* (Boston, 1696), p. 13.

8. Quoted in Henry Warner Bowden, *American Indians and Christian Missions* (Chicago, 1981), p. 188.

9. Paul J. Lindholt, ed., *John Josselyn, Colonial Traveler: A Critical Edition of Two Voyages to New-England* (Hanover, N.H., 1988), p. 101.

10. Nathaniel B. Shurtleff, ed., *Records of the Governor and Company of the Massachusetts Bay Colony,* 5 vols. (Boston, 1853–54), 5:59.

11. Rowlandson, *The Sovereignty and Goodness of God. . . .* (1682), in Alden T. Vaughan and Edward W. Clark, eds., *Puritans among the Indians: Accounts of Captivity and Restoration, 1676–1724* (Cambridge, Mass., 1981), p. 69.

12. Ibid., p. 45.

13. James Axtell, ed., "The Vengeful Women of Marblehead: James Rowles's Deposition of 1677," *William and Mary Quarterly,* 31 (1974), pp. 651–52.

14. John Hale, *A Modest Inquiry into the Nature of Witchcraft. . . .* (Boston, 1702), p. 25. Hale was the minister of nearby Beverly during the hysteria.

15. This is the argument of Mary Beth Norton's *In the Devil's Snare: The Salem Witchcraft Crisis of 1692* (New York, 2002). She provocatively examines the French-Indian frontier warfare connection to the hysteria. I draw on her work in my discussion that follows.

16. Mather, *Cases of Conscience concerning Evil Spirits Personating Men* (Boston, 1693), p. 24. The sermon had been delivered the previous October.

17. James F. Cooper Jr. and Kenneth P. Minkema, eds., *The Sermon Notebook of Samuel Parris, 1689–1694* (Boston, 1993), p. 184.

18. Quoted in Norton, *In the Devil's Snare,* p. 186.

FIVE    Saints and Strangers in the Eighteenth Century

1. J. Hector St. John de Crèvecoeur, *Letters from an American Farmer and Sketches of Eighteenth-Century America,* edited by Albert Stone (New York, 1981), p. 68. Crèvecoeur's book was published in 1782, but the letters were written before the Revolution.

2. Quoted in Richard Hofstadter, *America at 1750: A Social Portrait* (New York, 1971), p. 26.

3. Quoted in Stephen Foster, *Their Solitary Way: The Puritan Social Ethic in the First Century of Settlement in New England* (New Haven, Conn., 1971), p. 141.

4. Quoted in David W. Conroy, *In Public Houses: Drink and the Revolution of Authority in Colonial Massachusetts* (Chapel Hill, N.C., 1995), p. 141.

5. Cotton Mather, *Ornaments for the Daughters of Zion* (Boston, 1692), pp. 44–45.

6. Mary Beth Norton, *Liberty's Daughters: The Revolutionary Experience of American Women, 1750–1800* (Boston, 1980), pp. 126–30. Samuel Hopkins, *Memoirs of the Life of Mrs. Sarah Osborn* (Worcester, Mass., 1799).

7. Jean M. O'Brien, *Dispossession by Degrees: Indian Land and Identity in Natick, Massachusetts, 1650–1790* (New York, 1997), p. 211.

8. Daniel R. Mandell, *Behind the Frontier: Indians in Eighteenth-Century Massachusetts* (Lincoln, Neb., 1996), p. 61.

9. Carl Bridenbaugh, ed., *A Gentleman's Progress: The Itinerarium of Dr. Alexander Hamilton, 1744* (Chapel Hill, N.C., 1948), p. 98. My discussion of the Narragansett draws on John Wood Sweet's excellent study *Bodies Politic: Negotiating Race in the American North, 1730–1830* (Baltimore, 2003), ch. 1.

10. Quoted in David J. Silverman, "The Impact of Indentured Servitude on the Society and Culture of Southern New England Indians, 1680–1810," *New England Quarterly* 74 (Dec. 2001), p. 643.

11. Sewall, *The Selling of Joseph: A Memorial* (1700), edited by Sidney Kaplan (Amherst, Mass., 1969), p. 10.

12. Phillis Wheatley, "On Being Brought from Africa to America" (1773), in *Collected Works,* edited by John C. Shields (New York, 1988), p. 18.

13. Sarah Kemble Knight, *The Journal of Madam Knight,* in Perry Miller and Thomas H. Johnson, eds., *The Puritans: A Sourcebook of their Writings,* 2 vols. (New York, 1938), 2:437. Knight's journey took place in the fall and winter 1704–05, but the journal was not published until 1825.

14. Quoted in William D. Piersen, *Black Yankees: The Development of an Afro-American Subculture in Eighteenth-Century New England* (Amherst, Mass., 1988), p. 121. Piersen's book contains much useful information on black lives. Sweet's *Bodies Politic* is more incisive.

SIX  Provincial New England

1. Massachusetts House quoted in T. H. Breen, *The Character of the Good Ruler: A Study in Puritan Political Ideas in New England, 1630–1730* (New Haven, Conn., 1970), p. 199.

2. Quoted in Bruce Tucker, "The Reinvention of New England, 1691–1770," *New England Quarterly* (1985), p. 318.

3. Cotton Mather, *Magnalia Christi Americana, or the Ecclesiastical History of New England,* 2 vols. (1702; rpt. New York, 1967), 1:65.

4. Ibid., 1:75–76. Connecticut ministers quoted in Christopher Grasso, *A Speaking Aristocracy: Transforming Public Discourse in Eighteenth-Century Connecticut* (Chapel Hill, N.C., 1999), p. 40.

5. Thomas Prince, *The Peopling of New England* (Boston, 1730), p. 24. John Barnard, *The Throne of Righteousness* (1734), in A. W. Plumstead, ed., *The Wall*

*and the Garden: Selected Massachusetts Election Sermons, 1670–1775* (Minneapolis, 1968), pp. 230, 240.

6. Thomas Foxcroft, *Observations Historical and Practical on the Rise and Primitive State of New England* (Boston, 1730), p. 2. Barnard, *The Throne of Righteousness,* p. 230.

7. Benjamin Colman, *David's Dying Charge to the Rulers and People of Israel* (Boston, 1723), p. 29.

8. Prince, *The Peopling of New England,* p. 21.

9. T. H. Breen, *The Marketplace of Revolution: How Consumer Politics Shaped American Independence* (New York, 2004).

10. Quoted in Margaret Ellen Newell, *From Dependency to Independence: Economic Revolution in Colonial New England* (Ithaca, N.Y., 1998), p. 70.

11. Jeremiah Dummer, *A Defense of the New England Charters* (1721), in Alan Heimert and Andrew Delbanco, eds., *The Puritans in America: A Narrative Anthology* (New York, 1991), p. 68. The term *loyal consumers* is from Breen, *The Marketplace of Revolution,* p. 99.

12. See Patricia Cleary, *Elizabeth Murray: A Woman's Pursuit of Independence in Eighteenth-Century America* (Amherst, Mass., 2000), pp. 47, 57, for the handbill and other references.

13. On the rural Connecticut store's inventory, see T. H. Breen, "An Empire of Goods: The Anglicization of Colonial America, 1690–1776," *Journal of British Studies* 25 (October 1986), pp. 484–93. The writer in the *Connecticut Courant* is quoted in Breen, *The Marketplace of Revolution,* p. 157. I have also drawn information about the growth of advertising from Breen.

14. Edwards, "Some Thoughts Concerning the Present Revival of Religion in America," in C. C. Coen, ed., *The Great Awakening,* vol. 4 of *Works of Jonathan Edwards* (New Haven, Conn., 1972), p. 507.

15. *George Whitefield's Journals* (London, 1960), p. 480.

16. Frank Lambert, *Inventing the "Great Awakening"* (Princeton, N.J., 1999), p. 88. See also Lambert, *"Pedlar in Divinity": George Whitefield and the Transatlantic Revivals* (Princeton, N.J., 1994).

17. *George Whitefield's Journals,* p. 462; Whitefield, *The Marriage of Cana* (1742), in Richard L. Bushman, ed., *The Great Awakening: Documents on the Revival of Religion, 1740–1745* (New York, 1970), p. 33.

18. The quotations above, from Edwards's unpublished sermons, are cited in Mark Valeri, "The Economic Thought of Jonathan Edwards," *Church History* 60 (March 1991), pp. 43, 49.

19. Charles Chauncy, *Enthusiasm Described and Cautioned Against* (1742), in Alan Heimert and Perry Miller, eds., *The Great Awakening: Documents Illustrating the Crisis and its Consequences* (New York, 1967), p. 241.

20. Quoted in John Wood Sweet, *Bodies Politic: Negotiating Race in the American North, 1730–1830* (Baltimore, 2003), p. 133.

21. *George Whitefield's Journals,* p. 523.

22. Edwards quoted in Gerald R. McDermott, *One Holy and Happy Soci-*

*ety: The Public Theology of Jonathan Edwards* (University Park, Penn., 1992), p. 23n.

23. Edwards quoted in ibid., p. 20.

24. Harry S. Stout, *The New England Soul: Preaching and Religious Culture in Colonial New England* (New York, 1986), p. 234.

25. Mayhew, "A Sermon Preach'd in the Audience of His Excellency William Shirley, Esq. . . . ," in Plumstead, ed., *The Wall and the Garden,* pp. 308, 310.

26. Fred Anderson, *Crucible of War: The Seven Years' War and the Fate of Empire in British North America* (New York, 2000), p. 406.

27. Solomon Williams, *The Relations of God's People to Him. . . .* (New London, 1760), p. 19.

28. Thomas Foxcroft, *Grateful Reflections on the Signal Appearances of Divine Providence* (Boston, 1760), pp. 10–12.

29. Belknap quoted in George B. Kirsch, *Jeremy Belknap: A Biography* (New York, 1982), p. 49. Editor quoted in T. H. Breen, "Ideology and Nationalism on the Eve of the American Revolution: Revisions Once More in Need of Revising," *Journal of American History* 84 (June 1997), p. 28n.

EPILOGUE    From the City upon a Hill to Plymouth Rock

1. David Hackett Fischer, *Paul Revere's Ride* (New York, 1994), pp. 109–10.

2. "Yankee Doodle, or (as now christened by the Saints of New England) The Lexington March," (1777), Harris Rare Books, John Hay Library, Brown University. This 1777 printed version clearly documents the British use of the song during the French and Indian War. See Joseph Conforti, *Imagining New England: Explorations of Regional Identity from the Pilgrims to the Mid-Twentieth Century* (Chapel Hill, N.C., 2001), pp. 152–53.

3. "Records of the Old Colony Club," *Proceedings of the Massachusetts Historical Society* 3 (1887), pp. 400, 404–5.

4. Charles Turner, *A Sermon Preached at Plymouth, December 22, 1773* (Boston, 1774), p. 12, n. 9; Boston newspaper, quoted in Albert Mathews, "The Term Pilgrim Fathers and Early Celebrations of Forefathers' Day," *Publications of the Colonial Society of Massachusetts* 17 (1914), p. 305.

# Essay on Sources

PROLOGUE    City upon a Hill

With its abundance of published and documentary sources, colonial New England has long been one of American historians' preferred areas of research. Historians have produced a voluminous and impressive body of work on early New England that stands as one of the most sophisticated scholarly achievements in the academic study of American history. Many of these works have the label "colonial New England" in their titles, but most focus on the Puritans in Massachusetts. There is no up-to-date overview of New England that examines the region as a whole from the precontact era to the end of the colonial period.

For a discussion of the dominant narratives that have shaped our understanding of the colonial past, see Joseph A. Conforti, *Imagining New England: Explorations of Regional Identity from the Pilgrims to the Mid-Twentieth Century* (Chapel Hill: University of North Carolina Press, 2001). For an analysis of how nationalistic narratives have influenced the understanding of colonial development, see the essays in Robert St. George, ed., *Possible Pasts: Becoming Colonial in Early America* (Ithaca, N.Y.: Cornell University Press, 2002). For a different view, which focuses on the Middle Colonies and stresses the process of Americanization, see Jon Butler, *Becoming America: The Revolution before 1776* (Cambridge, Mass.: Harvard University Press, 2000). Alan Taylor, *American Colonies* (New York: Viking, 2001) offers a sweeping narrative that places New England and other British, Spanish, and French colonies in Atlantic and continental contexts.

The background and context of Winthrop's famous sermon are discussed in Francis J. Bremer, *John Winthrop: America's Forgotten Founding Father* (New York: Oxford University Press, 2003), and Theodore Dwight Bozeman, *To Live Ancient Lives: The Primitivist Dimension in Puritanism* (Chapel

Hill: University of North Carolina Press, 1988). See also Sacvan Bercovitch, *The Puritan Origins of the American Self* (New Haven, Conn.: Yale University Press, 1975).

ONE   Native New England

Over recent decades, historians, anthropologists, and archaeologists have produced many studies of Native people in New England and the Northeast during the Colonial Era. Neal Salisbury, *Manitou and Providence: Indians, Europeans, and the Making of New England, 1500–1643* (New York: Oxford University Press, 1982) is a major standard work that is more balanced than the lively earlier study by Francis Jennings, *The Invasion of America: Indians, Colonialism, and the Cant of Conquest* (Chapel Hill: University of North Carolina Press, 1975). Howard S. Russell, *Indian New England before the Mayflower* (Hanover, N.H.: University Press of New England, 1980) is a nonacademic study that is particularly informative about Native material culture. In his classic *Changes in the Land: Indians, Colonists, and the Ecology of New England* (New York: Hill and Wang, 1983), William Cronon examines the conflicting environmental practices of Native people and colonists. For a varied collection of essays on New England, see Alden Vaughan, ed., *New England Encounters: Indians and Euroamericans, ca. 1600–1850* (Boston: Northeastern University Press, 1999). For a good overview of Native Americans in the Colonial Era, see Colin G. Calloway, *New Worlds for All: Indians, Europeans, and the Remaking of Early America* (Baltimore: Johns Hopkins University Press, 1997). See also Nancy Shoemaker, *A Strange Likeness: Becoming Red and White in Eighteenth-Century North America* (New York: Oxford University Press, 2004).

Ethnohistory has transformed our understanding of Native life. James Axtell, *Natives and Newcomers: The Cultural Origins of North America* (New York: Oxford University Press, 2001) is an important study from the author of a series of pioneering works of ethnohistory. For an excellent synthesis of ethnohistorians' findings, see Daniel Richter, *Facing East from Indian Country: A Native History of Early America* (Cambridge, Mass.: Harvard University Press, 2001). Kathleen J. Bragdon, *Native People of Southern New England, 1500–1650* (Norman: University of Oklahoma Press, 1996) is an informative anthropological study. Roger Williams is one of the principal sources of information on early New England Native life. Archaeologist Patricia E. Rubertone assesses Williams's observations in *Grave Undertakings: An Archaeology of Roger Williams and the Narragansett Indians* (Washington, D.C.: Smithsonian Institution Press, 2001). Two standard works on folklore and warfare are William S. Simmons, *Spirit of the New England Tribes: Indian History and Folklore, 1620–1984* (Hanover, N.H.: University Press of New England, 1986) and Patrick M. Malone, *The Skulking Way of War: Technology and Tactics among New England Indians* (Baltimore: Johns Hopkins University Press, 1993). On the Pequot War, see Alfred F. Cave,

*The Pequot War* (Amherst: University of Massachusetts Press, 1996). Native depopulation as a result of disease rather than warfare has received much attention, though it is often examined in a simplistic way. For an excellent analysis informed by a contemporary understanding of epidemiology, see David S. Jones, "Virgin Soils Revisited," *William and Mary Quarterly*, 3d ser., 60 (2003): 704–42.

Most relevant studies of Native people focus on the tribes of southern New England. For the Abenaki, see Bruce Bourque, *Twelve Thousand Years: American Indians in Maine* (Lincoln: University of Nebraska Press, 2002); essays in Emerson W. Baker et al., eds., *American Beginnings: Exploration, Culture, and Cartography in the Land of Norumbega* (Lincoln: University of Nebraska Press, 1994); and Emerson W. Baker and John G. Reid, "Amerindian Power in the Early Modern Northeast: A Reappraisal," *William and Mary Quarterly* 61 (2004): 77–106.

For Native-Anglo cultural exchange involving foodways and domestic animals, see Keith Stavely and Kathleen Fitzgerald, *America's Founding Food: The Story of New England Cooking* (Chapel Hill: University of North Carolina Press, 2004) and Virginia DeJohn Anderson, *Creatures of Empire: How Domestic Animals Transformed Early America* (New York, Oxford, 2004).

TWO    Puritan New England, 1620–1660

The best recent study of life in Plymouth Colony, which offers an informative discussion of the first Thanksgiving, is James Deetz and Patricia Scott Deetz, *The Time of Their Lives: Life, Love, and Death in Plymouth Colony* (New York: W. H. Freeman, 2000). This book is an update and expansion of James Deetz's classic study of material life in Plymouth, *In Small Things Forgotten: The Archaeology of Early American Life* (New York: Anchor Books, 1977). Another classic work on Plymouth is John Demos, *A Little Commonwealth: Family Life in Plymouth Colony* (New York: Oxford University Press, 1970).

On developments in England and the rise of Puritanism, see Mark Kishlansky, *A Monarchy Transformed: Britain 1603–1714* (New York: Penguin, 1996); Patrick Collinson, *The Birthpangs of Protestant England: Religious and Cultural Change in the Sixteenth and Seventeenth Centuries* (London: Macmillan, 1988); and William Hunt, *The Puritan Moment: The Coming of Revolution in an English County* (Cambridge, Mass.: Harvard University Press, 1983). On connections between English and American Puritanism, see Stephen Foster, *The Long Argument: English Puritanism and the Shaping of New England Culture* (Chapel Hill: University of North Carolina Press, 1991).

The literature on American Puritanism is voluminous and continues to grow. Perry Miller did more than any other scholar to spark the revival of Puritan studies in the postwar era. His two most accessible early works are *Orthodoxy in Massachusetts, 1630–1650* (Cambridge, Mass.: Harvard University Press, 1933) and *The New England Mind: From Colony to Province* (Cambridge,

Mass.: Harvard University Press, 1953). Miller has been sharply criticized for the limited sources he used and for depicting Puritanism as a monolithic body of thought. Recent works on English and American "puritanism" sometimes drop capitalization of the label to underscore the diversity of Protestant religious dissent that has sometimes been masked by reliance on "Puritanism." A helpful discussion can be found in David Hall, "Narrating Puritanism," in Harry S. Stout and D. G. Hart, eds., *New Directions in American Religious History* (New York: Oxford University Press, 1997), 51–83. The following works are among the most important post-Miller religious studies of early New England: Michael P. Winship, *Making Heretics: Militant Protestantism and Free Grace in Massachusetts, 1636–1641* (Princeton, N.J.: Princeton University Press, 2002); David Hall, *Worlds of Wonder, Days of Judgment: Popular Religious Belief in Early New England* (New York: Oxford University Press, 1989); Theodore Dwight Bozeman, *To Live Ancient Lives: The Primitivist Dimension in Puritanism,* already cited; and Charles F. Hambrick-Stowe, *The Practice of Piety: Puritan Devotional Disciplines in Seventeenth-Century New England* (Chapel Hill: University of North Carolina Press, 1982). Edmund S. Morgan, *The Puritan Dilemma: The Story of John Winthrop* (Boston: Little Brown, 1958), remains a classic study of tensions within Puritanism.

On the relationship between religion and economics, see Margaret Ellen Newell, *From Dependency to Independence: Economic Revolution in Colonial New England* (Ithaca, N.Y.: Cornell University Press, 1998) and two excellent works by Stephen Inness, *Creating the Commonwealth: The Economic Culture of Puritan New England* (New York: Norton, 1995) and *Labor in a New Land: Economy and Society in Seventeenth-Century Springfield* (Princeton, N.J.: Princeton University Press, 1985).

For informative studies that examine migration to New England in a transatlantic context and discuss the role of religious and material motives and patterns, see Alison Games, *Migration and the Origins of the English Atlantic World* (Cambridge, Mass.: Harvard University Press, 1999); Virginia DeJohn Anderson, *New England's Generation: The Great Migration and the Formation of Society and Culture in the Seventeenth Century* (New York: Cambridge University Press, 1991), David Cressy, *Coming Over: Migration and Communication between England and New England in the Seventeenth Century* (New York: Cambridge University Press, 1987); and David Grayson Allen, *In English Ways: The Movement of Societies and the Transferal of English Local Law and Custom to Massachusetts Bay in the Seventeenth Century* (Chapel Hill: University of North Carolina Press, 1981).

Historians have produced numerous studies of individual communities and of the process of town-founding. Two of the best are John F. Martin, *Profits in the Wilderness: Entrepreneurship and the Founding of New England Towns in the Seventeenth Century* (Chapel Hill: University of North Carolina Press, 1991), and Philip Greven Jr., *Four Generations: Population, Land, and Family in*

*Colonial Andover* (Ithaca, N.Y.: Cornell University Press, 1970). Two informative recent studies synthesize the findings of many social historians; see Gloria L. Main, *Peoples of a Spacious Land: Families and Cultures in Colonial New England* (Cambridge, Mass.: Harvard University Press, 2001) and Richard Archer, *Fissures in the Rock: New England in the Seventeenth Century* (Hanover, N.H.: University Press of New England, 2001).

For women and issues of gender, see Jane Kamensky, *Governing the Tongue: The Politics of Speech in Early New England* (New York: Oxford University Press, 1997); Cornelia Hughes Dayton, *Women Before the Bar: Gender, Law, and Society in Connecticut, 1639–1789* (Chapel Hill: University of North Carolina Press, 1995); Laurel Thatcher Ulrich, *Good Wives: Image and Reality in the Lives of Women in Northern New England, 1650–1750* (New York: Alfred A. Knopf, 1982); and Anne S. Lombard, *Growing Up Male in Colonial New England* (Cambridge, Mass.: Harvard University Press, 2003).

THREE    Beyond Puritan New England

Works by Stephen Inness, already cited, offer important discussions of labor, servants, and the non-Puritan human capital that helped build New England. For the world of the profane, see Richard P. Gildrie, *The Profane, the Godly, and the Civil: The Reformation of Manners in Orthodox New England, 1679–1748* (University Park: Pennsylvania State University Press, 1994). For sexual behavior and court actions, see Richard Godbeer, *Sexual Revolution in Early America* (Baltimore: Johns Hopkins University Press, 2002); Roger Thompson, *Sex in Middlesex: Popular Mores in a Massachusetts County, 1649–1699* (Amherst: University of Massachusetts Press, 1986); and Edgar J. McManus, *Law and Liberty in Early New England: Criminal Justice and Due Process, 1620–1692* (Amherst: University of Massachusetts Press, 1993). Early America's tavern culture has drawn the attention of recent historians. The best New England study is David W. Conroy, *In Public Houses: Drink and the Revolution of Authority in Colonial Massachusetts* (Chapel Hill: University of North Carolina Press, 1995).

There are two helpful works that deal with New England geography. D. W. Meinig, *The Shaping of America: A Geographical Perspective on 500 Years of History,* vol. 1, *Atlantic America, 1492–1800* (New Haven, Conn.: Yale University Press, 1986); and Douglas R. McManis, *Colonial New England: A Historical Geography* (New York: Oxford University Press, 1975). There is useful information about maritime geography in the general history by Robert Albion et al., *New England and the Sea* (Middletown, Conn.: Wesleyan University Press, 1972).

We have no good scholarly history of New England and the sea in the Colonial Era. In *Creating the Commonwealth,* Stephen Inness has an excellent chapter on "The Making of Maritime New England." Daniel Vickers, *Farmers and Fishermen: Two Centuries of Work in Essex County, Massachusetts, 1630–1850* (Chapel Hill: University of North Carolina Press, 1994) is a highly informative study. Other important works include Christine Leigh Heyrman, *Commerce and Culture: The Maritime Communities of Colonial Massachusetts in the Seventeenth Century* (Cambridge, Mass.: Harvard University Press, 1985). Also see Peter E. Pope, *Fish into Wine: The New Foundland Plantation in the Seventeenth Century* (Chapel Hill: University of North Carolina Press, 2004).

A standard work on the West Indies is Richard S. Dunn, *Sugar and Slaves: The Rise of the Planter Class in the English West Indies* (Chapel Hill: University of North Carolina Press, 1972). For an excellent study of Puritan settlement in the Caribbean, see Karen Ordahl Kupperman, *Providence Island, 1630–1641: The Other Puritan Colony* (New York: Cambridge University Press, 1993). See also Sidney W. Mintz, *Sweetness and Power: The Place of Sugar in Modern History* (New York: Viking, 1985).

For a good introduction to slavery and race in colonial America, see Ira Berlin, *Generations of Captivity: A History of African-American Slaves* (Cambridge, Mass.: Harvard University Press, 2003). See also Winthrop D. Jordan, *White over Black: American Attitudes toward the Negro, 1550–1812* (Chapel Hill: University of North Carolina Press, 1968); and Lorenzo J. Greene, *The Negro in Colonial New England, 1620–1776* (New York: Columbia University Press, 1942).

The best general study of northern New England remains Charles E. Clark, *The Eastern Frontier: The Settlement of Northern New England, 1610–1753* (New York: Knopf, 1970). There are also excellent essays in Emerson W. Baker et al., eds., *American Beginnings: Exploration, Culture, and Cartography in the Land of Norumbega,* cited earlier. On New Hampshire, see Jere R. Daniell, *Colonial New Hampshire: A History* (Millwood, N.Y.: KTO Press, 1981) and David Van Deventer, *The Emergence of Provincial New Hampshire, 1623–1741* (Baltimore: Johns Hopkins University Press, 1976).

The most detailed study of Rhode Island's early history is Sydney V. James, *Colonial Metamorphoses in Rhode Island: A Study of Institutions and Change* (Hanover, N.H.: University Press of New England, 2000). He offers some suggestive comments about similarities between Rhode Island and New Hampshire. Three older studies are also informative: Bruce C. Daniels, *Dissent and Conformity on Narragansett Bay: The Colonial Rhode Island Town* (Middletown, Conn.: Wesleyan University Press, 1983); William G. McLoughlin, *Rhode Island: A Bicentennial History* (New York: W. W. Norton, 1978); and Carl Bridenbaugh, *Fat Mutton and Liberty of Conscience: Society in Rhode Island, 1636–1690* (Providence, R.I.: Brown University Press, 1974). For religious radicalism and its impact on Rhode Island, see Philip F. Gura, *A Glimpse of Sion's Glory: Puritan Radicalism in New England, 1620–1660* (Middletown, Conn.: Wesleyan University Press, 1984). For women prophesying and Anne Hutchinson, see Marilyn J. Westerkamp, *Women and Religion in America, 1600–1850: The Puritan and Evangelical Traditions* (New York: Routledge, 1999); and Amy Schrager Lang, *Prophetic Woman: Anne Hutchinson and the*

*Problem of Dissent in the Literature of New England* (Berkeley: University of California Press, 1987).

FOUR    New England Besieged, 1660–1700

Generational analysis, declension, and the jeremiad are among the hallmarks of Puritan studies. Mark A. Peterson, *The Price of Redemption: The Spiritual Economy of Puritan New England* (Stanford, Calif.: Stanford University Press, 1997) offers perhaps the best recent challenge to the familiar narrative of decline. See also Andrew Delbanco, *The Puritan Ordeal* (Cambridge, Mass.: Harvard University Press, 1989); Harry S. Stout, *The New England Soul: Preaching and Religious Culture in Colonial New England* (New York: Oxford University Press, 1986); and Robert Middlekauff, *The Mathers: Three Generations of Puritan Intellectuals, 1596–1728* (New York: Oxford University Press, 1971). In a superb analysis of the "invention of New England," Middlekauff argues that "the fathers may have founded the colonies but the sons invented New England" (p. 98). For a nationalistic view of the jeremiad that extends the work of the influential Perry Miller, see Sacvan Bercovitch, *The American Jeremiad* (Madison: University of Wisconsin Press, 1978).

Informative recent studies of Native conversion include Richard Cogley, *John Eliot's Mission to the Indians before King Philip's War* (Cambridge, Mass.: Harvard University Press, 1999); Jean M. O'Brien, *Dispossession by Degrees: Indian Land and Identity in Natick, Massachusetts, 1680–1790* (New York: Cambridge University Press, 1997); and Dane Morrison, *A Praying People: Massachusetts Acculturation and the Failure of Puritan Mission, 1600–1690* (New York: Peter Lang, 1995). On the era of King Philip's War, see James D. Drake, *King Philip's War: Civil War in New England, 1675–1676* (Amherst: University of Massachusetts Press, 1999); Jill Lepore, *The Name of War: King Philip's War and the Origins of American Identity* (New York: Alfred A. Knopf, 1998); and Alden Vaughan, *New England Frontier: Puritans and Indians, 1620–1675,* 3d ed. (Norman: University of Oklahoma Press, 1995). For the role of two key Native individuals in the origins and prosecution of the war, see Michael L. Oberg, *Uncas: First of the Mohegans* (Ithaca, N.Y.: Cornell University Press, 2003); and Yasuhide Kawashima, *Igniting King Philip's War: The John Sassamon Murder Trial* (Lawrence: University of Kansas Press, 2001). On the Indian captivity narrative, see Alden Vaughan and Edward W. Clark, eds., *Puritans among the Indians: Accounts of Captivity and Redemption, 1676–1724* (Cambridge, Mass.: Harvard University Press, 1981).

For the Glorious Revolution in general, see Jack M. Sosin, *English America and the Revolution of 1688* (Lincoln: University of Nebraska Press, 1982) and David S. Lovejoy, *The Glorious Revolution in America* (New York: Harper and Row, 1972). For the Glorious Revolution's impact on New England, see Richard Johnson, *Adjustment to Empire: The New England Colonies, 1675–1715* (New Brunswick, N.J.: Rutgers University Press, 1981); and T. H.

Breen, *The Character of the Good Ruler: A Study of Puritan Political Ideas* (New Haven, Conn.: Yale University Press, 1970).

Work on colonial witchcraft and especially Salem is voluminous and growing. For the connection between French-Indian frontier warfare and the hysteria, see Mary Beth Norton, *In the Devil's Snare: The Salem Witchcraft Crisis of 1692* (New York: Alfred A. Knopf, 2002). Norton also offers an excellent analysis of King Philip's War in northern New England. For an informative study of the hysteria's many dimensions, see Peter Charles Hoffer, *The Devil's Disciples: Makers of the Salem Witchcraft Trials* (Baltimore: Johns Hopkins University Press, 1996). For the village origins of the outbreak, see Paul Boyer and Stephen Nissenbaum, *Salem Possessed: The Social Origins of Witchcraft* (Cambridge, Mass.: Harvard University Press, 1974). For women and witchcraft, see Carol F. Karlsen, *The Devil in the Shape of a Woman: Witchcraft in Colonial New England* (New York: W. W. Norton, 1984). On witchcraft before and outside of Salem, see John P. Demos, *Entertaining Satan: Witchcraft and the Culture of Early New England* (New York: Oxford University Press, 1982) and Richard Godbeer, *Escaping Salem: The Other Witch Hunt of 1692* (New York: Oxford University Press, 2004).

FIVE   Saints and Strangers in the Eighteenth Century

For an informative study of New England migration and "serial town" settlement, see David Jaffee, *People of the Wachusett: Greater New England in History and Memory* (Ithaca, N.Y.: Cornell University Press, 1999). See also Bruce C. Daniels, *The Connecticut Town: Growth and Development, 1635–1790* (Middletown, Conn.: Wesleyan University Press, 1979). For developments in Newport and Rhode Island, see Lynne Withey, *Urban Growth in Colonial Rhode Island: Newport and Providence in the Eighteenth Century* (Albany: State University of New York Press, 1984). On the larger context of eighteenth-century migrations, see Marianne S. Wokeck, *Trade in Strangers: The Beginnings of Mass Migrations to North America* (University Park: Pennsylvania State University Press, 1999); Marilyn C. Baseler, *"Asylum for Mankind": America 1607–1800* (Ithaca, N.Y.: Cornell University Press, 1998); and Bernard Bailyn, *Voyagers to the West: A Passage in the Peopling of America on the Eve of the Revolution* (New York: Alfred A. Knopf, 1986).

For the effects of colonial expansion on Native relations in New England, see Evan Haefeli and Kevin Sweeney, *Captors and Captives: The 1704 French and Indian Raid on Deerfield* (Amherst: University of Massachusetts Press, 2003); Colin G. Calloway, *The Western Abenakis of Vermont, 1600–1800: War, Migration, and the Survival of an Indian People* (Norman: University of Oklahoma Press, 1990); and Kenneth M. Morrison, *The Embattled Northeast: The Elusive Ideal of Alliance in Abenaki-European Relations* (Berkeley: University of California Press, 1984).

For poverty, gender, social welfare, the strolling poor and warning out, see Ruth Wallis Herndon, *Unwelcome Americans: Living on the Margin in Early*

*New England* (Philadelphia: University of Pennsylvania Press, 2001); Elaine Forman Crane, *Ebb Tide in New England: Women, Seaports, and Social Change, 1630–1800* (Boston: Northeastern University Press, 1998); Douglas Lamar Jones, *Village and Seaport: Migration and Society in Eighteenth-Century Massachusetts* (Hanover, N.H.: University Press of New England, 1981); Gary B. Nash, *Urban Crucible: Social Change, Political Consciousness, and the Origins of the American Revolution* (Cambridge, Mass.: Harvard University Press, 1979); Robert A. Gross, *The Minutemen and Their World* (New York, 1976); and Stephen Foster, *Their Solitary Way: The Puritan Social Ethic in the First Century of Settlement* (New Haven, Conn.: Yale University Press, 1971).

For women's spirituality and the deficiencies of the declension model, see Ann Braude, "Women's History *is* American Religious History," in Thomas A. Tweed, ed., *Retelling U.S. Religious History* (Berkeley: University of California Press, 1997), 87–107; and Harry S. Stout and Catherine Brekus, "Declension, Gender, and the New Religious History," in Philip R. Vandermer and Robert P. Swierenga, eds., *Belief and Behavior: Essays in the New Religious History* (New Brunswick, N.J.: Rutgers University Press, 1991), 15–37. See also Patricia U. Bonomi, *Under the Cope of Heaven: Religion, Society, and Politics in Colonial America* (New York: Oxford University Press, 1986); Susan Juster, *Disorderly Women: Sexual Politics and Evangelicalism in Revolutionary New England* (Ithaca, N.Y.: Cornell University Press, 1994); and Rebecca Larson, *Daughters of Light: Quaker Women Preaching and Prophesying in the Colonies and Abroad, 1700–1775* (New York: Alfred A. Knopf, 1999).

In addition to Jean M. O'Brien, *Dispossession by Degrees,* on Native American survival and adaptation in the eighteenth century, see John Wood Sweet, *Bodies Politic: Negotiating Race in the American North, 1730–1830* (Baltimore: Johns Hopkins University Press, 2003); Ann Marie Plane, *Colonial Intimacies: Indian Marriage in Early New England* (Ithaca, N.Y.: Cornell University Press, 2000); David J. Silverman, " 'We Choose to be Bounded': Native American Animal Husbandry in Colonial New England," *William and Mary Quarterly* 60 (2003): 511–48; Silverman, "The Impact of Indentured Servitude on the Society and Culture of Southern New England Indians, 1680–1810," *New England Quarterly* 74 (2001): 622–66; Colin G. Calloway, ed., *After King Philip's War: Presence and Persistence in Indian New England* (Hanover, N.H.: University Press of New England, 1997); and Daniell Mandell, *Behind the Frontier: Indians in Eighteenth-Century Eastern Massachusetts* (Lincoln: University of Nebraska Press, 1996). On Native people and the whaling industry, see Daniel Vickers, "The First Whalemen of Nantucket," *William and Mary Quarterly* 40 (1983): 560–83.

New Englanders' role in the Atlantic slave trade is closely examined in Jay Coughtry, *The Notorious Triangle: Rhode Island and the African Slave Trade* (Philadelphia: Temple University Press, 1981). See also Herbert S. Klein, *The Atlantic Slave Trade* (New York: Cambridge University Press, 1999) and

Robin Blackburn, *The Making of New World Slavery: From Baroque to the Modern, 1492–1800* (New York: Verso, 1997).

On slavery and race in eighteenth-century New England, in addition to Sweet, *Bodies Politic,* see William D. Piersen, *Black Yankees: The Development of an Afro-American Subculture in Eighteenth-Century New England* (Amherst: University of Massachusetts Press, 1988); W. Jeffrey Bolster, *Black Jacks: African American Seamen in the Age of Sail* (Cambridge, Mass.: Harvard University Press, 1998); Erik R. Seeman, " 'Justise Must Take Plase': Three African Americans Speak of Religion in Eighteenth-Century New England," *William and Mary Quarterly* 56 (1999): 393–414; David R. Mandell, "Shifting Boundaries of Race and Ethnicity: Indian-Black Intermarriage in Southern New England, 1760–1880," *Journal of American History* 85 (1998): 466–501; and Mark J. Sammons and Valerie Cunningham, *Black Portsmouth: Three Centuries of African-American Heritage* (Hanover, N.H.: University Press of New England, 2004).

SIX   Provincial New England

For political developments surrounding the Glorious Revolution in England and America, see Craig Rose, *England in the 1690s: Revolution, Religion, and War* (Oxford, Eng.: Oxford University Press, 1999); and Stephen Saunders Webb, *Lord Churchill's Coup: The Anglo-American Empire and the Glorious Revolution Reconsidered* (New York: Alfred A. Knopf, 1995). On eighteenth-century colonial politics, see Edmund S. Morgan, *Inventing the People: The Rise of Popular Sovereignty in England and America* (New York: W. W. Norton, 1988); Richard L. Bushman, *King and People in Provincial Massachusetts* (Chapel Hill: University of North Carolina Press, 1985); Jack P. Greene, *Peripheries and Center: Constitutional Development in the Extended Politics of the British Empire and the United States, 1607–1788* (Athens: University of Georgia Press, 1986); Bernard Bailyn, *The Origins of American Politics* (New York: Alfred A. Knopf, 1968); and John J. Waters Jr., *The Otis Family in Provincial and Revolutionary Massachusetts* (Chapel Hill: University of North Carolina Press, 1968).

On the development of British nationalism and imperialism, see Lawrence Stone, ed., *The Imperial State of War: Britain from 1689 to 1815* (London: Routledge, 1994); Linda Colley, *Britons: Forging the Nation, 1707–1837* (New Haven, Conn.: Yale University Press, 1992); and John Brewer, *The Sinews of Power: War, Money, and the English State* (New York: Alfred A. Knopf, 1989).

For the commercial empire, see Elizabeth Mancke and Carol Shammas, *The Creation of the British Atlantic World* (Baltimore: Johns Hopkins University Press, 2005); T. H. Breen, *The Marketplace of Revolution: How Consumer Politics Shaped American Independence* (New York: Oxford University Press, 2004); Carol Shammas, *The Pre-Industrial Consumer in England and America*

(Oxford, Eng.: Oxford University Press, 1990); and John J. McCusker and Russell R. Menard, *The Economy of British America, 1607–1789* (Chapel Hill: University of North Carolina Press, 1985). On "she-merchants" in Boston, see Patricia Cleary, *Elizabeth Murray: A Woman's Pursuit of Independence in Eighteenth-Century America* (Amherst: University of Massachusetts Press, 2000). On the domestic use of imported and homemade goods, see Laurel Thatcher Ulrich, *The Age of Homespun: Objects and Stories in the Creation of an American Myth* (New York: Vintage, 2001).

For the Anglicization of colonial life, see John E. Crowley, *The Invention of Comfort: Sensibilities and Design in Early Modern Britain and Early America* (Baltimore: Johns Hopkins University Press, 2001); Richard L. Bushman, *The Refinement of America: Persons, Houses, Cities* (New York: Random House, 1993); and Wayne Craven, *Colonial American Portraiture* (New York: Alfred A. Knopf, 1992). On religious Anglicization, see John Corrigan, *The Prism of Piety: Catholick Congregational Clergy at the Beginning of the Enlightenment* (New York: Oxford University Press, 1991). For re-Anglicization, the covenant, and the Enlightenment, see Bruce Tucker, "The Reinvention of New England, 1691–1770," *New England Quarterly* 63 (1985): 315–40; Christopher Grasso, *A Speaking Aristocracy: Transforming Public Discourse in Eighteenth-Century Connecticut* (Chapel Hill: University of North Carolina Press, 1999); Michael P. Winship, *Seers of God: Puritan Providentialism in the Restoration and Early Enlightenment* (Baltimore: Johns Hopkins University Press, 1996); and Ned C. Landsman, *From Colonials to Provincials: American Thought and Culture, 1680–1760* (Ithaca, N.Y.: Cornell University Press, 2000).

For lay piety, revivalism, and the background to the Awakening, see Erik R. Seeman, *Pious Persuasions: Laity and Clergy in Eighteenth-Century New England* (Baltimore: Johns Hopkins University Press, 1999) and Michael J. Crawford, *Seasons of Grace: Colonial New England's Revival Tradition in its British Context* (New York: Oxford University Press, 1991). The most informative general history of the Awakening is Frank Lambert, *Inventing the "Great Awakening"* (Princeton, N.J.: Princeton University Press, 1999). On how the "greatness" of the Awakening has been exaggerated, see Jon Butler, *Awash in a Sea of Faith: Christianizing the American People* (Cambridge, Mass: Harvard University Press, 1990) and Joseph Conforti, *Jonathan Edwards, Religious Tradition, and American Culture* (Chapel Hill: University of North Carolina Press, 1993). On transatlantic piety, see W. R. Ward, *The Protestant Evangelical Awakening* (Cambridge, Eng.: Cambridge University Press, 1992).

Jonathan Edwards and George Whitefield are the subjects of excellent broad biographical studies. See Philip F. Gura, *Jonathan Edwards: America's Evangelical* (New York: Hill and Wang, 2005); and George Marsden, *Jonathan Edwards: A Life* (New Haven, Conn.: Yale University Press, 2003). Frank Lambert, *"Pedlar in Divinity": George Whitefield and the Transatlantic Re-*

*vivals, 1737–1770* (Princeton, N.J.: Princeton University Press, 1991); and Harry S. Stout, *The Divine Dramatist: George Whitefield and the Rise of Modern Evangelicalism* (Grand Rapids, Mich.: William B. Eerdmans, 1991).

On radical awakeners and the revival in northern New England, see Douglas L. Winiarski, "Souls Filled with Ravishing Transport: Heavenly Visions and the Radical Awakening in New England," *William and Mary Quarterly* 61 (2004): 3–41; Timothy D. Hall, *Contested Boundaries: Itinerancy and the Reshaping of the Colonial Religious World* (Durham, N.C.: Duke University Press, 1994); Clarence C. Goen, *Revivalism and Separatism in New England, 1740–1800* (New Haven, Conn.: Yale University Press, 1962); Douglas L. Winiarski, " 'A Journal of Five Days at York': The Great Awakening on the Northern New England Frontier," *Maine History* 42 (2004): 47–85; and Elizabeth C. Nordbeck, "Almost Revived: The Great Revival in New Hampshire and Maine, 1727–1748," *Historical New Hampshire* 35 (1980): 24–58.

On women and revivalism, see Catherine Brekus, *Strangers and Pilgrims: Female Preaching in America* (Chapel Hill: University of North Carolina Press, 1998); Susan Juster, *Disorderly Women: Sexual Politics and Evangelicalism in Revolutionary New England* (Ithaca, N.Y.: Cornell University Press, 1994); and Barbara Lacey, "Gender, Piety, and Secularization in Connecticut," *Journal of Social History* 24 (1991): 799–821.

For blacks and Indians in the Awakening, in addition to Sweet, *Bodies Politic,* and Piersen, *Black Yankees,* already cited, see Hilary E. Wyss, *Writing Indians: Literacy, Christianity, and Native Community in Early America* (Amherst: University of Massachusetts Press, 2000) and William S. Simmons, "Red Yankees: Narragansett Conversion in the Great Awakening," *American Ethnologist* 10 (1983): 253–71.

For the sensory side of the Awakening, see Peter Charles Hoffer, *The Sensory Worlds of Early America* (Baltimore: Johns Hopkins University Press, 2003). On the Awakening's legacy, see the suggestive discussions in James F. Block, *A Nation of Agents: The American Path to a Modern Self* (Cambridge, Mass.: Harvard University Press, 2002) and Allen C. Guelzo, "God's Designs: The Literature of the Colonial Revivals of Religion," in Harry S. Stout and D. G. Hart, eds., *New Directions in American Religious History* (New York: Oxford University Press, 1997), 141–72.

For the eighteenth-century European empires, see Anthony Pagden, *Lords of All the World: Ideologies of Empire in Spain, Britain, and France* (New Haven, Conn.: Yale University Press, 1995). On the French, see Allan Greer, *The People of New France* (Toronto: University of Toronto Press, 1997) and W. J. Eccles, *The French in North America* (East Lansing: Michigan State University Press, 1990). On midcentury imperial warfare, see Fred Anderson's two fine books *Crucible of War: The Seven Years' War and the Fate of Empire in British North America* (New York: Alfred A. Knopf, 2000) and *A People's Army: Massachusetts Soldiers and Society in the Seven Years' War* (Chapel

Hill: University of North Carolina Press, 1984). On New Englanders' re-action to imperial victory, see Nathan O. Hatch, *The Sacred Cause of Liberty: Republican Thought and the Millennium in Revolutionary New England* (New Haven, Conn.: Yale University Press, 1977) and Ruth Bloch, *Visionary Re-public: Millennial Themes in American Thought, 1756–1800* (Cambridge, Eng.: Cambridge University Press, 1985).

EPILOGUE    From the City upon a Hill to Plymouth Rock

For an excellent study of the shift from a British to an American iden-tity in the life of one prominent New England native, see Gordon S. Wood, *The Americanization of Benjamin Franklin* (New York: Penguin, 2004). See also T. H. Breen, "Ideology and Nationalism on the Eve of the American Revolution: Revisions Once More in Need of Revising," *Journal of Ameri-can History* 84 (1997): 13–39 and Bernard Bailyn, *Ideological Origins of the American Revolution* (Cambridge, Mass.: Harvard University Press, 1967). On the mythology of Plymouth, see John Seelye, *Memory's Nation: The Place of Plymouth Rock* (Chapel Hill: University of North Carolina Press, 1998).

# Index

Abenaki, 7, 24, 89, 115, 116, 121, 131, 136, 148, 149
Adams, John, 205
African Americans: in colonial New England, 4, 133, 155–162; festivals for, 161–162; intermarriage and, 149, 155; religious revivalism and, 190–191; social interaction between colonists and, 159–162; social interaction between Native Americans and, 155
Agawam, 28
agriculture. *See* farming
alcohol consumption: in Native New England, 18–19, 27; Puritan regulation of, 72
Alden, John, 39
Algonquians: hunting, fishing, and gathering by, 6, 7, 15; material life among, 16; overview of, 6–7; spiritual beliefs of, 24, 110; wampum use by, 15; warfare and, 22, 115, 116. *See also* Native Americans; Native New England
almshouses, 141, 143
American Revolution, 200
Amoskeag, 28
Andros, Edmund, 118–120
Anglicization, 163–164

Antinomianism, 93–94
Apponaug, 28
Attucks, Crispus, 155
Awashunkes, 20–21

baptist churches: in Connecticut, 147; in Massachusetts, 147; in Rhode Island, 92, 147, 148; women in, 148
Battle of Quebec, 197
Belknap, Jeremy, 198
birthrate, 149
bodily ornamentation, 19
bordellos, 73
*Boston Evening Post,* 177
Boston Massacre of 1770, 155, 202
*Boston Weekly News-Letter,* 176
Braddock, Edward, 196
Bradford, William, 22, 40, 67
Bradstreet, Anne, 61–64, 66, 100, 101
Bradstreet, Simon, 61, 62
Brattle Street Church, 172, 178, 179
Brown, Obadiah, 140
Burroughs, George, 129

Calvin, John, 36, 101
Calvinism, 181, 183, 193
*Cambridge Platform (1648),* 65

William of Orange, 120, 131, 171
Williams, Eunice, 132
Williams, John, 132
Williams, Roger, 22, 24, 67, 91–92, 94, 95, 100, 108, 114
Winthrop, John, 30–31, 37, 40–43, 45, 46, 55, 85, 93, 100, 105–170, 173, 200
witchcraft hysteria: climate preceding, 121–123; executions during, 2, 122, 125, 126; historical records of, 125–126; Native Americans and, 129–130; Puritanism and, 98, 99, 130; responses to, 123–129
Wolfe, James, 197

women: literacy among, 60; premarital pregnancy among, 63, 144; in Puritan congregations, 58, 59; Puritanism and, 60–64, 127; religion and, 144–148; religious revivals and, 187; responsibilities of Native American, 11–12, 15, 17; as sachems, 20–21; witchcraft accusations and, 126–127
work culture, 41–43
workhouses, 141, 143

"Yankee Doodle," 201–202, 205